Leading Strategic Change

Why do some companies continue to be successful while others experience difficulties and even failure? In *Leading Strategic Change*, Eric Flamholtz and Yvonne Randle demonstrate that the key to long-term organizational success is the ability to adapt to and manage different types of change. Drawing on over thirty years' consultancy experience within major firms, they combine theoretical and practical models of organizational change, together with a new theory of leadership, to build a framework for understanding, planning, and leading change. The scope and value of this framework are then shown in relation to nine real-world case studies, ranging from relatively small companies (IndyMac Bank, Infogix) to large multinationals (Starbucks, Westfield). The focus throughout is to provide practical guidance to those concerned with managing and leading change in organizations. This book is an excellent guide to the many lessons to be learned about successful organizational change.

ERIC FLAMHOLTZ is Professor of Human Resource Management and Organizational Behavior in the Anderson Graduate School of Management and a faculty research fellow in the Harold and Pauline Price Center for Entrepreneurial Studies at the University of California, Los Angeles (UCLA). He is also President of Management Systems Consulting Corporation, which he co-founded in 1978.

YVONNE RANDLE is Vice-president of Management Systems Consulting Corporation. She has extensive consulting experience with companies ranging in size from small entrepreneurships to multi-billion-dollar enterprises and is a lecturer in executive education programs in the Anderson Graduate School of Management, University of California, Los Angeles.

Leading Strategic Change

Bridging Theory and Practice

ERIC FLAMHOLTZ and YVONNE RANDLE

CAMBRIDGE
UNIVERSITY PRESS

CAMBRIDGE UNIVERSITY PRESS
Cambridge, New York, Melbourne, Madrid, Cape Town, Singapore, São Paulo, Delhi

Cambridge University Press
The Edinburgh Building, Cambridge CB2 8RU, UK

Published in the United States of America by Cambridge University Press, New York

www.cambridge.org
Information on this title: www.cambridge.org/9780521849470

© Cambridge University Press 2008

First published 2008

Printed in the United Kingdom at the University Press, Cambridge

A catalogue record for this publication is available from the British Library

Library of Congress Cataloguing in Publication data
Flamholtz, Eric.
  Leading strategic change: bridging theory and practice / Eric Flamholtz and
Yvonne Randle.
    p. cm.
  Includes bibliographical references and index.
  ISBN 978-0-521-84947-0 (hardback)
  1. Organizational change–United States. 2. Organizational change–United
States–Case studies. 3. Leadership–United States. I. Randle, Yvonne. II. Title.

  HD58.8.F5455 2008
  658.4'06–dc22

                                                                        2008010879

ISBN 978-0-521-84947-0 hardback

Contents

Exhibits

Preface

The inevitability of change

Nothing lasts for ever. Not people, not redwood trees, not empires, not climatic conditions, not even the Sun and Earth themselves. And certainly not an organization's success formula.

Regardless of how strong and successful an organization is, and regardless of how long a period of success the organization has had, the need for change is inevitable. In some instances, the need for change occurs because of changes in the environment. This can be due to changes in customers' tastes and preferences, changes in technology, changes in the nature of competition, or other external factors beyond the control of management. The need for change can also occur because of the organization's own success. Changes in organizational size and complexity as a result of growth and market success create the need for changes in organizational structure and, possibly, culture.

The "secret" of long-term success is the ability to adapt to change. Organizations develop "success formulas" or "winning business models" that last for a period of time. Then, as the environment changes or conditions within the organization itself change, the enterprise must adapt. If it does so successfully, it will continue to exist and flourish. If it does not adapt successfully, however, it will experience difficulties and perhaps failure, regardless of how strong it appears at a moment or how many resources it has. The decline can occur swiftly or agonizingly slowly over a long period of time. The decline of General Motors, AT&T, Xerox, Reuters, and Mövenpick are just a few examples.

The ability to adapt to change

Some organizations are better than others at adapting to change. Some have successfully "reinvented" themselves, while others have perished. For example, IBM, under the leadership of Lewis Gerstner, was able to transform from a company based upon "Big Iron" to an information solutions company with a product mix of hardware, software, and services. Unfortunately, AT&T, under the leadership of C. Michael Armstrong, spent almost $100 billion in a futile effort to change its business model. Although AT&T still exists as a corporate entity, it was purchased by one of its offspring (the so-called "Baby Bells") and is no longer what it once was: a proud and successful company with a magnificent technological heritage.

We believe that the difference in outcomes at IBM and AT&T was not due just to chance or luck. There were systematic reasons why one company was successful and the other experienced difficulties and ultimately wasted almost $100 billion in a vain effort to change. One of the major reasons was the leadership capabilities of the two people who led the change efforts.

Our purpose

This book deals with leading strategic and organizational change. This issue is critical to virtually all organizations at some stage of their life cycle.

For the past thirty years we have been working with and studying companies engaged in strategic and organizational change. We believe that much can be learned about successful and unsuccessful change by studying what companies have actually done.

Our approach is a combination of theory and practice, and our intent is to bridge theory and practice from both directions. This means that we look to theory to provide content for practice, but we also look to practice to provide insights and lessons for theory. We believe in what might be termed "practical management theory," which we define as theory that is empirically sound but relevant and actionable by practicing leaders and managers. Hence, this book is heavily oriented to practitioners. Our intent is to provide a useful "tool" to enable them to deal with the issues and problems of strategic and organizational change.

Scope and limitations

Our strategy is to draw heavily upon our own experience as participant observers in the process of leading strategic and organizational change. Each of us has been working with companies for very many years.

Although we present a conceptual framework for understanding, planning, and leading change efforts, it is *not* our intention to summarize the vast literature related to this topic. Other authors have adopted a similar approach.[1] We have drawn upon some concepts and research in this area and incorporated them into the working framework we use to guide change efforts. Some of these are classic concepts and research; other aspects are based upon our own previously published or unpublished work. We do, however, provide a list of references related to the theories and concepts of others as a resource for interested practitioners and scholars; this is in the appendix at the back of the book. It includes both scholar-oriented and practitioner-oriented references.

Structure

In Part I we present an "integrated" framework for understanding, thinking about, planning, and leading strategic and organizational change. The aim of this conceptual framework is to provide the reader with the tools that we have used in many of the case studies presented in Part II. Our intent is not to suggest that this is the only way to look at strategic and organizational change. It is, nonetheless, our approach to examining change, and for us it has proved useful.

Chapter 1 deals with the nature of change and presents a framework for understanding change. The literature on managing change is vast and replete with references to various types of changes. It lacks a coherent framework for classifying or categorizing different types of change issues, however. The purpose of chapter 1, then, is to present a typology for classifying change issues that should prove useful to practitioners, and possibly to scholars as well. The typology includes different aspects of change based upon the magnitude of change, types of change, and the organizational levels that are the target of change. By putting these various aspects together, this provides a conceptual or theoretical framework for understanding the nature and process of change.

---

[1] For example, see Kotter, J. P., 1996, *Leading Change*, Boston, Harvard Business School Press. This book is based upon his article published in the March/April 1995 issue of *Harvard Business Review* and does not summarize or cite any of the literature of change management.

Chapter 2 presents a "lens" for planning and leading strategic and organizational changes. This framework builds upon a construct termed the "Pyramid of Organizational Development™," which we have used for many years in working with companies on strategic and organizational change. It provides an actionable model for a change management plan. This framework and approach to planning change has been used in most of the case studies presented in Part II of this book.

Chapter 3 deals with some aspects of leadership, and the leadership requirements and capabilities for successful change. In this chapter we identify the key leadership competencies required for planning and leading organizational change. Based upon this model of these competencies, we also propose a construct termed the "molecule theory of leadership," which has been derived from our work with companies. This theory suggests that a leadership team rather than a single individual is the key unit for planning and leading strategic changes.

The three chapters comprising Part I of the book together provide a set of theoretical constructs and tools, a template for the change management planning process, and a discussion of the leadership skills required for leading successful strategic and organizational change.

In Part II we examine a number of examples of the process of leading strategic and organizational change in a variety of actual companies. The selected companies differ widely in terms of their size, their geographic locations, and in terms of the types of strategic and organizational issues they are dealing with. We have intentionally selected examples of changes in organizations ranging in size from relatively small to giants, because the readers of this book will also inhabit organizations of varying sizes, and the problems differ according to size and complexity. For example, Countrywide Financial Corporation, IndyMac Bank, Infogix, and Tashman are all dealing with changes in strategy caused by environmental changes and opportunities; the nature of the change process is very different in each company, however, at least in part because of the organizations' different sizes and complexity.

We have also selected examples of companies dealing with a variety of organizational changes such as structural issues, performance management issues, and cultural issues. The case of Infogix, for example, deals with performance management issues. Pardee Homes is a case dealing with structural change in response to growth and additional strategic opportunities. The Tata Steel case deals with the role of cultural change as a strategy of adapting to the need for increasing competitiveness. Our intent is to demonstrate the nature of leading change with each type of issue.

While there is a primary focus on change in all the cases, these and other companies usually find themselves dealing with two or more aspects of change simultaneously. For example, they might be dealing with changes in strategic direction *and* changes in structure, or changes in strategic direction *and* the need to transform from entrepreneurship to professional management (organizational change). Dealing with these compound changes makes things more complex, but that is what happens in "the real world." As a result, we have several case examples of companies dealing with similar (but typically not identical) phenomena, and we can see the subtleties of how their approach differed.

Many of the case examples are companies in which the authors have personal experience as facilitators of the change efforts. Similarly, many of these companies have applied the strategic lens we present in chapter 3. We treat each of these examples as independent, self-contained "case studies" in Part II. We term this a "vertical" analysis.

Then, in Part III, we step back from the details of each of the case examples and do a "horizontal analysis" across all these case examples, in order to try and distill some common insights and lessons.

In chapter 13, the final chapter, our approach is to use the case studies as "data" so as to derive insights and lessons with respect to the leadership and management of strategic and organizational change. We examine the different but related aspects of the cases, including the catalyst for change, the overall purpose or objective of the change process, the type of change (including the focus and magnitude of change), and the duration of change. We also examine aspects of the barriers to change that are encountered. Finally, we identify – for researchers and scholars – areas for further investigation of the framework described in Part I.

Acknowledgments

Most of the cases that appear in Part II of this book are co-authored with members of the management of the companies or other researchers. The names of these individuals are shown in each chapter. These co-authors include: Stanford Kurland, formerly chief operating officer (COO) and currently a member of the board of directors of Countrywide Financial Corporation; Dr. N. G. Kannan, formerly Director (Marketing) Indian Oil Corporation Limited, and Ms. Rangapriya Kannan-Narasimhan, who co-authored the case on Indian Oil; Madhavan Nayar, founder and Company Leader of Infogix; Mr. B. Muthuraman, Managing Director, Tata Steel, and Shalini Lal, who co-authored the case on Tata Steel; and Michael McGee, chief executive officer (CEO) of Pardee Homes. In addition, we are also grateful to the following individuals for their support in developing cases on their companies: Rich Tashman, President and CEO, Stan Tashman, founder and Chairman, and Ty Olson, Senior Vice-president of Tashman and Associates; Michael Perry, CEO IndyMac Bank; and Frank Lowy and Peter Lowy, for the Westfield Group. Kathy Schreiner, Senior Associate Consultant, Management Systems Consulting Corporation, also provided assistance for the case on Tashman and Associates.

We are also indebted to Rangapriya Kannan-Narasimhan and Shalini Lal, both PhD students in the Anderson School of Management, UCLA, for their assistance in preparing the list of key references for additional reading on change management and leadership shown in the appendix.

An integrative framework for leading strategic and organizational change

There is a great deal of literature on change. Unfortunately, the literature is fragmented and requires both scholars and practitioners to create the connections. Part I of this book presents the key dimensions of a framework for leading strategic and organizational change. The proposed integrative framework is intended to be helpful as a context for understanding, planning, leading, and studying change. As shown in exhibit I.1, this framework consists of three levels and five components.

Level 1 consists of theoretical concepts/frameworks upon which a model for managing change can be built. This level has three components: (1) identifying the nature/type of change needed; (2) understanding the phases in the change process; (3) identifying ways to measure the outcome of change. In brief, the foundation of managing change is understanding the theory underlying the change management process. These three theoretical concepts are the focus of chapter 1. In this chapter we also present tools that can be used by leaders of change in applying these concepts in practice within their organizations. Taken together, the three components comprise a "theory of change" that we have found most relevant and of practical value in strategic and organizational change. Although there are other concepts and theories available, the ones presented here are the core ideas that we have actually used in our practice of change management.

Level 2 builds upon the "theory of change" and converts it to an actionable model in the form of a "strategic organizational development plan." Effective development and implementation of this plan can take an organization and its members from "where they are" to "where they want to be." In brief, this plan identifies the types of change needed, what needs to be done to move through the phases in the change process, and how results of the change effort will be measured. Chapter 2 presents a framework and approach for

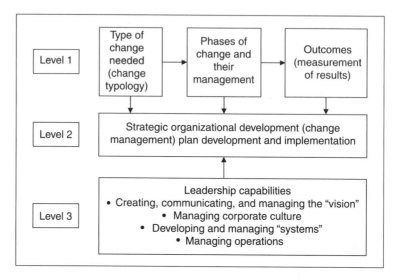

Exhibit I.1 Integrative framework for leading strategic and organizational change

developing and implementing change management plans – based upon an approach to building successful organizations that has been validated by recent empirical research.

Level 3 consists of the "change management" capabilities possessed by those who need to lead the change effort. These capabilities include: (1) creating, communicating, and managing the company's **vision**; (2) managing the company's **culture**; (3) developing the **systems** needed to support the change effort; and (4) designing, implementing, and effectively managing day-to-day **operations** in a way that supports the change effort. As explained in chapter 3, it is rare to find these four skills/ capabilities in a single individual. Hence, we suggest that successful change depends upon having a management team whose members possess these four skills. The absence of any one of these four skills will adversely affect the implementation of the change management plan (level 2) and, as a result, will affect the success of the change effort.

This section of the book, then, focuses upon each level of the framework:

- chapter 1: theoretical constructs and tools;
- chapter 2: the change management plan process; and

- chapter 3: the leadership skills/capabilities needed to support successful change.

Taken together, these three levels and their related components comprise an integrative framework for leading strategic and organizational change. It can be used as a lens to plan, lead, and evaluate the results of change programs – as will be illustrated in many of the case studies presented in Part II.

1 | *Understanding organizational change*

Clearly, there are vast differences in the types of change that organizations face and make. Some change is incremental, other change is substantial, and some is even transformational. Some change is strategic, while other change is operational or tactical. The need to change can be brought about by external factors (e.g., changes in customer preferences, changes in technology that make the company's existing products/services obsolete, changes in the regulatory environment, etc.), internal factors (e.g., the company's own growth, changes in technology, retiring leaders, etc.), or a combination of factors. While there are significant differences in the types of change that an organization might face, much of the existing literature about organizational change treats it homogeneously, as though "change is change is change." Given this approach and definition (that "all change is created equal"), strategies for managing change frequently focus on one versus many phenomena.

Regardless of the source or causes of change, all organizations are regularly faced with the need to do just that: change. The process of leading change successfully is not a trivial issue, however. It is fraught with difficulties, and sometimes the results are unsuccessful even for relatively small incremental changes.

The purpose of this book is to bring about a better understanding of the nature of change – offering a practical but theoretically sound guide to strategic and organizational change. It is intended for practicing leaders and managers as well as scholars. Its intent is to provide a framework for understanding, planning, and leading strategic and organizational change while simultaneously providing real-life examples of companies that have actually dealt with a variety of strategic and organizational change.

Purpose of this chapter

The specific purpose of this chapter is to present a framework for understanding and leading organizational change. This includes a typology of different aspects of change based upon the magnitude of change, types of change, and the organizational levels at which change is to be implemented. The chapter presents two different but complementary approaches to treating change as a process with defined phases. It also defines the nature of successful change and provides a set of criteria for it. Finally, it deals with the measurement of the results of change efforts.

Organizational change

This section examines the nature of organizational change. It provides a conceptual framework for understanding change as a prerequisite for the process of designing and leading change.

What is change?

There are many different definitions, but they all carry the connotation of "making something different in some particular way." The difference can be small (incremental) or radical (transformational). It can involve shifting from one (or the current/equilibrium) state or phase to another, which, in turn, results in a "transformation" or "transition." While change can result in a transformation, a transformation is different from change per se. Change involves anything that is different from the norm, while transformation involves a "metamorphosis" from one state to another. As a caterpillar grows, it changes; when it becomes a butterfly, however, a metamorphosis or transformation has occurred. This distinction is an important one when we turn, later in this chapter, to examining the typology of organizational change.

Why is change so difficult?

Within organizations, the ultimate target of change is behavior – whether the change itself involves a system, a process, or the company's structure. It moves people, their team, or their company from what is familiar and, in a very real sense, comfortable to that which is unfamiliar and uncomfortable. This discomfort leads people, teams, and organizations as a whole to resist rather than embrace change (although there are exceptions to this "rule").

There are a number of factors that can lead an organization either to resist or to embrace change. One factor consists of the values and norms (formed over a number of years) that influence the ways that people behave in the organization. In a very real sense, these values and norms can promote or detract from an organization's willingness to embrace change. Universities, for example, are comprised of the faculties, students, and administrative staffs who are there; but they are also influenced by the legions of past faculties, students, and administrators who have gone before. The culture of some universities supports change and innovation – in curricula, in student activities, in alumni relations, and other factors. In other universities – particularly those that have been successful for some time (measured in terms of rankings by various publications, the prestige of their alumni, donations/grants, academic awards, or other factors) – there may be resistance to change. In these institutions, faculty and administrators – who have spent their careers in the culture – may individually or collectively feel threatened by the change or feel that the change will adversely affect continued success.

Similarly, in business enterprises such as Hewlett-Packard, IBM, Wal-Mart, Ford, Johnson & Johnson ("J & J"), and Disney, the culture of the company – reflecting, in many cases, the people who founded the business – has an impact on what people believe and how they behave with respect to change. At 3M, for example, the culture of the company promotes change and innovation. Employees are encouraged to pursue their ideas for new products and, if successful, are rewarded for their efforts. One product that resulted from this focus on innovation was the Post-it note.

Another factor that can affect an organization's willingness to embrace change is the degree of success it has or is experiencing. Extended success tends to breed inertia, because it leads to a mindset of "don't rock the boat." For example, long-term success at Eastman Kodak, once a great company, led to a culture of avoiding hasty action. While this seems reasonable on the face of it, it became a formidable barrier to innovation, and Kodak avoided acting hastily while competitors innovated with instant photography, 36mm cameras, and VCRs.

A third factor that can contribute to organizational resistance to change is the level of investment made in existing systems, even if they are not functioning effectively. It promotes the belief that "it will cost us too much to change." As a result, companies will continue using computer systems, accounting systems, planning systems, etc. that do not meet their needs simply because of the costs and risks of change. This is, of course, not entirely irrational. There is much invested in existing knowledge and a degree of comfort with existing operations, systems, processes, etc. Unwillingness to change these systems can severely hamper a company's ability to continue its growth and success, however. For example, when it was a start-up, a $50 million manufacturer had purchased a computer system/platform that was considered state-of-the-art. Over a period of five years, however, this system became outdated to the point where there were very few IT professionals or programmers who possessed the expertise to use it effectively. Instead of replacing the system with one that was more generally accepted, the company spent time and resources finding IT professionals who possessed the knowledge needed to keep the existing system working. The false belief was that it would cost more to replace the system than to hire people to "fix it."

A less rational reason for resistance to change is a corporate culture that promotes fear of failure, hypercriticism, and even arrogance. There are many examples of companies that have unintentionally created cultures with these characteristics – making change extremely difficult. For example, one large entertainment company was described by insiders as a "one-mistake company." The belief was that any mistake – even if made in the context of trying to improve per-formance – would result in termination. As a result, ideas were seldom challenged, new ideas were seldom offered, and employees basically did what they were told to do (because, if a mistake was made in this case, they could blame their manager).

Resistance to change can exist not just at the corporate level but also at the group and individual levels. For example, while IBM as a whole understood the competitive threat of microcomputers (PCs), the company found it difficult to adapt to change. In part, the problem was the mindset of people and the overall culture that existed in the mainframe division. This division – and, to a certain extent, the company as a whole – believed that IBM was, and should continue to be, in the "Big Iron" business: that is, it should continue to focus on producing large mainframe computers. The division did not embrace the need for the company to transform itself and this led to a decade of turmoil, a change in leadership at the top, and the departure/ termination of more than 250,000 workers before the dust had settled with a "new" IBM under the leadership of an outsider (Louis Gerstner).

One of the barriers to change at the group level is what Irving Janis has termed "groupthink,"[1] or the tendency of a group to develop a common mindset that is not open to outside ideas or influences. This was thought to be a cause of the Challenger disaster (January 28, 1986), where the group involved in the launch decision was so invested in its decision that it could not be changed even by members of the group. This is why an "outside" leader is often needed to serve as a catalyst for change. It is interesting to note that Louis Gerstner, who came from RJR Nabisco and whose knowledge of "chips" was probably limited initially to potato snacks, was capable of the revitalization of IBM, while other leaders from inside the company could not achieve this.

Ultimately, the behavior of individuals is a critical ingredient in any organizational change. If people cannot be persuaded to change their behavior they will resist, either actively or passively. Individual barriers to change include fear, apathy and indifference, loss of control, and personal vulnerability. The typical individual, group and organizational barriers to change are summarized in exhibit 1.1.

Proactive and reactive change

Another aspect to change that is significant concerns whether the strategic or organizational change that occurs is a proactive or a reactive response to something in the environment or the organizational situation. Some of the changes described in the cases in this book are proactive while others are reactive.

"Proactive change" can be defined as a change initiated by an organization as a result of its assessment of the anticipated future environment or organizational situation. It is an opportunistic change, in which the organization wants to create a strategic advantage because of something present or anticipated in the environment. For example, as discussed in chapter 5, Howard Schultz at Starbucks

---

[1] See Janis, I. L., 1972, *Groupthink: Psychological Studies of Policy Decisions and Fiascoes*, Boston, Houghton Mifflin.

Organizational barriers

- Extended success, which breeds inertia
- Investments made in existing systems, even if they
  are not functioning effectively ("It will cost us too much
  to change")
- Knowledge and comfort with existing operations,
  systems, processes, etc.
- A corporate culture that promotes:
  - o fear of failure
  - o hypercriticism
  - o arrogance

Group barriers

- A culture of "we" versus "them" (that is, functional silos)
- Knowledge and comfort with existing operations, systems,
  processes, etc.
- Groupthink ("We have been successful in the past and
  this will continue")

Individual barriers

- Fear
- Apathy and indifference
- Loss of control
- Personal vulnerability

Exhibit 1.1 Barriers to change that lead to resistance

perceived the opportunity to create an American version of the classic Italian coffee bar, and set up Starbucks in order to achieve that vision. Similarly, Madhavan Nayar, founder and Company Leader of Infogix, perceived the need for a new paradigm of "information integrity" (as described in chapter 9), and took steps to position his company for this emerging opportunity.

"Reactive change" can be defined as responses to changes in the environment or organizational situation that have already occurred, rather than those that are anticipated in the future. For example, if the company has already experienced increased competition, such as Indian Oil Corporation and Tata Steel, it will need to react to this change. Similarly, Tashman and Associates, a relatively small entrepreneurial firm, needed to respond to the changing dynamics of its industry and the behavior of a major customer (Home Depot), as examined in chapter 7.

A typology for change

A first step in managing change is to understand what **type** of change is needed. Change in organizations can be classified according to three factors – which, in a very real sense, form a typology of organizational change:

- magnitude of change – incremental to "transformational";
- focus of change – strategic or operational; and
- level of change – individual, group, or organizational.

These factors are examined, in turn, below.

Magnitude (scale) of change

The first dimension of the organizational change typology is the magnitude or scale of change. This scale of change can be viewed in terms of three levels: *incremental*, *major*, and *transformational* change.[2]

Incremental changes are small changes that are sometimes barely noticeable. They are not material or significant. Operationally defined, incremental changes are changes involving less than 5 percent of existing operations (content). Examples of incremental changes include:

- changing a product formula in such a way that customers would notice no difference (e.g., Neutrogena changes the formula for one of its shampoo products – adding more aloe);
- outsourcing a function such as payroll (provided it doesn't lead to a large layoff of personnel); and
- changing the format (not content) of written documents (such as policies and procedures or job descriptions).

Major changes are substantial changes in the organization, its operations, etc. Operationally defined, these changes involve greater

---

[2] A version of this typology of change has actually been used by Johnson & Johnson to monitor and motivate its business units to enhance product innovation.

than 10 percent of the content of the change. Examples of major changes include:

- creating a new product line through either internal development or acquisition that boosts revenues by more than ten percent;
- revising job descriptions to reflect changes that have occurred in the organization through growth;
- converting to a new computer platform;
- adding a new location (warehouse, store, etc.) to an existing operation;
- bringing in a new member of the executive team; and
- changing organizational structure.

For example, a change in company structure from a functional one to a divisional or matrix structure will undoubtedly be a major change. A case study of this type of change is presented in chapter 10.

As suggested earlier, transformational change is change in "kind." Operationally, transformational change involves or approaches 100 percent of the content of the change. When an organization adds a product line it involves change, but not necessarily transformation. When it changes the basic concept of its business, a transformation is likely to be involved. For example, if PepsiCo acquires another beverage such as "Gatorade" it is still a beverage company; but when it acquires Frito-Lay it transforms into a "snack food company" from a beverage business. Similarly, if Starbucks adds a coffee-flavored cold drink such as Frappuccino to its menu it is still a "café" business; but when it begins to sell coffee through the grocery channel it is transforming itself from a retail business into a "coffee business."

A special type of transformational change occurs when an organization makes the change from an entrepreneurship to a "professionally managed" firm. This typically occurs in response to a significant change in organizational size, and involves developing the management systems and culture required to operate a larger, more complex company. This will also involve the development of management systems such as planning, organizational structure, management development, and performance management. We shall examine a number of examples of companies that have engaged in this type of transformation in this book, including Countrywide Financial Corporation (chapter 4), Starbucks (chapter 5), Pardee Homes (chapter 10), and Westfield (chapter 12).

Johnson & Johnson, the leading health care organization, uses this aspect of the typology for monitoring purposes and to motivate its constituent companies to enhance innovation. In the mid-1990s J & J asked all its operating units to prepare a report on the sales revenues that had originated from product innovations during the past three years. These increases were to be further classified as deriving from (1) incremental innovations, (2) major innovations, and (3) transformational innovations in new products. Examples were provided for each category.

Although all J & J did was to ask for the data, the message to the organization was clear: senior leadership now wanted its companies to focus on major and transformational product innovations. Further, the extent to which a company effectively developed and launched innovative products would be an important criterion for evaluating performance. This led to significant strategic changes in one J & J company, Neutrogena. Under the leadership of the CEO, Jeff Nugent, Neutrogena reexamined its business and made the strategic decision to broaden the company's business concept and launch a cosmetics business. Although this was a stretch for the Neutrogena brand, and it was considered a transformational strategic change, it was successful and resulted in a doubling of the company's revenues and a quadrupling of its profits.

Focus of change

The second dimension of the organizational change typology is the focus of change – *strategic* or *operational*. Strategic change involves a shift of direction or vision. Operational change involves anything affecting day-to-day operations. When PepsiCo divested its restaurant business – which included KFC (Kentucky Fried Chicken), Pizza Hut, and California Pizza Kitchen – it was a strategic change designed to enable the company to focus on its beverage and snack food businesses. When Taco Bell redesigned its stores to provide more space for customers and provide many of the ingredients of its menu in prepackaged form rather than made to order, it was an operational change. The example of Neutrogena's launch of cosmetics was, of course, a combination of both strategic and operational changes requiring different products, different manufacturing techniques, and different distribution and advertising.

We shall examine two different examples of this type of change in the case of Westfield (chapter 12). Westfield, which is today one of the two largest shopping center companies in the world and the largest global player, engaged in a change strategy to diversify into a different business (media) from shopping centers. This diversification was ultimately unsuccessful. It also engaged in strategic diversification from its roots as an Australian company to become a global enterprise. This diversification was ultimately successful.

Organizational level of change

The third dimension of the organizational change typology is the level of the change process – *individual, team/unit,* or *organization* as a whole. The targets for this dimension of change are behavior, skills, knowledge, and/or attitudes. Although the three levels are related, changes affecting each require different strategies and tactics, and ought to be viewed independently. In addition, this dimension of change can also act like a "waterfall." What is meant by this is that, if the target of change is the organization as a whole, the change effort will frequently "waterfall" down to the teams/units that make up the larger entity, and down to the individuals who make up the team/unit. If the target of change is the team/unit, the change effort will frequently waterfall down to the individuals who make up the team/unit.

Examples of individual change efforts include:

- one-on-one coaching provided to executives; and
- on-the-job training or mentoring.

Examples of group change efforts include:

- team building;
- team/unit policy/procedure changes;
- team training; and
- implementation of new team/unit systems.

Examples of organizational change efforts include:

- implementation of new company-wide systems/processes (e.g., planning, management development); and
- formal corporate culture management efforts.

Bringing the three factors together: the change typology matrix

Exhibit 1.2 presents a matrix that can be used to identify the type of change being focused upon within an organization. This matrix combines the three dimensions – magnitude (scale), focus of change (strategic or operational), and level of change (individual, team/unit, and/or organizational) – just discussed.

This matrix can be used by leaders in planning for and effectively implementing change. In brief, the matrix can help leaders identify the level, magnitude, and focus of their change efforts. It can also be used as a tool to communicate the scope and direction of the change program undertaken at a company. Since change is unsettling to people, anything that can help them understand the changes taking place can be useful in reducing anxiety, and possibly in reducing resistance to change as well.

Using the change typology: the case of AMEX[3]

This section uses American Express (AMEX) as a case example to illustrate how to use this matrix. This is shown in Exhibit 1.3 and explained below. Although the matrix was not actually used at American Express, it might have been a useful tool to plan and communicate the nature of the changes undertaken.

When Harvey Golub assumed leadership of American Express in 1991, he was faced with the need to make major changes. Brought about by both internal and external challenges, these included:

- increased competition from other card companies, such as MasterCard and Visa, which was leading to a loss of market share;
- erosion in the company's core business – the number of active American Express cards was decreasing; and
- problems in accounts receivable – 11 percent of the company's portfolio had to be written off as bad debts.

To overcome these problems, Golub led American Express through a number of changes in several phases. The changes that occurred illustrate all types of changes included in the change typology presented above, as seen in exhibit 1.3.

[3] See Harvard Business School Case no. 396212, "Harvey Golub: recharging American Express," 1996.

Magnitude of change	Focus of change	
	Strategic	Operational
Transformational • Organizational • Team/unit • Individual		
Major • Organizational • Team/unit • Individual		
Incremental • Organizational • Team/unit • Individual		

Exhibit 1.2 Change typology matrix

	Operational	Strategic
Transformational	Move to web-based transactions	Change from a "financial supermarket" business concept to a strategy of leveraging the AMEX brand as core focus
Major	Reduce operating costs by $1 billion	Spin off non-core business operations
Incremental	Specific areas of cost reduction	Add new credit card types

Exhibit 1.3 Change at American Express

At AMEX, the target for all the changes was the company as a whole. The technical objective of the changes during phase 1 was cost control. The strategic purpose was getting the American Express "house in order," stopping the "bleeding," and stabilizing the company. The specific objective was to reduce operating costs by $1 billion – the equivalent of a 100 basis point spread between American Express and bank card merchant fees. Golub articulated the goal, but did not tell people where to make the cuts. The changes made to achieve this were largely operational in nature, and the change was major in scope.

As a result of this change initiative, Golub reduced the cost of the Travel Related Services Division (the core AMEX business unit) by $1 billion. He also succeeded in sending a message throughout American Express that change was necessary and possible.

The second phase of the change process led by Golub was transformational in magnitude. It involved redefining the company's strategic direction. Golub mandated that the core strategy of the company would be to leverage the AMEX brand; he viewed the brand as the company's biggest asset. Given this brand focus, Golub made decisions to spin off non-core businesses. This was a major change. As a result, he moved the company away from the concept of being a "financial supermarket" that had been articulated and pursued by his predecessor, James Robinson – a transformational change.

In addition to this transformational change in the strategic direction of American Express, Golub made some other major and transformational changes as phase 2. For example, he made major changes in the culture at American Express. He changed the culture from a "debating society," where people scored points for raising ideas, to one where ideas were examined critically and in depth. If people took one point of view on an issue such as whether fees on American Express cards should be reduced, Golub might well take the opposite viewpoint (i.e., perhaps fees ought to be raised) to make sure that the reasoning was sound. Golub also emphasized the role that the Internet would play in American Express's business, and launched initiatives to explore how the company could change the way it did business using the Internet. This move of AMEX to web-based transactions was transformational. Moreover, to convey the message of how important the Internet initiative was, he became personally involved in the effort.

Golub also made other incremental but significant changes. He targeted specific areas of additional cost reduction. He also added new credit card types as part of the brand extension.

These changes were important not only in themselves but as a means to support the larger aim of changing strategic direction and the organizational culture at American Express.

Compound change

One of the things seen in this example at American Express is that the change is what might be termed a "compound change," or multi-dimensional change, rather than a simple or single-dimension change. American Express was engaged in a number of different types of changes simultaneously. They were engaged in changing their vision, reducing operating costs, introducing new products, and changing operations (i.e., web-based transactions). As seen in exhibit 1.3, the changes at AMEX were complex and significant. The change matrix could have been used during the change process as a communications tool to help people understand the magnitude and direction of the changes in progress. In addition, the process of planning the changes at American Express was somewhat ad hoc, and the change matrix could have been used as a tool to structure the plan for the changes.

Some of the changes at American Express occurred in phases, while others occurred simultaneously. We deal with the notion of phases in the change process in the next section.

Phases in the change process

Just as there are several dimensions (identified in the last section) that should be considered in identifying what type of changes are required, there are also distinct phases in the change process. This section presents and describes two different views of change as a process. The first was developed by Kurt Lewin,[4] who envisioned a three-phase process. The second is proposed by the current authors, who envision

---

[4] See Lewin, K., 1947, "Frontiers in group dynamics 1. concept, method, and reality in social science: social equilibria and social change," *Human Relations*, 1, 5–41.

Lewin's phases of change	Management Systems' phases of change
(1) Unfreezing • Surfacing unmet organizational needs, unanswered opportunities • Developing the need for change	**(1) Planning** • Identifying "where we are" (need for change, barriers to change, etc.) • Identifying "where we want to or need to be" (the goal of the change process) • Developing a plan to move from where we are to where we want to or need to be (that is, the steps that will be taken to make the overall "goal" of the change process a reality)
(2) Moving • Activities to support the change(s) including communicating the change and reinforcing the change through rewards and recognition	**(2) Getting started** • Beginning to implement the plan (developed in phase 1) **(3) Letting go** • Letting go of the "old ways" of doing things and embracing the change (as identified in the plan) • Monitoring progress against the plan and making adjustments, as needed (e.g., to overcome resistance to the plan)
(3) Refreezing • Stabilizing the change and beginning to plan for the next round of change(s)	**(4) Completion** • Completing the change and beginning to plan for the next

Exhibit 1.4 Two models of the organizational change process

a four-phase process. As we shall see, the two views of the change process are complementary.

Kurt Lewin's paradigm of organizational change

As shown in exhibit 1.4, Lewin's model of organizational change consists of three phases: (1) unfreezing, (2) moving, and (3) refreezing.

Recognizing that resistance to change exists, Lewin proposed that the first step in the process of change is "unfreezing" old behaviors. Under this view behavior is set or frozen, and for change to occur it must be unfrozen. Once this has occurred, then change per se can occur. This is the second phase, but it cannot occur unless the old behavior is unfrozen. The final phase is to "refreeze" the "new" behavior and have it become the new norm.

We accept the model of change proposed by Lewin as a valid conceptual model of change. We have developed an alternative model, however, which adds specificity to our understanding of the change process and, in turn, might make it more useful for application in organizations.

The Management Systems model

We have developed an alternative model for leading change, based upon our experience in working with companies for over thirty years. Our alternative model (the Management Systems model) proposes that change occurs in four, rather than three phases: (1) planning, (2) getting started, (3) letting go, and (4) completion.[5] Consistent with our orientation toward practical management theory, our model is intended to help leaders plan the operational aspects of the change process, rather than just deal with it conceptually. These four phases are defined below.

Phase 1: planning
This involves several stages.

- Identifying the need for change (including the underlying factors that are contributing to the need for change).
- Identifying potential barriers to change that must be managed in the change process.
- Identifying the "type" of change required (using the typology of change presented earlier in this chapter).
- Developing a plan (typically a written plan) to move the organization, team, and/or individual from the current state to

---

[5] Management Systems Consulting Corporation is our organizational development firm, and this model is thereby called the "Management Systems model."

the "new" state. This plan should define the overall goal of the change process, identify specific action steps to be taken to achieve this goal, and specify who is responsible for completing each step.

Phase 2: getting started
This involves beginning to implement the change management plan. Simply having a plan is not enough. For the change to become a reality, those involved in the change process need to begin working to complete their "action steps." The leader of the change process needs to create enthusiasm for the change and hold people accountable for results.

Phase 3: letting go
This is the most difficult phase in the change process, because it is the phase when the organization, team, and/or individual must "give up" the old ways of doing things and embrace the new ways that represent **the change**. Leaders need to recognize that this is a very "emotionally loaded" phase and that these emotions need to be managed as a part of the change process. It is in this phase that strategies for managing resistance to change become very important. Leaders need to identify the sources of resistance and manage them as a part of the overall change management plan.

During this phase there needs to be continued monitoring of the extent to which overall and supporting goals in the change management plan are being achieved. When problems arise – typically resulting in resistance to change – the leader(s) of the change process need(s) to take steps to address them. In other words, during this phase there needs to be sustained monitoring of performance against the plan.

Phase 4: completion
A change is completed when the goal of the change process (identified in phase 1) has been achieved. The assessment of whether the change has or has not been successful is evaluated based on the goals outlined in the plan – created in phase 1. In brief, phase 4 occurs when the organization, team, and/or individual has moved to the "new state" and that state is now the norm.

We have found that this model is more operational than the Lewin model – in part because it involves developing, implementing, and monitoring performance against a more formal (typically written) change management "plan." This plan should identify the target of change, the overall goal of the change process, and the steps that need to be taken to make this goal a reality. The plan provides the basis for those involved in implementing the change – that is, the leaders of the change process – to continually evaluate the progress being made and to take steps to increase the likely success of the change management process. It also provides the basis for evaluating, once the plan has been completed, the success of the change management process.

In brief, the Management Systems model of the change process provides an operational template for planning the specific phases of change. This can be useful as a tool for dealing with a process as complex as change management.

Exhibit 1.4 shows a comparison of both models and their relationship to one another. In brief, the Lewin model explains what is necessary to move from the current to the desired state, while the Management Systems model provides a more operational template for executing the change process.

The bottom line: the nature of successful change

So far, we have examined the nature of change and the change process. How do we know when the change has been successful, however? This section presents some criteria for assessing the success of change efforts.

Criteria for successful change

For the change to be truly successful – at the highest level – it needs to meet at least four criteria:

- the organization has moved from the current to the desired state;
- the functioning of the organization in the desired state meets expectations (i.e., it works as planned);
- the transition is accomplished without undue cost to the organization; and
- the transition is accomplished without undue cost to individuals in the organization.

One of the simplest criteria for assessing the success of change is whether there has been a movement from the current to the desired state. For example, if we aimed to introduce a new customer service practice, has it happened? The extent to which this criterion has been met can be assessed by comparing the goal of the change process with the actual results achieved.

Another criterion is whether the change has met expectations. For example, if the new customer service practice has been implemented (that is, it meets the first criterion), is it actually producing the desired results (e.g., fewer customer complaints, higher customer service ratings, etc.)? There can be situations in which the overall goal of the change process has been implemented but the results it is producing are less than optimal.

The remaining two criteria relate to the cost of the change to the organization and its members. For example, the new customer service system may have been effectively implemented and it may be producing the desired results, but if the system is resulting in higher costs without the accompanying higher benefits it may not be successful. In addition, if the new system – for whatever reason – is resulting in turnover of key employees (e.g., because of declining satisfaction or morale), the cost associated with the change may result in its being classified as not highly successful.

If these are the four key criteria that should be used to measure the success of a change, then time needs to be devoted during phase I of the change process to identifying ways to measure performance against each of them. We deal with the process of planning strategic and organizational changes in the next chapter. Issues related to measuring performance against these criteria are discussed below.

Measuring the results of change

The measurement of results can be a powerful tool in a change program. It can be used to assess the results of the current change effort while at the same time facilitating further change. In order to assess the results of a change program, we need to measure the changes that occur. The tools to measure change can vary from the simple to the very sophisticated.

Changes can be measured in quantitative terms at different levels of measurement or in monetary terms. The most powerful measurement level is monetary measurement, because it has relevance to the "bottom line" of business. When measurement in monetary terms is not feasible, however, other forms (or levels) of measurement can be used as a tool to measure the results of changes. The principal levels of measurement that can be used are: nominal, ordinal, interval, and ratio.

Nominal changes are changes in classification. For example, we can "measure" whether a program to train people was done by answering "yes" or "no." Yes, it happened, or no, it did not. We can also measure nominally by counting. For example, how many people graduated from a program to train people as "black belts" in quality improvement programs? Ordinal measurement involves assigning numerals to indicate rank order. We can use ordinal measurement to rank change programs in terms of their perceived impact upon organizational productivity. Interval measurement involves the assignment of numbers to indicate the degree of improvement. A classic "Likert scale" can be used to assess improvement from change efforts. For example, in response to the question "To what extent did the change program have the desired results?" the answers may be (1) "To a very slight extent," (2) "To a slight extent," (3) "To some extent," (4) "To a great extent," or (5) "To a very great extent." These responses are "coded" 1 to 5 and achieve an interval level of measurement.

We can use ratio measurement if it is possible to assign an empirically meaningful "zero" to the change program. This means that the program had no, or zero, impact. All monetary measurement achieves a ratio level of measurement. When we measure the monetary impact of a training program, for example, a zero impact is possible. A change program designed to impact employee turnover can also have a zero, or no, impact.

Measuring the results of a change program can be a powerful tool to facilitate further change. This can be seen in the case of American Express cited above, where Harvey Golub invested a great deal of effort in measuring the results of the change process. He set up an elaborate and relatively sophisticated process of tracking and measuring the results of the changes. He was able to show that there had been a reduction of $1 billion in operating costs, the equivalent of a 100 basis point spread between American Express card fees and the fees charged by bank card merchants. This was a powerful measurement of the effectiveness of the results of the change process he had led. It would also be possible to "measure" the effects of the transformation from the old business concept of a "financial supermarket" under Jim Robinson to the new concept of a company based upon the core American Express brand by "counting" the spin-offs (divestitures) of companies that did not fit the new business concept.

Some sophisticated instruments have been developed and validated for use with organizational change programs. For example, in our consulting firm we have developed several measurement tools to assess the effects of individual and organizational changes. These include the Growing Pains Survey© and the Organizational Effectiveness Survey©.[6] We have used these measurement tools to assess the impact of organizational change programs for more than a decade. These tools were used in some of the case studies presented in Part II of this book.

Summary

This chapter has presented a framework or "lens" that leaders of change can use to understand and manage the change process. The framework includes a typology of different aspects of change based upon the magnitude of change, focus of change, and the organizational levels that are the target of change. We have also presented two different, but complementary, approaches to treating change as a process with defined phases. It identifies some of the most common barriers that must be overcome by those who are the leaders of change. It also defines the conditions for effective or successful change and provides a set of criteria for it. Finally, we have examined the issue of measuring change.

Ultimately, change is created through a process of leadership in organizations. This involves the planning and execution of change programs. Building upon the concepts presented in this chapter, the next chapter presents an approach to planning for and implementing change.

---

[6] For a discussion of the Growing Pains Survey©, see Kannan-Narasimhan, R., and E. G. Flamholtz, 2006, "Growing pains: a barrier to successful corporate entrepreneurship," *Silicon Valley Review of Global Entrepreneurship Research*, 2(1), 4–24.

2 | *A framework for planning strategic and organizational change*

Introduction

In chapter 1 we defined change, identified common barriers to change, and presented a typology for classifying the target of change. We also described the phases in the change process. This chapter builds upon these constructs to create a framework or "lens" for developing an effective change management plan. We first present the framework and then describe how to use this framework in planning for and successfully implementing the change process. We also summarize some of the empirical research that has been done and assess its validity and usefulness in an appendix.

This framework is presented for two major reasons. First and foremost, it can be used to plan and lead strategic and organizational change. It is also important as a perspective for this book, however, because most of the case analyses of actual change efforts described in subsequent chapters are from companies that have used this framework.

Key components of the framework

The framework for planning and implementing change is based on an organizational effectiveness (or success factors) model. Derived from a combination of empirical research and "clinical" experience in working with organizations, this model identifies the key factors upon which an organization needs to focus in order to maximize long-term success. Hence, these are the factors that an organization and its management need to focus upon in the context of planning for and implementing change.

The basic premise underlying this framework is that all economic enterprises (whether for- or not-for-profit) are comprised of two

26

things: (1) a "business foundation" and (2) a set of six key "strategic building blocks" of organizations. These two components need to be effectively designed and managed – both as organizations grow and develop and, more importantly for the purpose of this book, as organizations plan for and implement change. The nature of the business foundation and the six key strategic building blocks are described below. In the next section we describe the role that each of these components can and should play in the change process.

The business foundation

A "business foundation" consists of three key dimensions: (1) a "business concept or definition," (2) a "core strategy," and (3) a "strategic mission." Each of these constructs is defined below.

Business concept

A business concept defines what the overall purpose of the business is. It answers the question "What are we?" It defines the space that an organization seeks to occupy as a player in a market.

It is a fundamentally important strategic concept, because it gives focus to what the organization is – in a sense, defining for employees what the boundaries are within which the business will operate. It is not necessarily an easy concept to articulate. For example, is Starbucks in the "coffee" business, the "specialty retail business," or the "café" business? The appropriate answer to this question is strategic rather than descriptive. This means that the answer is a decision, not just a description, requiring that management spend time thinking about the opportunities and threats presented by the market in which the organization operates, identifying the organization's internal strengths and weaknesses, and then deciding how best to define the business so as to maximize results.

From a strategic standpoint, a business definition needs to avoid being either too broad or too narrow. If it is too broad, it has no strategic value. For example, to say that AT&T is in the "telephone business" has little or no strategic value. If it is too narrow it will be unduly restrictive. The classic example of this was the US railroads at the end of the nineteenth century, when most companies defined themselves as being in the railroad business as opposed to the transportation business.

Core strategy

A core strategy is the central or core theme around which the organization plans to compete to achieve its strategic mission. To maximize effectiveness, the core strategy should build upon those factors that truly differentiate the organization from its competitors – that is, upon those things that make it unique. For example, an organization might choose to compete on price with the desire to become the low-cost producer, or on quality with the desire to be the provider of the highest-quality product. Organizations can also build their core strategy around the quality of their sales force, the effectiveness of their planning process, or the strength of their company's culture.

Strategic mission

A strategic mission broadly defines what an organization wants to achieve over the long term (three to five years out). The strategic mission provides a sense of direction for decisions and actions. Ideally, a strategic mission should be capable of being stated in both qualitative and quantitative terms. In other words, ideally, the strategic mission should have a component that is measurable. This is important because the organization, its management, and its employees need to be able to assess the progress they are making and whether or not they are achieving desired results. For example, the (qualitative) strategic mission of Starbucks for the period from 1994 to 2000 was to become the "leading brand of specialty coffee in the United States by the year 2000." Quantitatively, it was to achieve $2 billion in revenues and more than 2,000 locations by the end of fiscal year 2000; or, as it was stated internally, "$2 billion + 2000 = 2000."

Six key strategic building blocks

The second component of this model (which should build upon the first) consists of six key "strategic building blocks" of strategic organizational development. The six building blocks of strategic organizational development, all of which have been supported by previous research, are:

(1) the identification and definition of a viable market segment and creation of a "niche," if possible;[1]

---

[1] As explained below, the term "niche" is used here in its ecological sense of a place in the environment where an organism has created a protected place.

(2) the development of products or services for the chosen market segment/niche;
(3) the acquisition and development of the resources required to operate the firm, and to facilitate growth;
(4) the development of the day-to-day operational systems required to operate the organization;
(5) the development of the management systems necessary for the long-term functioning of the organization; and
(6) the development and management of the organizational culture that leadership believes is necessary to guide the firm.

Each of these key tasks is now discussed in detail below.

Identification of market segment and niche

The first building block involves identifying a market need for a service or product.[2] This involves identifying the customers that the organization wants to serve and the customer needs that the organization wants to meet through the products and/or services that it offers or will offer. The chances of organizational success are enhanced to the extent that the organization is successful in this step.[3]

The challenge is not merely to identify the market but also, if possible, to identify and capture a "market niche." A market niche is a place within the market that the organization "controls," based on the sustainable competitive advantages it possesses. The term "niche" is being used here in its ecological sense. It does not necessarily refer to a small space, though it sometimes has that connotation. A true niche can be a very large space. For example, Microsoft has created a niche in this sense with its software for desktop PCs. It has a "virtual," if not legal, monopoly.[4]

---

[2] Aldrich, H. E., 1979, *Organization and Environment*, Englewood Cliffs, NJ, Prentice-Hill; Brittain, J. W., and J. Freeman, 1980, "Organizational proliferation and density-dependent selection," in J. R. Kimberly, R. H. Miles, and associates (eds.), *The Organizational Life Cycle: Issues in the Creation, Transformation and Decline of Organizations*, San Francisco, Jossey-Bass, 291–338; Freeman, J., and M. T. Hannan, 1983, "The liability of newness: age dependence in organizational death rates," *American Sociological Review*, 48, 692–710.

[3] Flamholtz, E. G., 1995, "Managing organizational transitions: implications for corporate and human resource management," *European Management Journal*, 13, 1, 39–51.

[4] Microsoft's virtual monopoly is not illegal, but is simply not awarded by legislative charter, having instead been created through competition.

Identifying the market in which an organization is or should be competing involves developing a strategic market plan. This includes clearly identifying present and potential customers and their needs, and, using this information, creating a competitive strategy.[5]

Development of products and services

The second strategic building block involves the development of products and/or services to meet present and potential customer needs.[6] This process can also be called "productization," which refers to the process of analyzing the needs of customers in the target market, designing the product, developing the ability to produce it, and identifying how it will be distributed to its designated customers.[7] For a production firm this involves product design, the development of effective manufacturing processes, and distribution systems. For service firms, this involves identifying the services to be provided and creating the system through which customers will be provided with these services.[8]

Successfully developing products/services is highly related to the previous critical task, proper definition of the market niche.[9] Unless a firm fully understands the needs of the market, it cannot satisfy those needs in productization.

The output of this task is to demonstrate "proof of concept." This means that the organization can create and provide a product or service that will be acceptable to a set of customers who will pay for it. This is not a trivial issue, and the failure to do this led to the dot.com debacle of the early part of this decade. Although it would seem obvious, it was clearly not recognized that a company cannot "produce" a product or service and sell it at a price less than incremental cost. This operating margin loss cannot be made up with volume!

[5] Flamholtz, "Managing organizational transitions."
[6] Burns, T., and G. M. Stalker, 1961, *The Management of Innovation*, London, Tavistock; Midgley, D. F., 1981, "Toward a theory of the product life cycle: explaining diversity," *Journal of Marketing*, 45, 109–15.
[7] Flamholtz, E. G., and Y. Randle, 2007, *Growing Pains: Transitioning from an Entrepreneurship to a Professionally Managed Firm*, San Francisco, Jossey-Bass.
[8] Flamholtz and Randle, *Growing Pains*.
[9] Flamholtz, "Managing organizational transitions."

Acquiring resources

The third strategic building block consists of the resources – human, technological, physical (e.g., facilities), and financial – that an organization has and can acquire to support its continuing operations and growth.[10] Success in identifying a market niche and in productization will create increased demand for a company's products or services. Consequently, the company's resources will be spread very thin.[11] The organization will require additional physical, technological, financial, and human resources. Further, the type of resources required to support effective operations may change over time as the organization grows. For example, as the company grows, it may need people with different skills from those possessed by current employees, it may need to upgrade its computer system, and it may need more or different types of facilities. Management, then, needs to focus an appropriate amount of attention on identifying, acquiring, and effectively managing company resources.[12]

In building Starbucks, for example, financial resources were necessary to scale up operations and take advantage of market opportunities. Scale-up meant adding a roasting plant, investing in information systems, hiring people ahead of the growth curve, and acquiring real estate leases. Thus it is fair to say "No bucks, no Starbucks!" – or at least a much smaller version of the company.

Development of operational systems

The fourth building block involves developing systems to support effective and efficient day-to-day operations. These "operational systems" include accounting, billing, collections, advertising, personnel recruiting and training, sales, marketing, production, delivery, customer service, and related systems.[13] As small organizations grow and change, they quickly tend to outgrow the administrative systems available to operate them. Therefore, it is necessary to develop

---

[10] Pfeffer, J., and G. R. Salancik, 1978, *The External Control of Organizations: A Resource Dependence Perspective*, New York, Harper & Row; Brittain and Freeman, "Organizational Proliferation;" Carroll, G. R., and P. H. Yangchung, 1986, "Organizational task and institutional environments in ecological perspective: findings from the local newspaper industry," *American Journal of Sociology*, 91, 838–73.

[11] Flamholtz, "Managing organizational transitions."

[12] Flamholtz and Randle, *Growing Pains*.

[13] Flamholtz, "Managing organizational transitions."

effective operational systems, on time, in order to build a successful organization.[14] In contrast, large established companies sometimes have overly complicated operational systems. In this case, the success of the organization depends on the reengineering of operational systems.[15]

Development of management systems

The fifth building block involves creating and effectively managing the "management systems" that will support the long-term development of the organization.[16] Management systems include systems for planning, organization, management development and control.

The "planning system" includes:

- the process an organization uses to plan for its overall development;
- the product developed as the outcome of this process (that is, the "plan");
- how the plan is communicated to the organization's members;
- how the plan is translated into "action;"
- how performance against the plan is monitored; and
- the company's budgeting system – including how the budget is prepared and how the budget is monitored.

In brief, the planning system includes strategic planning, operational planning, and contingency planning.[17] The mere existence of planning activities does not indicate that the organization has a planning system. A planning system ensures that planning activities are strategic and ongoing.

We shall review the role of planning systems in facilitating strategic and operational changes through this book.

---

[14] Starbuck, W. H., 1965, "Organizational growth and development," in J. G. March (ed.), *Handbook of Organizations*, Chicago, Rand McNally, 451–533.

[15] Flamholtz, "Managing organizational transitions."

[16] Child, J., and A. Keiser, 1981, "Development of organizations over time," in P. C. Nystrom and W. H. Starbuck (eds.), *Handbook of Organizations: Adapting Organizations to Their Environments*, New York, Oxford University Press, 28–64; Tushman, M. L., B. Virany, and E. Romanelli, 1985, "Executive succession, strategic reorientation, and organization evolution: the minicomputer industry as a case in point," *Technology in Society*, 7, 297–313; Flamholtz and Randle, *Growing Pains*.

[17] Flamholtz, "Managing organizational transitions."

Organizational structure consists of the ways people are organized and activities are coordinated. Structure includes:

- the "boxes" on organization charts and how they are arranged;
- how the roles and responsibilities of each position are defined; and
- systems – including operational systems, systems for developing managers, reward systems, etc. – that support the effective operation of the structure.[18]

As with the planning activities, success depends not on the mere existence of a structure but on the match between the structure and business strategy.[19] Pardee Homes (see Part II, chapter 10) is a good example of the role of organizational structure in supporting growth and strategic change.

The management development system consists of the process an organization uses to develop the **management/leadership** capabilities needed to support effective current operations and continued growth and development. It includes:

- identifying/acquiring future managers;
- identifying the skill sets that managers in each position and at each level of the organization need to have to be effective;
- evaluating the extent to which each manager or potential manager possesses the skills needed to be effective in his or her role;
- designing and implementing "formal" programs/processes that support the development of needed skills; and
- developing strategies and processes for continuously enhancing the company's management/leadership capabilities.

The Countrywide Financial Corporation case, in chapter 4, examines the role of leadership and management development in supporting strategic change.

A control or performance management system is the set of processes (budgeting, goal setting) and mechanisms (performance appraisal) that promote behavior consistent with the organization's objectives.[20]

---

[18] Flamholtz and Randle, *Growing Pains.*
[19] Flamholtz and Randle, *Growing Pains.*
[20] Flamholtz, E. G., 1996, *Effective Management Control: Theory and Practice*, Nowell, MA, Kluwer Academic Publishers; Flamholtz, "Managing organizational transitions."

Control/performance management systems consist of the following.

- **Objectives** and **goals** that identify the results an organization, team, or individual should be working to achieve.
- **Measurement** systems that provide information that can be used to assess performance against objectives and goals.
- A system for providing continuous **feedback** – using the outcome of the measurement process – to the organization, team, or individual, on progress being made toward achieving goals and objectives. Ongoing feedback provides those responsible with the opportunity to adjust their behavior so as to increase the probability that objectives and goals will be achieved.
- A formal **evaluation** process during which overall performance against objectives and goals is assessed.
- **Rewards** that are used to recognize performance against objectives and goals.

We examine several cases of how companies developed and used performance management systems in Part II of this book.

Developing and managing corporate culture

The final building block is developing systems to identify, communicate, and effectively manage corporate culture.[21] Just as people have personalities, organizations have cultures, which are composed of shared values, beliefs, and norms. Shared values refer to the importance the organization attaches to the aspects of product quality, customer service, treatment of employees, performance standards, and other factors. Beliefs are the ideas that the people in the organization hold about themselves and the organization. Lastly, norms are the unwritten rules that guide interactions and behavior.[22]

Case studies of culture change are examined in Part II, including at IndyMac Bank, Indian Oil Corporation, and Tata Steel.

The model as a whole

Taken together, the business foundation and the six building blocks comprise the business model or business design of an economic

---

[21] Peters, T. J., and R. H. Waterman, 1982, *In Search of Excellence*, New York, Harper & Row; Walton, R. E., 1986, "A vision-led approach to management restructuring," *Organizational Dynamics*, 14, 1, 9–16.

[22] Flamholtz, "Managing organizational transitions."

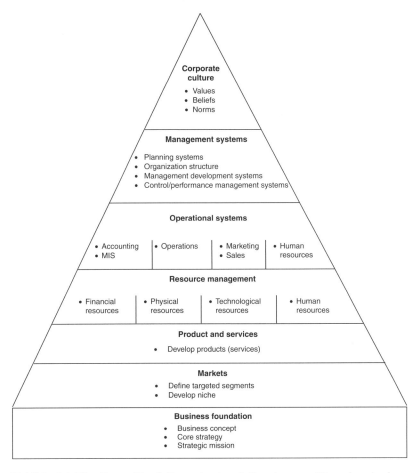

Exhibit 2.1 The Pyramid of Organizational Development™ – the six key building blocks of successful organizations

enterprise called the Pyramid of Organizational Development™, which is shown in exhibit 2.1. This model can serve as a strategic lens for building and, more importantly, in the context of this book, for changing an organization.

It should be noted that the pyramid shape does not imply that the business foundation and each of the six building blocks are independent components of the model. While it is important to focus on the design and implementation of each component, it is equally important that all components "fit" together as an integrated whole.

This means that a change in one aspect of the business model (e.g., at the operational systems level) will probably result in changes in other aspects of the model (e.g., at the corporate culture, management systems, resources levels). This is discussed further later in this chapter.

Empirical support for the model

Research has been conducted to assess the relationship between the six building blocks and organizational success. Research to date has shown that these six variables are linked to financial performance and demonstrate a strong correlation to approximately 55 percent of "EBIT" (earnings before interest and taxes).[23] Stated differently, they are drivers of financial performance, as shown graphically in exhibit 2.2. This research is summarized in the appendix to this chapter.

Implications of the model

Organizations compete on more than markets and products

One key implication of the model is that organizations compete not just in products and technology but in terms of all aspects of their business design, including business foundation and the organization's infrastructure (resources, operational systems, management systems, and corporate culture).

Sustainable competitive advantages exist at the top levels

A related and very critical implication is that the top four levels of the pyramid, which form the "infrastructure" of the firm, are less susceptible to imitation[24] and, accordingly, provide the basis for long-term sustainable competitive advantage. For example, Wal-Mart sells the very same products as K-mart, but has attained a dominant position in the United States as a retailer. It has done this by creating logistics and information technology (IT) systems that are vastly superior to those of

---

[23] Flamholtz, E. G., and W. Hua, 2002, "Strategic organizational development and the bottom line: further empirical evidence," *European Management Journal*, 21, 1, 72–81.

[24] Flamholtz, "Managing organizational transitions;" Flamholtz, E. G., and W. Hua, 2003, "Searching for competitive advantage in the black box," *European Management Journal*, 21, 2, 222–36.

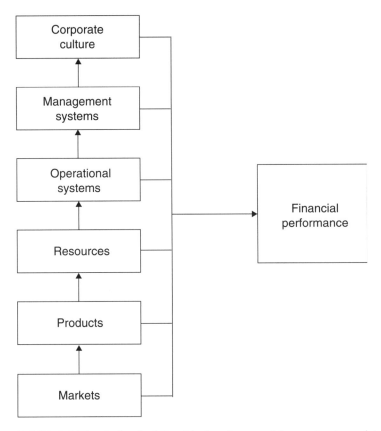

Exhibit 2.2 The six key building blocks of successful organizations: drivers of financial performance

K-mart and other competitors. As a result, Wal-Mart can require its suppliers to have "plug in" adaptability to its supply chain operations. K-mart cannot require this. This gives Wal-Mart significant operational and cost advantages vis-à-vis K-mart. Thus, although competition between firms takes place at all levels, long-term sustainable advantage is primarily found at the top three or possibly four levels of the pyramid. These comprise the infrastructure.

This perspective is a fundamental challenge to conventional wisdom (and practice), which has companies looking for competitive advantage in markets and products. In the short term these can be sources of competitive advantage. For example, being first to market can be an advantage. Over the longer term, however, success will create competition, and later entrants can take away market share.

Reuters, which lost share to Bloomberg; PowerBar, which lost share to many competitors, including Clif Bar and Metrex; and Netscape, which was driven out of business by Microsoft, are only a few examples of companies that focused too heavily on proprietary products as the source of competitive advantage. In contrast, Wal-Mart, which sells nothing that is not sold by K-mart and Sears, has totally come to dominate the retail market with essentially commodity products, *because* Wal-Mart has competitive advantages that exist well beyond just the products it offers.

The same thing is true for Starbucks and other companies that sell "commodity-like" products. These companies ultimately win with infrastructure, not with products or being first to market. The role of infrastructure rather than product per se is demonstrated in the decision by Dedrich's Coffee to sell its cafés to Starbucks. Dedrich's at one point had 400 company-owned and franchised stores, "but the company was unable to manage a large network and has steadily lost money and shrunk."[25] The company finally sold its forty company-owned stores to its arch-rival, Starbucks. We examine a case study of how Starbucks developed its dominant strategic position in chapter 5.

Using the model in planning and managing change

The Pyramid of Organizational Development™ can be used as a platform or template for planning and managing organizational change. There are four steps in this process.

- Step 1: assessing/identifying the need for change.
- Step 2: developing a change management plan – to move the organization from where it is to the desired end state.
- Step 3: implementing the plan.
- Step 4: monitoring performance against the plan.

Effectively executing these steps promotes the movement through the four phases of the change process described in chapter 1: planning (steps 1 through 2 above), getting started and letting go (step 3 and

---

[25] Hirsch, J., "Dedrich to sell cafes to rival," *Los Angeles Times*, September 15, 2006, C2.

step 4), and completion (the result of all four steps). Each of these steps is described below.

Step 1: assessing/identifying the need for change

Step 1 consists of formally or informally completing an "environmental scan" and an "organizational assessment." Completing the environmental scan involves collecting and analyzing information on the "market" (that is, present and potential customers and their needs), competitors, and key trends that might positively or negatively affect the organization's continued success. Completing the organizational assessment involves identifying the company's strengths and limitations at each level in the Pyramid of Organizational Development™.

If step 1 is carried out formally and is part of ongoing planning efforts, the result will be the identification of changes that the organization needs to make in its internal operations – that is, changes that need to be made to one or more levels of the Pyramid of Organizational Development™. The changes identified may be needed to improve organizational effectiveness (that is, to overcome limitations), to help the organization take advantage of environmental opportunities, and/or to minimize possible threats posed by the environment. Typically this will result in a "proactive" approach to managing change, which can be a source of significant competitive advantage.

If step 1 is carried out in an informal manner – that is, there is no systematic process in place to monitor environmental changes and/or there is limited focus on evaluating the organization's strengths and limitations at *all* levels in the Pyramid of Organizational Development™ – the organization can be placed at a significant competitive disadvantage. The organization will be reacting to environmental changes and doing so in the absence of a complete understanding of its own strengths and limitations. The organization, in essence, will be operating in a reactive mode and be doing so very ineffectively.

Even when there is a systematic process in place to complete step 1, there will be times when an organization needs to react to change that could not have been anticipated. These changes include the introduction of competitive products that make current products obsolete, major shifts in a competitor's strategy (that could not be foreseen), natural disasters, and the loss of key managers from within the organization. In these situations, organizations that have a formal process to assess internal strengths and limitations will be better equipped to make the necessary changes at each level in the Pyramid of Organizational Development™ than those whose understanding of their internal operations is less than clear.

The outcome of step 1 will be the identification of specific aspects of the organization's infrastructure that need to be changed.

Step 2: developing a change management plan

The change management plan should not be a separate plan. Instead, it should be embedded in an organization's overall **written** strategic plan. In fact, organizations that are effective at strategic planning are continually managing change in the context of their planning processes.

The Pyramid of Organizational Development™ can be used as the framework for developing these plans – which, more properly, might be called "strategic organizational development" plans. In brief, strategic plans constructed around the pyramid include the following elements.

- Current business model assessment. A brief overview of key findings from the environmental scan and organizational assessment (described in Step 1) – that is, the most significant environmental opportunities and threats, as well as the organization's most significant strengths and limitations. It should also include an assessment of the extent to which the current business foundation supports the company's long-term development and success.
- Business foundation. The business concept, core strategy, and strategic mission on which the organization will focus as it looks to the future (three to five years out). Detailed examples of how to do this will be provided in several of the case chapters in Part II.[26]
- Six building blocks design/definition. A description – typically in the form of strategic initiatives or objectives – of what each building block should "look like" in the long term (three to five years out) to support the business foundation effectively.
- Strategies and tactics. How the organization will move from the current state to the future state – as defined by the business foundation and definition of six building blocks.

[26] See, for example, chapter 4 on Countrywide Financial Corporation.

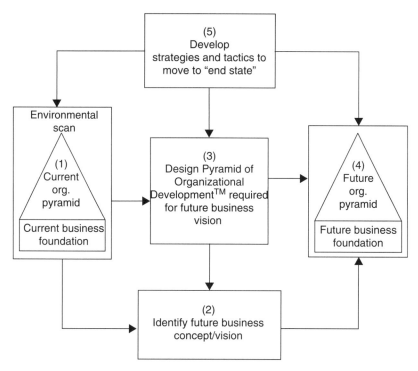

Exhibit 2.3 A model for planning change

The process for creating a strategic organizational development plan is shown graphically in exhibit 2.3. This process is different from typical strategic planning in a few subtle, yet critical ways. First, the typical strategic planning approach tends to focus only on markets, products, and strategy, rather than the entire set of building blocks necessary for organizational success over the long term. Second, the pyramid provides an explicit lens to view the integrated development of the entire enterprise – from the business foundation through the development of corporate culture.

It should be clear that this approach to planning very much supports change and change management. The "end state" of the change process will be reflected in the plan in how the business foundation is defined and/or in how one or more levels in the future Pyramid of Organizational Development™ are designed. In addition, it is frequently useful for those involved in the change management process to classify the nature of the changes that they are making in the context of their planning process – using, for example, the change typology presented in chapter 1. This can assist the leaders of the change process in understanding what will be involved in moving from the current to the desired state.

Transformational, strategic, organizational changes, for example, occur most often when the target of change is the business foundation. In brief, changes in this component (particularly changes to the business concept) can lead to the organization becoming a significantly different entity. Further, changes in the business foundation typically require changes in each of the six building blocks.

In the special case of companies making the transition from an entrepreneurship to a professionally managed firm (illustrated in several cases throughout this book), the focus of the changes will typically be on the top two building blocks – management systems and culture. This type of change is also transformational, strategic, and organizational in nature.

Major and incremental operational changes tend to occur most frequently at the operational systems and resource levels of the pyramid – although some changes at these levels can also be strategic in nature. For example, changing hiring practices so that they more effectively identify people who will embrace the company's culture and who have the skills needed to support the company's vision might be viewed as a strategic versus an operational change.

Identifying the nature of the change being undertaken and clearly defining the desired end state is important, because it helps all those involved understand "where we are going" and the impact (transformational, major, incremental; organizational, team/unit, individual; strategic or operational) that the change will have on the organization. If done effectively, it paints the picture – in a very real sense – of the future state of the organization, team/unit, or individual. The definition of these end states will be embedded in the strategic plan as part of the business foundation or in the definition of one or more of the building blocks.

The "change planning matrix" – a tool for developing the change management plan

Exhibit 2.4 shows a template to make the organizational development planning model (and, in turn, the change management plan)

Key areas	From: Old Banner	To: New Banner
Business concept	• Iron foundry business • Parts supplier	• Multiple metals and multiple technologies • Component supplier
Markets	• Many accounts • Willing to sell to any buyer	• Fewer accounts • More large accounts, through targeted selling to major customers
Product mix	• Primarily gray and ductile iron castings	• More diverse product mix • Different manufacturing technologies
Resources and operational systems	• Each division with its own resources and operational systems • Common use of Banner costing systems	• More emphasis on sharing "best practices" among divisions • More corporate standards for division operating systems
Management systems	• Divisional management systems • Corporate bonus plan based on divisional performance	• Corporate and divisional management roles and systems • Bonus plan based on divisional performance against key goals and contribution to group
Culture	• Lack of defined Banner culture • Autonomous divisions, each with its own culture • Informal culture management, with minimal corporate involvement	• A "core" Banner culture, with emphasis on shared values, beliefs, and norms • Formal culture *management* at corporate, group, and divisional levels

Exhibit 2.4 The change planning matrix – Banner Corporation

operational. This is termed the "change planning matrix." It is intended to clearly present information on the nature of changes that need to occur at the business foundation level and/or in one or more of the building blocks. In brief, it shows where the organization is today and creates a picture of where it wants to or needs to be in the future.

This sets the stage for developing strategies and tactics to move from the current to the desired state.

The matrix shown in exhibit 2.4 is based upon an actual example of a company in the foundry business. The matrix summarizes the changes that need to occur within the business foundation and within each building block. It shows that Banner Corporation is moving from a business concept of being a parts supplier in the iron foundry business to a "components" supplier with multiple metals and multiple technologies, not just iron. This represents a change in business concept and, thus, a transformational, organizational, strategic change.

As stated previously, when there is a change within the business foundation, there are typically changes within all building blocks. As can be seen, this is true at Banner Corporation, where the company is moving from:

- focusing on a large number of accounts of many types to targeted selling to fewer, large accounts;
- emphasizing primarily gray and ductile iron castings to using different manufacturing technologies to develop and offer more diverse products;
- having each division develop and manage its own resources and operational systems to utilizing more standard practices for resource management and operational systems throughout the company;
- "divisional" management systems to corporate and divisional management systems that work effectively together as a comprehensive system; and
- no common "Banner corporate culture" or culture management process to a common Banner culture and formal culture *management* at corporate, group, and divisional levels.

This matrix, then, can be used in the context of the strategic planning/ change management planning process as a tool that shows, in a very concise manner, where the organization is and where it needs to be.

The change planning matrix can also be used at the team/unit or individual level. The "Key areas" column will need to be adapted to the specifics of the team/unit or individual, however. For example, at the team/unit level for a sales organization, key areas might include training processes, the management of accounts, customer service processes, sales administration processes, target accounts, and other factors. At the individual sales rep level, for example, key areas might include selling skills, customer service, teamwork, sale targets, time management, and other factors. The same process – identifying where the team/unit or individual is and then identifying where the team/unit individual needs to be in the matrix – would be used.

Preparing for resistance to change
While it is important to define clearly where the organization is going, it is equally important that those who are leading the change effort devote time to identifying and developing strategies to overcome barriers to change (see chapter 1). The identification of barriers should be one outcome of step 1 (assessing/identifying the need for change), and the strategies for addressing these barriers should be included in the change management plan.

Step 3 and step 4: implementing and monitoring performance against the plan

As stated in chapter 1, just having a plan is only the first step in managing the change process. The next steps involve "getting started" (beginning to implement the plan) and helping the organization and the individuals that make up the organization "let go" of the old ways of doing things and work toward the achievement of the desired end state.

The first step in the implementation process is to communicate the plan effectively to all those who need to be involved in helping to achieve desired results. This involves helping those who are not necessarily leaders of the change process to "see" the picture of the end state clearly and understand just what their roles will be in making this a reality.

The next step in the implementation process is to find ways to maximize the involvement of people in changes that will affect them. This is discussed in more detail in chapter 3.

Finally, effective implementation involves understanding and effectively managing resistance to change that is brought about by people not wanting to "let go." Not all resistance can be predicted during the planning step of the change process. Therefore, leaders need to be vigilant in identifying resistance as it arises and in finding ways to deal with it effectively.

For any planning process to be effective, there needs to be a formal way to monitor progress against the plan. The more measurable the results of the change process are the easier it will be for leaders to assess this progress. We recommend that leaders of the change process meet on a quarterly basis to review and discuss progress against the plan, identify any problems in achieving desired results, and develop strategies for addressing any problems encountered. This review process provides the change leaders with the opportunity to adjust their plans, as needed, to increase the probability of achieving the desired end state. Moreover, if additional changes are required because of changes in the environment or organization's capabilities, leaders can proactively take steps to plan for and manage them. In brief, ongoing monitoring of progress against the plan makes change and change management a part of the organization's continued operations. It helps to increase the extent to which an organization can proactively manage change, and thus boosts its probability of long-term success.

Summary and conclusion

This chapter has presented a framework for planning and leading strategic and organizational change. The framework is based upon the Pyramid of Organizational Development™ paradigm. This framework, or "lens," can be used to help visualize, plan, and lead strategic and organizational change. We have shown how the pyramid can be used not only to assess the situation an organization finds itself in but also to plan what it wants to become over time. We have also presented a tool termed "the change planning matrix," which can be used to translate the conceptual framework into action.

In Part II we examine several actual case studies where this framework was used by companies to plan and lead strategic and organizational changes, and the results of the changes. For example, we shall see in chapter 4 how Countrywide Financial Corporation responded to its growth and industry consolidation by changing both its strategic vision and its organizational capabilities. Similarly, in Chapter 7 we shall see how a much smaller company (Stan Tashman and Associates) responded to another version of the same problem (changing industry dynamics) by transforming to a professionally managed firm.

Appendix: Empirical research to assess validity of framework

In the following section, the method used to evaluate the predictive ability of the Pyramid of Organizational Development™ framework is summarized.

Flamholtz and Aksehirli (2000)[27]

Eric Flamholtz and Zeynep Aksehirli (2000) performed the first empirical test of the proposed model. The paper proposes a link between the organizational development model and the financial success of organizations. To test this hypothesized relationship, financial and non-financial information relevant to the hypothesized model was analyzed for eight pairs of companies in different industries. Each company was evaluated in terms of the six key strategic building blocks, and scores were assigned to indicate the degree of the organization's development. These organizational development scores and measures of financial performance were used in a Friedman two-way analysis of variance as well as in a regression analysis to test the predictive validity of the framework.

The results of both the Friedman and regression analyses suggest that there is a statistically significant relationship between the development of the six critical success factors and the overall financial success of organizations.

Flamholtz and Hua (2002)[28]

Eric Flamholtz and Wei Hua (2002) provide another empirical test of a holistic model of organizational success. This paper builds upon the previous research and provides additional empirical evidence of the hypothesized link between the organizational development model and financial performance. This paper reports the results of a test within a *single* firm (a foundry business), however, using a set of fifteen relatively comparable divisions. A related research question concerns the

---

[27] Flamholtz and Aksehirli, "Organizational success and failure."
[28] Flamholtz, E. G., and W. Hua, 2002, "Strategic organizational development and the bottom line: further empirical evidence," *European Management Journal*, 20, 1, 72–81.

thresholds of strategic organizational development for the profitability of individual companies or operating units.

Each division was evaluated in terms of the six key strategic building blocks. Scores were assigned to indicate the degree of each division's "strategic organizational development." These scores and measures of financial performance (EBIT) were used in a regression analysis to test the predictive validity of the framework.

The results of the regression analysis suggest that there is a statistically significant relationship between the development of the six critical success factors and the overall financial success of organizations. The analysis explained approximately 55 percent of the financial performance of the divisions.

Flamholtz and Kurland (2006)[29]

Eric Flamholtz and Stanford Kurland (2006) provide another empirical test of a holistic model of organizational success. This paper builds upon the previous research and provides additional empirical evidence of the hypothesized link between the organizational development model and financial performance. The paper also reports the results of a test within a *single* firm (the research site was a financial services business), using a set of seven relatively comparable divisions.

Each division was evaluated in terms of the six key strategic building blocks. Scores were assigned to indicate the degree of each division's "strategic organizational development." These scores and measures of financial performance (gross margin) were used in a regression analysis to test the predictive validity of the framework.

The results of the regression analysis suggest that there is a statistically significant relationship between the development of the six critical success factors and the overall financial success of organizations. The analysis explained approximately 73 percent of the financial performance of the divisions.

[29] Flamholtz, E. G., and S. Kurland, 2006, "Strategic organizational development, infrastructure and financial performance: an empirical test," *International Journal of Entrepreneurial Education*, 3, 2, 117–42.

3 | *Leading change*

In chapter 2 we presented a framework to plan for and manage strategic and organizational change. Building upon this framework, this chapter examines the nature of the leadership tasks and skills required for leading change. It examines the nature of change leadership, identifies four "key drivers of change," and identifies the skills that leaders need to develop to use these drivers in successfully managing change. Finally, the chapter examines some recent research that is relevant to leading successful change efforts.

Leadership required to create change

What kind of leadership is required to create change? Many scholars and writers approach this question by looking at the style or personality of the leader. There is a popular notion that leaders of change are people with bold vision, and that there is a set of leadership characteristics – including charisma – that are important determinants of leadership effectiveness. This school of thought might be termed the "heroic school of leadership." Examples of heroic leaders are Lee Iacocca, who rescued Chrysler; Steven Jobs, of Apple and Pixar; Jack Welch, who led GE to the next level of greatness; Howard Schultz, who led Starbucks to become a coffee colossus; and Louis Gerstner, who led the revitalization of IBM. Undoubtedly these larger than life leaders do exist, and they were each successful in creating change; but it is not necessarily correct to assume that their results were the fruits of their efforts alone or that they personify the model or mode of leadership required to create change.

Three things are important to note. First, none of these individuals worked alone to create the changes required in their companies. Second, charisma alone does not an effective leader of change make. Finally, there is no one "best" style for leading change. Instead, successful change leadership is the result of having the skills and capabilities to manage four key drivers of organizational success, which are identified below.

Change leadership: understanding the four key drivers of organizational change

Based upon our experience in working with organizations for many years, we have formulated a four-factor model of the key tools or "drivers" of organizational change. According to this view, there are four primary drivers of change: vision, culture, systems, and operations. We term this the "VCSO theory," where the letters represent the four different drivers of change, as shown in exhibit 3.1. The basic notion is that these four factors are critical to helping organizations, teams, and individuals move through the change process that was described in chapter 1. Therefore, leaders of the change process need to focus on these four factors if they are to maximize the potential for success. Each of these factors and the role that leaders should play with respect to each is examined below.

Vision

A vision is both a requirement of effective leadership of change and a tool as well. Effective change, whether operational or strategic, requires a vision of what the leader is trying to achieve as the end result of the change process. This involves defining what the end state will "look like" – that is, what the business foundation is and/or how each of the six strategic building blocks (markets, products, resources, operational systems, management systems, culture) should be designed. It also involves communicating this vision effectively to all those who will need to be involved in making the vision a reality.

Unless people can '"visualize" what the end result of the change will be, they will be uncertain. They will also be more likely to resist the change. As discussed in chapter 2, creating a vision of the desired end state is an essential first step in the change management process. Having a well-defined vision is, in fact, critical to the success of moving an organization, team, or individual from phase 1 (planning) to phases 2 and 3 (getting started and "letting go") of the change process. This means that leaders of change must understand how to define, communicate, create buy-in for, and reinforce their vision. As

> **Vision**
>
> - Creating a "picture" of what the future state will be like (that is, results to be achieved)
> - Clearly communicating the vision to all involved
> - Continually reinforcing the vision through words and actions
>
> **Culture**
>
> - Identifying what the current culture is with respect to innovation, risk taking, change, etc.
> - Defining the "desired" culture with respect to change
> - Managing the culture so that it promotes valuing and embracing change (as opposed to resisting change)
>
> **Systems**
>
> - Identifying targets of change within existing systems
> - Evaluating the costs and benefits of changing existing systems
> - Developing new systems (operational and management) to support vision and culture changes
> - Helping others "let go" of the old ways of doing things
>
> **Operations**
>
> - Using day-to-day operations of a business, business unit, or administrative unit to support change
> - Influencing the behavior of people on a day-to-day basis to operate in ways consistent with changes to the vision, culture, and/or systems

Exhibit 3.1 Summary of the key drivers of change: VCSO theory

described in chapter 2, one tool that can be used in defining and communicating the vision is the "change management matrix."

Definition and communication of a vision, however, are not enough to ensure success. Effective leaders also need to find ways to help those who must support the vision accept and embrace it as a desired end state. This means understanding and addressing possible resistance to change. It also means helping others understand how achieving the vision will benefit them. Finally, leaders need to find ways to reinforce their vision – through their own words and actions and through recognizing those whose behavior is consistent with moving the organization, team/unit, or individual target of change to the desired end state.

Culture

Some organizational cultures are more likely than others to promote the idea that change should be embraced (rather than resisted). A requirement of effective change management is to be able to create and manage a culture that is supportive of change, innovation, appropriate risk taking, etc. This is a characteristic of successful, growing, entrepreneurial companies. Support for change is also something that needs to be fostered and maintained in larger companies, where a variety of factors (discussed in chapter 1) may contribute to a culture that promotes resisting versus embracing change.

In the absence of a culture that promotes openness to change, change efforts can be ignored or resisted. Ignoring change is a form of passive aggressive resistance. There isn't outright resistance. Instead, people adopt the attitude that "this will eventually pass, so we'll just wait and see." They may give "lip service" to the change, but they do not embrace it. As discussed previously, resistance involves actively working against the change.

Leaders of the change process, then, need to understand how to create and manage a culture that promotes openness to change. Promoting this value needs to be a focus of leaders on an ongoing basis, as opposed to something that is addressed only when there is a need to change. In small organizations, leaders can promote this value through direct contact with employees – through their own words and actions and through the recognition that they give to others who support change efforts.

As the organization grows, the value placed on change can start to decline – unless there is a focus on preserving it. Direct contact with employees can no longer be the principal mechanism for communicating and reinforcing this value because the organization is simply too large. Therefore, leaders need to find less direct ways to help employees continue to embrace the need for and recognize the value of change. This can be done through creating processes or systems that support or promote innovation (such as 3M's "skunk works"), through finding ways to recognize and reward innovation and appropriate risk taking, through implicit or explicit communication, and through other means.

Organizations of all sizes should include strategies for maintaining the focus on innovation and change in their strategic organizational development plans (as described in chapter 2). In brief, embedded in the strategic plan should be a "culture management plan."[1] A first step in developing this aspect of the plan involves collecting information on what the current culture is with respect to change, innovation, risk taking, etc. (the "current culture"). This might be done using a culture survey or interviews. Next, leaders need to identify what the culture should be with respect to these factors (the "desired culture"). Leaders then need to identify the steps that can be taken to move from the current to the desired culture. These steps should be reflected in the company's strategic plan. Since culture affects and is affected by all other aspects of the Pyramid of Organizational Development™, moving from the current to the desired culture will typically involve making changes in other components of the business model. Again, these will be reflected in the strategic plan. A final step in this "culture management process" is to monitor performance against the plan. Again, this will occur in the context of the overall strategic planning process.

While developing, implementing, and monitoring performance against a culture management plan is important, it is not enough to ensure success in terms of this driver of change. As is true of other drivers, leaders of the change process need to continually serve as role models for the value placed on change. Leaders' words and actions will serve as signals to employees about what is and is not valued with respect to change.

Systems

Systems – both operational and management systems – are important tools in creating and supporting change. These systems provide the infrastructure required to support ongoing operations and promote

---

[1] Flamholtz and Randle, *Growing Pains*, chap. 12.

long-term growth and development. They are also important elements in the successful change process.

As described in chapter 2, operational systems consist of all the systems required to facilitate the operations of the business on a daily basis. They include sales and marketing, production or service delivery, accounting, human resource management (recruiting, selection, training), and information systems. Management systems are the systems required for the growth and development of a business. They include the planning system, organization structure, management development processes and systems, and control/performance management systems.

Step 1 of the strategic organizational development planning process (assessing the need for change) should assist leaders in identifying the strengths and limitations of these systems. This assessment should involve identifying specific changes that may need to be made to these systems to support long-term growth – including changes that will help the organization maximize external opportunities and minimize external threats; and support specific changes within other components of the Pyramid of Organizational Development™ business model. Since changing systems can be costly (e.g., changing a computer platform), leaders of the change process need to evaluate carefully the costs and benefits associated with possible changes on both a short- and long-term basis. They also need to be sure to take a comprehensive view of their organization – rather than simply focusing on what might be best for their unit or business team. Finally, leaders (like all those the change will affect) need to be willing to "let go" of the old way of doing things and embrace the "new" system. This is, perhaps, the most difficult aspect to manage with respect to this driver of change.

Once the targets of change – that is, the specific systems that need to be changed – have been identified, the "new" systems need to be clearly defined in the organization's strategic plan. In brief, they need to be reflected in the future business design (as described in chapter 2). Leaders and all those who who will be affected by the change need to understand what the new system will look like or do. Further, leaders need to recognize that changing systems can lead to a cascade of organizational changes. Changes in technology or operations flow can lead to changes in roles and organizational structure. Changes in management systems such as planning can lead to changes throughout an organization.

This means that the leaders of the change process need to have an understanding of organizational systems, their relationship to each other, and the impact that changing systems can have on overall operations. This is not to suggest that leaders need to understand all the technical details of all organizational systems. Instead, they need to have a more holistic understanding of how the various systems relate to one another. They can bring in technical experts to assist with the details.

Once the picture of the future system has been "painted," leaders then need to identify the steps that will be taken to implement the new system fully. This involves creating a clear plan for how the organization will move from the current to the end state of the change process. It also involves identifying and developing plans to deal with possible resistance to these changes.

Operations

Operations may be either a driver of change or the element that is affected by other changes. In this context, "operations" refer to the day-to-day activities that take place in a business. The term relates to, among other things, how information flows through a business, how products move from idea through launch, how people are trained and coached daily by their managers, how "orders" flow from customers through shipping, how the company tracks its financials on a day-to-day basis, and many other processes and systems. At its most basic level, operations relates to how systems and processes are actually implemented and used, and how people behave within their roles and within the company.

As a driver of change, operations is, in a very real sense, on the "front line" of the change process. It is the most visible outcome of efforts to change the behavior of an organization, team/unit, or individual. Changes in the other drivers – vision, culture, systems – will ultimately be reflected in changes in operations, which, in turn, will be reflected in changes in people's behavior.

Systems and operations are, in a sense, the most closely related drivers of change. The systems driver relates to the design and implementation of new operational or management systems, which, in turn, affect operations. The operations driver relates to influencing the behavior of people on a daily basis so that they embrace and operate in ways consistent with the new systems, processes, etc. Therefore, it is typically the case that the leaders of the systems "driver" will be different from the leaders of the operations "driver." One example of this is how the successful implementation of American Express's shift to an Internet-based approach to operations (developed by systems people) depended on the ability of leaders in operations to help their team members accept and embrace the change. Another example is the adoption of the "just in time" inventory management philosophy of operations, which had a profound impact on inventory management operations in the automobile and other related industries in the 1980s. A third example is the shift from a "point-to-point" operational approach in the airline industry to a "hub and spoke" approach to operations. In each example, leaders focused on operations were important to the successful implementation of the change.

Leaders focused on the operations driver of change need to understand how to translate the changes made to the organization's business model – that is, changes made within the Pyramid of Organizational Development™ – into changes in daily behavior. In a sense, they need to break these changes down into the concrete steps that will be taken by teams/units or individuals to implement the change fully. This can involve changing team/unit or individual roles and responsibilities, providing training, changing reward/recognition systems, and other factors. Leaders also need to find ways to show – through their words and actions – that they understand and embrace the "new" way of operating.

Developing change management leadership capabilities

Becoming an effective leader of change involves the following:[2]

- understanding and embracing the role of leader in the change process (role concept);
- developing the skills needed to implement this role effectively (skills); and

---

[2] The three factors described in this section – role concept, skills, and managerial psychology (the "inner game") – represent three critical determinants of "management/leadership" effectiveness. This framework is explained in more depth in chapter 9 of Flamholtz and Randle, *Growing Pains*.

- managing one's "mindset" or psychology so that it supports, rather than detracts from, the ability to implement the leadership role effectively in the context of the change process (the "inner game").

Each of these factors is explained below.

Understanding and embracing the "leadership" role

For an individual to be an effective leader of change, he or she needs to understand the nature of this role. The role of "change leader" involves, among other things, devoting time to:

- continually monitoring the need for change at the organizational, team/unit, and individual levels of the enterprise;
- developing change management plans;
- creating buy-in on the proposed changes and the change management plan;
- implementing and monitoring performance against these plans; and
- identifying and dealing with resistance to change.

In brief, the change leader needs to spend time differently from a "traditional" manager. This may mean, in some cases, that certain tasks previously performed by this individual need to be delegated to others. In other cases, the role of the leader may have been defined from the very beginning as that of a "change agent."

In addition, the role of change leader involves behaving in ways that are consistent with moving the organization, team/unit, and/or individual to the desired end state. The change leader needs to be a role model for what behavior consistent with the desired end state "looks like."

Finally, the change leader needs to accept that his or her role involves focusing on and helping the organization, team/unit, and/or individual team members understand and embrace change. The final section of this chapter presents research findings that can assist those already in or making the transition to change leadership roles in understanding what they can do to increase the probability of a successful change effort.

Skills

Developing effective change leadership skills means having the skills needed to deploy the four drivers of change presented in the last section – "visioning," corporate culture management, systems development and implementation, and the management of day-to-day operations. Being able to deploy these four drivers involves, at its broadest sense, developing what might be termed "organizational development skills." In brief, what this means is that skilled change leaders need to understand and be able to implement effectively the strategic organizational development process (described in chapter 2). In addition, the ability to deploy these four drivers is also dependent upon leaders developing certain supporting skills.

To use the "visioning" driver effectively, an individual needs to understand how to define clearly the future state of the change process and create buy-in to this vision. Since visioning should begin with an understanding of the situation the organization, team/unit, and/or individual team members currently find themselves in, the individual needs to be able to analyze and use as input to decision making information about the environment and the organization's own capabilities. In brief, the change leader needs to possess effective decision-making skills – including understanding how to make decisions as a member of a team. Deploying the visioning driver effectively also involves having effective communication skills. The change leader needs to be able to communicate this vision effectively to all those it will affect and be able to listen to feedback carefully. Finally, deploying the visioning driver involves understanding how to motivate others to embrace the change and be willing to work toward its realization. This involves possessing the skills of motivation and performance management – including understanding the role the leader needs to play in driving behavior.

Deploying the culture driver effectively involves understanding and being able to use a "culture management process." Change leaders need to understand how to identify the organization's or unit's/team's current culture as it relates to change. This involves collecting and analyzing information about what employees believe the company's values are and about how employees actually behave. Using this information, change leaders need to be able to identify what the culture should be and what aspects of the existing culture need to be changed. Finally, change leaders need to understand and be able to use culture management "tools" such as recruiting/selection, systems redesign, communication, rewards/recognition, structure redesign, and others to support the culture change process. As is true of the visioning driver, fully deploying the culture driver involves understanding how to

motivate others to embrace the change and be willing to work toward
its realization.

The skills needed to deploy the systems driver effectively can range
from high-level "strategic" design of the systems required to support
the change effort to more detailed design and implementation of these
systems. The strategic aspect of design involves understanding the
framework for organizational effectiveness and development
described in chapter 2 and being able – individually or with a team –
to identify the systems, processes, etc. that need to be in place at each
level in the Pyramid of Organizational Development™ to support the
continued success of the enterprise. This does not mean that change
leaders operating at this level need to understand all the details of the
design of these systems. Instead, it means that they need to be able
to define and communicate clearly what the "new" system needs to do
(i.e., the "end state"). As is true of being able to deploy the visioning
driver, deploying the systems driver effectively involves having and
using effective decision-making and communication skills.

There will be some change leaders in the systems area who *do*
operate as experts in the detailed design of required systems. For
example, the unit leader of the IT function might be a key member of
the team who is developing and implementing a new computer system; or the head of manufacturing might be involved in the design and
implementation of new, innovative manufacturing processes. In these
cases, the individual needs to possess not only the skills needed to
manage and work as a member of a team but also the technical
knowledge needed to assist in system design and implementation.

Deploying the operations driver effectively involves developing and
using a variety of skills. First, change leaders need to have the skills to
translate plans into action. This typically involves understanding how
to develop and work with others to develop detailed action plans.
Second, change leaders need to understand how to create buy-in to the
changes in behavior that are involved in using the operations driver.
This means understanding how to motivate team members and using
performance management systems as tools to promote desired
behavior. Third, to deploy the operations driver effectively, change
leaders need to have effective communication skills – including lis-
tening. They need to be able to help others understand what needs to
be done or done differently and, at the same time, need to be able to
listen to and address others' concerns. Finally, as is true of deploying

the other drivers, it is important that change leaders demonstrate behavior consistent with the new ways of operating.

Utilizing the key drivers of change: need for a leadership team

Based upon our experience in working with organizations, we have observed that it is rare for a single individual to have the skills needed to deploy effectively all four drivers of change. Even when a single person can use all four drivers, it becomes increasingly difficult to do so alone and remain effective as the organization increases in size. In larger organizations that have been successful in managing growth and change, it is, therefore, most typical to find a core leadership team of three people who perform these functions as a team. We call this the "leadership molecule."

The "leadership molecule"

A "leadership molecule" is an organizational unit of two or more leaders who function as a team and perform the key functions of creating a vision, managing the culture, developing systems, and managing operations. This leadership team typically consists of three people. Three is not a magic number, however. Sometimes it is a team of two, and occasionally a team of four.

These core leadership teams are always recognized by the organization, and sometimes, but not always, have a nickname. They might be known as "the Three Musketeers," "the Dynamic Duo," "the Four Musketeers," or other creative names. At Starbucks, the core team of Howard Schultz, Howard Behar, and Orin Smith were known as "H_2O," a play both on their initials and on the chemical formula for water, which is the foundation for coffee. At another company, there were two groups with nicknames: the "Three Musketeers" and the "Four Musketeers." In this company, people recognized that there was an inner core of three people and a fourth member who was an "insider," but not quite the equal of the other three.

An illustration: Starbucks

To make this concept more concrete, we now examine how it operated at Starbucks. As we shall see in chapter 5, for many years Howard

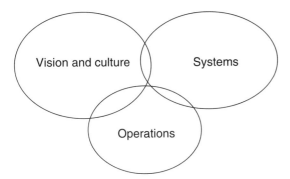

Exhibit 3.2 The "molecule" theory of leadership: the four functions exist as an integrated unit

Schultz was the CEO of Starbucks, and he performed the functions of vision and culture management. He had two major "sidekicks:" Orin Smith and Howard Behar. Smith, then the chief financial officer (CFO), was largely responsible for the development of support systems – not just financial management systems, but information systems and management systems as well. Howard Behar was the head of Starbucks operations. He ran the day-to-day operations of the largest component of the business: the retail stores or cafés. He was also a key person in transmitting the corporate culture throughout Starbucks.

Although many people contributed to the development of Starbucks, for years these three would have a weekly dinner to discuss the business. One of the authors of this book, who was consulting with Starbucks, was invited to sit in on one of these dinners and observe the dynamics. The three clearly operated as a team. This does not mean that there was not conflict. There was conflict and a clashing of opinions, but it was clear that they saw themselves as a team.

This notion of a leadership team as a molecule is shown schematically in exhibit 3.2. Exhibit 3.3 shows some examples of companies where we have observed the existence of this type of effective leadership molecule. These include Countrywide Financial Corporation and PacifiCare, as well as Starbucks.

When the four functions are not a "molecule"

We have observed many situations in which there is no molecule. This can be because a piece is missing (e.g., there is no one focused on

---

PacifiCare (early 1990s)

- Culture: Terry Hartshorn, CEO
- Vision and systems: Alan Hoops, COO
- Operations: Rich Lapellis, Head of California HMO

Starbucks

- Culture and vision: Howard Schultz, CEO
- Systems: Orin Smith, CFO
- Operations (and culture) : Howard Behar, SVP, Retail Stores

Countrywide

- Vision and culture: Angelo Mozilo, CEO
- Vision and systems: Stanford Kurland, COO
- Operations: Dave Sambol, EVP

Exhibit 3.3 Examples of companies where the leadership molecule exists
Note: HMO = health maintenance organization;
       SVP = senior vice-president;
       EVP = executive vice-president.

culture) or because the team is not functioning as a true molecule. This can best be viewed as three atoms in search of a molecule, as shown in exhibit 3.4.

When the four functions are not performed effectively by a leadership team, one or more of the following can occur:

- success will be "suboptimal";
- there will be significant conflict;
- the organization will be overly "cautious"; and/or
- people will resist change because of the danger of "crossfire."

All or any of these can significantly undermine the organization's ongoing success.

Research on leading change: creating buy-in

As discussed throughout this chapter, one of the key skills that change leaders need to possess is the ability to help others understand and

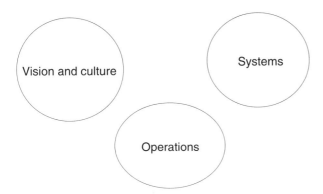

Exhibit 3.4 Three atoms in search of a molecule: the four functions exist, but not as a unit

"buy in" to the change. This section examines some of the research that is relevant to this skill.

Research on role of participation in change

There has been a great deal of research on the role of participatory leadership as a tool to enhance people's willingness to change. Although participation is not a panacea or silver bullet, there is substantial evidence that when people participate in planning changes they are more willing to change themselves. For leaders in the change process, this suggests that it is important to identify how those who will be affected can and should participate in planning for and implementing the change.

It also appears that the simple act of having people discuss something among themselves and reach an agreement about an intention to act is more effective than attempts at persuasive communication. For example, during World War II the US government was interested in having people eat different cuts of beef. Research was conducted on the relative effectiveness of persuasive communication versus group discussion. It was found that, when people were permitted to discuss it among themselves, and when they indicated an intention to try the different cuts of meat, it was more effective in producing changed behavior than persuasive communication. These findings suggest that leaders of the change process should identify ways to solicit input from those who will be affected early in the process. For example, in the context of the strategic planning process (described in chapter 2), this might mean asking people for input on the strengths and limitations of the organization at each level in the Pyramid of Organizational Development™ (part of step 1 of this process) and then sharing with those who provided input how this information was used in the development of the plan.

Risks of "pseudo-participation"
Unfortunately, the focus on the benefits of participation has led, at times, to the practice of "pseudo-participation." This is a spurious form of participation in which leaders give the illusion of a participative process. For example, one general manager of a major world-class pharmaceuticals company had learned about the benefits of participation when he received his MBA degree at a leading Ivy League university. His practice was to bring up an issue for discussion until his team reached a decision. Then, if he did not like the decision, he would bring up the issue again and again until the "correct" decision – one he agreed with – was reached. His team was aware of this practice, but did not confront him on it. They simply played along. Privately, however, one asked: "Why do we go through this charade? This is a waste of time. Why doesn't he just tell us what he wants to do?"

Leaders of the change process, then, need to be sure that if they ask people to participate in the change process – by providing input to decisions, actively working with a team to make decisions, and in other ways – the output of these efforts will actually be used and used effectively.

Research on data-based change

Another stream of research that is relevant to understanding how to communicate and create buy-in to change concerns the idea of "data-based change." This is the notion that people are more likely to change as a result of data rather than persuasive communication.

A great deal of research, particularly by researchers at the Center for Utilization of Scientific Knowledge at the University of Michigan, supports the notion of data-based change. In brief, when people are presented with data (either in qualitative or quantitative form) it allows them to formulate their own opinions about the need for change.

The authors of this book have had a great deal of experience with this strategy of change – both at the individual and organizational levels. In one instance, for example, the CEO of a mutual fund investment company refused to change the company's practice of being a "no minimum fund." Although virtually all the other senior executives in the company argued that the company was losing money on many of its clients, he refused to change the practice of there being no minimum amount in clients' accounts. Some of these arguments were quite heated, and the CEO was called stubborn. He held a strong belief that a young boy or girl who invested $50 in his or her account from a newspaper route or babysitting would continue to invest more as he or she earned more money. After several years of arguments, a project was conducted to address this issue. The company determined that the break-even point for a client investment was $5,000. If someone had less than $5,000, the company would lose money. Research was also conducted to obtain actual data on the practices of the company's clients. The data derived indicated that the CEO's belief was not correct, and he finally changed his views about the need for account minimums.[3]

For leaders of change, this research suggests that using data in the planning, implementation, communication, and monitoring stages of the change management process is important. For example, sharing information on environmental opportunities and threats as a part of the strategic planning process can help those the change will affect understand its importance. Further, during the implementation process, those affected should be provided with regular feedback (information) about progress in achieving desired results, problems in achieving desired results and the impact these problems are having on the organization and team, and how the organization or team will be addressing the problems identified.

---

[3] The CEO of this company had many strongly held views. Once he had changed his views on this issue, however, all other issues were then open for discussion.

The important role of planning in managing change

Research on change management is telling us that:

- a principle tool for managing change is participation in the planning process; and
- the key is creating congruence or alignment among the goals of different individuals or groups.

The value of planning is not just the plan per se but the process of creating the plans.

Summary

This chapter has examined the nature of the leadership tasks and skills required for leading change. We have also discussed the need for a leadership team or "molecule" as the key unit for leading complex strategic and organizational change. Finally, we have examined some research that is relevant to leading successful change efforts.

Leading strategic change in actual organizations

Part I of this book presented a framework for understanding and managing strategic and organizational change. It described the theory underlying the change management process and tools that can be used by leaders of change in applying these concepts in practice within their organizations. It also presented a framework and approach for planning for and managing the phases of change, and identified the capabilities that those in leadership positions need to possess to lead the change process successfully.

Part II consists of nine chapters, each presenting a case study of a company that successfully managed change. Some of these companies – Starbucks (chapter 5) and Westfield (chapter 12) – are global enterprises. Others are well known in their country of origin – Countrywide Financial Corporation (chapter 4), Indian Oil (chapter 6), and Tata Steel (chapter 11). Still others are known within their specific geographic area or industry – Stan Tashman and Associates (chapter 7), IndyMac Bank (chapter 8), Infogix (chapter 9), and Pardee Homes (chapter 10). What all these companies have in common, however, is that their leadership teams planned for and successfully managed strategic organizational change.

The types of changes that were the primary focus for management at each company range from changing or creating an entirely new business "concept" (Countrywide Financial Corporation, Starbucks, Tashman, IndyMac Bank, Infogix, Westfield), to changing the company's structure (Pardee Homes), to changing the company's culture (Indian Oil Corporation, Tata Steel). In all cases, however, these primary changes typically involved making changes in other aspects of the company's systems – including the planning, performance management, and management/leadership development systems. In other words, in many of the cases described in the following chapters, companies were really making "compound" changes – that is, they were simultaneously making changes in multiple aspects of their operations to support the movement from the current to the desired state.

In each chapter we present background on the company (in many cases including the company's history), define the "driver" or catalyst for change, identify the overall goal of the change process (that is, the desired end state), and describe how the company's management team worked to move the company from the current to the "desired" state. In many cases, we describe the "tools" that management used in planning for, implementing, and monitoring the effectiveness of the change process. Most case studies also include a description of the challenges or problems that company leadership faced and how they addressed these challenges.

In Part III, we identify and examine the specific lessons that can be learned from the experiences of the nine companies whose efforts in planning for and managing change are described in the case studies that comprise Part II.

4 | *Leading strategic and organizational change at Countrywide Financial Corporation*

Introduction

Recognizing the mounting threats to its leadership position, in late October 1999 Countrywide Financial Corporation invited Eric Flamholtz, Professor of Management at UCLA's Anderson School of Management and President of Management Systems Consulting Corporation, his own consulting firm, to its annual planning meeting. He was asked to present a strategic planning framework for building the organizational capability needed to sustain long-term success and to adapt to environmental changes. He was also asked to facilitate a preliminary planning session in which Countrywide's senior managers would be introduced to the concept of approaching planning in relation to longer-term business issues.

While Stanford Kurland, Countrywide's COO, was accustomed to considering longer-range issues for the company, most of the other members of Countrywide's senior management team were more focused on achieving competitive success in the current, as opposed to the future, market. The team also believed that they were very good at strategy, and the company's financial performance up until that point had validated their assertions.

Nevertheless, the session with Flamholtz triggered the realization that, though the company was performing well, it was necessary for management to extend its thinking beyond incremental performance improvement goals and to begin to address longer-term, environmental issues, as well as changing competitive dynamics.

This chapter gives an account of the process undertaken to respond to these changing industry dynamics. It also describes how the

This chapter was jointly authored with Stanford Kurland, then President and Chief Operating Officer Countrywide Financial Corporation, Chairman and Chief Executive Officer Countrywide Home Loans, Inc.

company made the subtle, yet profound, transformation from a small entrepreneurial venture to an entrepreneurially oriented, professionally managed organization. It is a case study involving a company that grew from a small, independent mortgage company into a large, complex organization, offering a full array of financial products and services. The case focuses, in particular, on the implementation of a systematic and integrated planning approach and the role of strategic planning in helping the company to evolve its culture and operational foundation from entrepreneurship to professional management. As related below, this transformation was driven by a combination of environmental changes as well as by the company's own growth.

About Countrywide

Countrywide Financial Corporation (CFC) is a diversified financial services provider. Since 1969 the company has grown from a small entrepreneurial venture to a very large (Fortune 150) international company. Today, CFC consists of more than twenty major business units, operating in five business segments: mortgage banking (including mortgage origination, mortgage servicing and loan-closing services), banking, insurance, capital markets, and investments. The company's 2004 revenues exceeded $8 billion and, as of the second quarter of 2005, it held more than $159 billion in total assets and employed roughly 50,000 people, globally.

The catalyst for change and transition to professional management

Spurred by the collapse of the thrift industry (the savings and loan – S&L – crisis), the late 1990s saw a period of consolidation within the mortgage industry as retail banking behemoths such as Wells Fargo and Washington Mutual entered the market, seeking to fill the void left by the S&Ls. Prior to this period Countrywide had achieved much of its success through its strategy of positioning itself as a branded "price leader." With the entry of the large retail banks into residential mortgage finance, however, the industry dynamics changed considerably. The company faced new, larger competitors, which had grown through acquisition (a strategy that was not available to CFC because of capital constraints). These new competitors, with greater financial resources, posed a significant challenge to CFC's core strategy of being the branded price leader. Consequently, by 1999, while still among the top players in the mortgage market, CFC had lost the leadership position it had enjoyed in the early 1990s.

Another challenge for Countrywide in the late 1990s was the company's own exponential growth. Between 1995 and 1999 the company had nearly tripled its employee base, almost tripled its mortgage volume, and more than doubled its mortgage servicing portfolio; as a result, it had increased earnings by more than seven times. Moreover, during the same four-year period the company had added new business segments, including subprime mortgage origin-ations, global operations, and additional insurance offerings, and had begun its entry into traditional banking.

This dramatic growth had the potential to become a liability for Countrywide, because it had not evolved its operational infrastruc-ture, culture, or strategies to foster the cross-functional and cross-divisional coordination necessary to achieve an integrated vision for the company, and to fuel its long-term competitive advantage.

Moreover, the growth and diversification that CFC experienced during the 1990s made the business more complex and created the critical need for management to address new industry segments and larger operating units. CFC's entrepreneurial spirit, combined with the measure of business unit autonomy that had long been part of the company's culture, now presented a management challenge. Previ-ously these hallmarks had helped to create a vibrant, nimble operating environment but, at this stage of CFC's organizational development, they had a greater potential to foster counterproductive organiza-tional "silos."

The case for long-term planning

One of the key themes of Flamholtz's presentation concerned industry consolidation and the possibility of a "winner take all" situation within the mortgage market. The argument was that there would ultimately be three major players in any business space or segment (a classic oligopoly), which, collectively, would control 70 percent or more of market share, distributed among them as follows: no. 1 at least 40 percent, no. 2 at least 20 percent, and no. 3 at least 10 percent. The remaining share would be divided among many smaller "boutique" players. Examples of industries that have consolidated in this manner include: the international airliner industry, in which Boeing and Airbus control the greatest share of the market; the US express package delivery industry, with UPS and FedEx emerging as the dominant two carriers; and Home Depot and Loews rising to the top of the US home improvement retail space.

There was a great deal of discussion about this scenario among Countrywide senior managers. Despite the growing influence of the retail banks in the mortgage arena, some believed that such a dramatic form of consolidation was unlikely to occur in financial services, and even less likely in mortgage banking, considering that no player held more than 4–5 percent of total market share at that time. Others, such as Kurland and Angelo Mozilo, CFC's Chairman and CEO, expressed a different perspective, believing that Flamholtz's consolidation theory might, in fact, be possible, particularly since CFC, at one time the largest mortgage banker, had by then slipped to fourth place. The growing insecurity of CFC's position at the apex of the mortgage industry served as the catalyst for shifting the senior management team's attitude toward planning for the long term.

At a minimum, the session encouraged senior management to think about the future of CFC, and convinced them of the need for a more formal and systematic approach to strategic planning and organizational development. As Mozilo stated, "We were focused upon the hedgerows; this got us thinking over the next hill."

A template for organizational assessment and development

During his session with the Countrywide executives, Flamholtz presented the Pyramid for Organizational Development™ template for organizational development and assessment (discussed in chapter 2). Flamholtz had developed the framework previously and had been exploring its effectiveness in assessing the organizational needs of companies. There has been a program on empirical research designed to assess the validity of this framework.[1]

---

[1] For a summary of this research, see Flamholtz, E. G., 2004, "Towards an integrative theory of organizational success and failure: previous research and future issues; *International Journal of Entrepreneurial Education*, 1, 3, 297–320.

This template was used to assess the strengths and areas requiring further development at Countrywide. The content of the discussions at this first session made it clear that the company was relatively competent in the areas associated with the bottom four levels of the pyramid: selecting appropriate markets, developing products and services, managing financial, physical, and technological resources, and hiring the right people. By contrast, the company required significant development in the competency areas associated with the top two levels of the pyramid – management systems and culture management. These two areas became the points of focus for the organizational development efforts that CFC would design and implement over the coming years to help it sustain its leadership position in the financial services arena.

The development of an enhanced strategic planning capability was seen as the first priority for organizational development at CFC, as a means of creating both a management system and as a means of managing its culture. Kurland became the sponsor or champion of the effort and hired Flamholtz and his firm to assist the company in building and integrating a sophisticated and consistent approach to planning across the company.

Taking strategic planning to the next level

Planning had always played a key role in Countrywide's culture and its ability to seize new opportunities in the market as they arose. The leaders of the company had always prided themselves on their strategic capabilities. With the organization becoming increasingly large and complex, however, the process that the company had implemented in the past was no longer effective.

Countrywide's "old" planning process

Prior to 1999 Countrywide employed a very traditional strategic planning process. Like most companies, it devoted a few days a year to planning. The company also conducted informal brainstorming sessions as needed, but the sessions usually centered on resolving "issues of the day" or urgent matters. As a consequence of its entrepreneurial culture and decentralized operations, there was great variation in the approaches taken to planning throughout the company.

Further, these diverse and disparate planning sessions were typically conducted with only a small nucleus of senior executives, creating an environment in which the "main" strategy was developed at the top of the company or operating divisions and then "pushed down" to the various departments and employees. These strategies also lacked continuity, as management demonstrated a penchant for establishing entirely new sets of priorities each year.

While CFC's relatively informal approach to planning had worked quite well for a considerable amount of time, as the organization grew in size and complexity, management realized that the company had outgrown its planning process. Some of the key issues with the "old" planning process were that: (1) the informal style of planning limited management's ability to achieve synergies and efficiency across the organization; (2) "herding" the divisions to work across organizational boundaries required a great deal of time and effort by the COO; (3) tracking initiatives was difficult; and (4) the constantly changing priorities caused senior managers to be less inclined to "fully engage" in the planning process.

The need for change in planning

Once Countrywide's senior management had made the decision to make planning a corporate priority, they were able to focus on the development of a rigorous approach. Management viewed the creation of this new strategic planning process as an opportunity to embed in the planning cycle principles that would foster better alignment and establish a common planning standard across business units. In a complex company such as CFC, there was a need to create alignment among all the business units to ensure that they all moved in concert to achieve the desired overall results.

For CFC, the goal was to use this new planning methodology as a tool for also managing the company's culture, in terms of breaking down silos, fostering management accountability and employee ownership, while also continuing to build on the cultural traits that had driven the company's earlier success (e.g., its entrepreneurialism).

Countrywide's "new" approach to strategic planning

Countrywide's evolution from a company that merely embraced planning to one that possessed a fully integrated and effective long-term planning process and system began with its initial recognition of planning as a corporate priority. The company's transformation continued with senior management's commitment to modifying the planning infrastructure and process, adopting a clearly defined planning methodology, and making the appropriate resources available to support the planning process. In this manner, senior management ensured that the organization maintained its focus on strategic planning as a corporate priority.

Planning as a corporate priority

Although there is no definitive explanation as to why planning fails at so many companies, one might suspect that the cause stems from a lack of proper attention, effort, and support. Countrywide's management made the process of planning important at every level within the company. The process was "sponsored" at the highest levels of the organization, with Kurland, the COO, playing a very visible role; this was critical to obtaining "buy-in" throughout the organization.

Dedicating resources to support planning

To ensure its success, Countrywide's management aggressively poured resources into the planning function. The Strategic Planning Department was charged with managing the high-level administration of the strategic planning process so that the executive team could focus on the big picture rather than getting mired in the details. Having a formal group of people to support the process relieved operating executives of routine process-oriented responsibilities and eliminated the resistance and barriers that typically arise when managers are asked to deliver more without additional resources.

Another function of the planning group was to provide analytical support for the newly created committees charged with overseeing the execution of high-priority initiatives – the Priority Objective Committees. The company also mandated that each division dedicate a trained staff member to serve as the liaison with the strategic planning group and to assist in creating the divisional plan. The Strategic Planning Department launched a "train the trainer" program, with the assistance of an outside consulting firm to prepare these key individuals – known as "Divisional Planners" – to assume their new planning responsibilities.

Restructuring the planning process

Initially, there were approximately sixty people involved in the corporate planning sessions. Since there were no consistent guidelines for determining who needed to be involved in the process, management erred on the side of including more people. Eventually, they concluded that the size of the group was too large to permit effective planning. As a result, the company formed two groups to spearhead the planning process: the Executive Committee and the Managing Directorate. The Executive Committee was charged with the task of supporting the CEO and COO in providing corporate-level oversight and leadership for the planning process throughout the entire company. Ultimately, the group was expected to become one of the leading sources of corporate-level strategy and vision. The committee's membership included the CEO, the COO and their direct reports (Senior Managing Directors) as well as a select group of Managing Directors.

While the Executive Committee maintained oversight for the corporate planning process, the Managing Directorate (comprised of all the company's Managing Directors) was held accountable for providing division-level oversight and leadership for the planning process.

Adopting a common planning template

Although there are many approaches to planning, Countrywide chose to adopt the method created by Flamholtz.[2] He had previously developed and deployed this methodology with such diverse companies as, among others, Starbucks, PacifiCare and Navistar International.

The approach implemented at CFC had two major components: (1) a planning framework or conceptual "platform," and (2) a planning process. The planning framework used is shown schematically in exhibit 4.1. The process begins with an environmental scan to assess the market, competition, and trends. Once this external assessment is completed, the next phase includes an organizational assessment, which involves an internal review of the company's resources and ability to capitalize on external trends. The organizational assessment component of this process enables management to determine the

---

[2] For further discussion of this method of strategic planning, see Flamholtz and Randle, *Growing Pains*, chap. 7.

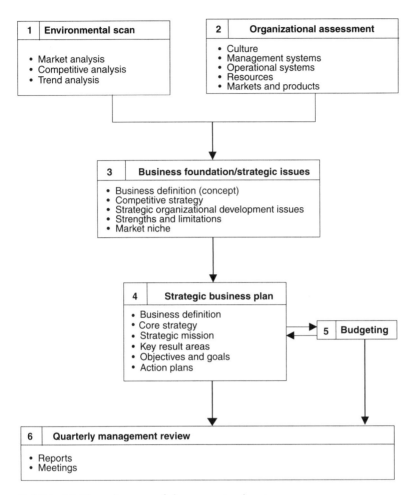

Exhibit 4.1 Flow diagram of the strategic planning process

company's strengths and limitations associated with the competencies included in each layer of the Pyramid of Organizational Development™.

Once these assessments have been completed, the organization then constructs its "business foundation." This process involves outlining the business concept (i.e., business definition), strategic mission (i.e., overriding corporate objective), and core strategy of the organization (i.e., fundamental approach to achieving a strategic mission). The business foundation then becomes the basis for the development of objectives and goals for areas that are critical to organizational success or performance – "key result areas" (or KRAs).

Key result areas are operationally defined as the six strategic building blocks contained in the Pyramid of Organizational Development™ plus financial results management. As discussed in chapter 2, research has shown that there are six key building blocks of successful organizations: markets selected, products or services offered, resources and how they are managed, operational systems, management systems (including the planning system), and corporate culture. Research has also shown a direct correlation between these building blocks and financial performance, impacting approximately 55 to 75 percent of a company's financial results, measured in terms of gross margin and EBIT.[3]

Objectives are developed in each of these KRAs according to what the organization wants to achieve. For example, an objective might be to increase market share or profitability. These key objectives are intended to be broad and relatively amorphous. They are supported by "SMART goals," which are specific, measurable, actionable, realistic, and time-dated.

Developing "priority objectives"

Although there are many objectives in any strategic plan, a well-thought-out set of "priority objectives" – objectives that are given critical management focus – is one of the "secret ingredients" that has made planning work at Countrywide. The priority objectives were derived from the strategic mission and were in line with CFC's overarching theme of striving for dominance in its business space. In addition, the priority objectives have been organized into an acronym (the word "dominance," as shown in exhibit 4.2), creating a mnemonic device that facilitates spreading the strategic message throughout the company.

---

[3] See Flamholtz and Aksehirili, "Organizational success and failure"; Flamholtz and Hua, "Strategic organizational development and the bottom line"; Flamholtz and Kurland, "Strategic organizational development, infrastructure, and financial performance."

Diversification expansion

    Operational efficiency

        Market share growth

            Internet supremacy

                New strategic alliances

                    Accountability and responsibility

                        Nullify capital disadvantage

                            CHL portfolio retention

                                Expense control and cost leadership

---

Exhibit 4.2 Countrywide's priority objectives: D.O.M.I.N.A.N.C.E.
Note: CHL = Credit Hi Lite.

Crafting an approach to issues of "linkage" and "follow-through"

Two critical challenges to making strategic planning work in any organization involve: (1) creating linkages across organizational units; and (2) ensuring that business units follow through on plans. These tasks are deceptively simple, but essential to extracting real value from strategic planning. Countrywide's solution was to create Priority Objective Committees – cross-functional teams responsible for providing corporate oversight of and continued focus on initiatives designed to support the priority objective, including tracking the progress of the initiatives and monitoring divisional plans to ensure that objectives were being adequately addressed.

Committee members were determined based on the organizational units most impacted by the objective. The Managing Director of the unit most affected by the objective was appointed to chair the committee. The head of the next most affected unit became vice-chair. Other members included interested parties from corporate functions and other parts of the company. Committee sizes ranged from five to ten members. These committees met regularly with the planning group to provide updates and reports on key metrics. Also, to emphasize further the importance of the priority objectives, the teams were required to make regular progress reports throughout the year to the CEO and COO.

Monitoring progress throughout the organization

Countrywide also developed electronic scorecards to facilitate monitoring the progress made against each priority objective. The scorecards measured key financial and non-financial metrics for each objective. They were designed to allow real-time performance tracking against established criteria for each objective. Scorecards also facilitated the mapping of responsibility and accountability for objectives and related measures to appropriate teams and divisions. In all, the scorecards represented a tangible reporting system that fostered communication among management.

Countrywide was able to accomplish the development of its strategic planning infrastructure and integration of the methodology over a period of about two years. The implementation of a strategic planning system is an evolutionary process, however, dependent on varying internal and external factors. By its nature, the strategic planning process can never be seen as entirely complete or perfected. As a result, Countrywide continues to refine its strategic planning process, and to date has delivered very significant results.

A shift in corporate strategic direction

To what extent can we conclude that Countrywide's adoption of a more sophisticated approach to strategic planning had value to the company? The new strategic planning process has led to some significant changes. The benefits that the company has derived from the strategic planning process have been both direct and indirect, as described below.

One of the most important changes resulting from the new planning process has been a subtle but profound strategic shift in corporate direction. Countrywide's business foundation was changed to better reflect the expected outcome of the company's diversification efforts. The former business foundation (see exhibit 4.3) was focused solely on the "mortgage banking business." Even though, by 2000, Countrywide's family of companies included a wide array of consumer and institutional financial products and services, management continued to view the company primarily in terms of its "mortgage banking business." This mindset implicitly diminished the importance of the non-mortgage aspects of its operation.

> **Business definition**
> Mortgage banking
>
> **Strategic mission**
> To become the dominant mortgage banking company
>
> **Core strategy**
> To be the low-price leader and have brand recognition

Exhibit 4.3 Countrywide's former business foundation

Countrywide's new business foundation

As a result of the planning process, Countrywide evolved its business foundation from having a singular focus on mortgages to incorporating a broader view of the company as a diversified financial services provider with mortgage banking at its core. Its mission reflected the need to complete the transition from a mortgage company to a fully diversified financial services company. The new business foundation is shown in exhibit 4.4.

Shift in business foundation led to name change

The subtle yet profound shift in its business definition also served as the impetus for the company's decision to change its name from

> **Business definition**
> A diversified financial services provider with mortgage banking at its core
>
> **Strategic mission**
> • To dominate residential mortgage lending and finance
> • To stabilize core earnings growth
> • To complete the transition to a fully diversified financial services company with mortgage banking at its core
>
> **Core strategy**
> To enable its employees to deliver best-of-class and value-added products and services to its customers through superior technology and processes

Exhibit 4.4 Countrywide's new business foundation

Countrywide Credit Industries to Countrywide Financial Corporation in 2002. This name change was symbolic of the evolution of the company's identity in terms of its vision and long-term strategy. The move signified to customers, shareholders, and employees that Countrywide was no longer just a mortgage company but, rather, a company that had truly transformed into a diversified financial services provider.

Other benefits from the new planning process

In addition to enabling CFC to embrace its business diversification fully as a strategic imperative, the successful integration of the planning system has also led to a variety of significant organizational benefits.

- A constructive forum for elevating management's focus from tactical and operational concerns to broader strategic challenges facing Countrywide.
- A shift away from "silo mentality," which now encourages divisional leadership to make decisions from a "Countrywide perspective" as well as a divisional perspective.
- A clear set of priorities to guide operating unit activities and decision making.
- Measurable objectives that emphasize coordination and linkages across organizational boundaries.
- "SMART goals" – the company learned to convert objectives into measurable initiatives and targets.
- Greater understanding and communication of the plan throughout the organization.
- A highly sophisticated planning process that is consistently applied throughout the company, which helps to promote organizational alignment.

Another benefit of the strategic planning system has been the development of the senior management team in terms of increased sophistication in strategic thinking.

External validation of Countrywide's planning system

In addition to the benefits that Countrywide has recognized internally as a result of its strategic planning system, the company has also received external validation of the process's value. In 2004 Countrywide's Strategic Planning Department was honored by the Association for Strategic Planning with the 2004 Richard Goodman Strategic Planning Award for large for-profit enterprises. The award honors organizations at the leading edge of strategic planning practice.

The bottom line: Countrywide Financial's performance

The ultimate test of any new business application is its impact on the "bottom line," or shareholder value. To what extent can we conclude that Countrywide's adoption of a more sophisticated approach to strategic planning had economic value to the company?

In May 2004 *Barron's Magazine* listed CFC as second on its list of the 500 largest companies in terms of their returns to stockholders.[4] Of course, the company's improved financial performance is not wholly attributable to its strategic planning. The strategic planning process directly impacted the shift in strategic direction and mindset, which, in turn, contributed to overall financial performance. Although Countrywide benefited from the effects of lower interest rates on refinancing, so did its competitors, and they did not fare as well in the *Barron's* rankings.

CFC growth

Additionally, Countrywide grew considerably between 2000 and 2005, following the institutionalizing of the planning system across the company. This is shown in exhibit 4.5.

CFC performance results

As a result, Countrywide has achieved the performance rankings shown in exhibit 4.6.

CFC shareholder returns

The strongest indication of results achieved is the outstanding shareholder returns that Countrywide delivered between 2000 and 2005. This is shown in exhibit 4.7.

---

[4] Racanelli, V. J., 2004, "Barron's 500 triple crown: the best companies for investors," *Barron's*, May 17, 31–2.

2000	2005
• $410 million net earnings • $2.95 billion market capitalization • $15.8 billion total assets • 6.5% mortgage market share • $250 billion servicing portfolio • Fortune 500 rank • 542 branches • 11,000 employees	• $2.2 billion net earnings[1] • $22 billion market capitalization[1] • $159 billion total assets[2] • 14.4% mortgage market share[2] • $964 billion servicing portfolio[2] • Fortune 150 rank • 1,278 branches • 50,000 employees

Exhibit 4.5 Countrywide Financial Corporation: growth, 2000 to 2005

Notes:

1 Year-end 2004.

2 Second quarter 2005.

• Largest mortgage originator
• Largest mortgage servicer
• 17th largest national bank

Exhibit 4.6 Countrywide's 2005 performance rankings

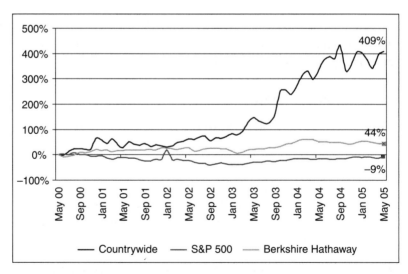

Exhibit 4.7 Countrywide Financial Corporation: five-year shareholder returns

Other organizational development initiatives

In addition to the development of enhanced strategic planning cap-ability based on the platform or strategic lens offered by the Pyramid of Organizational Development™, Countrywide has implemented other organizational development initiatives. These have included a formal culture management process and a program for leadership development (both championed by Kurland and assisted by Flamholtz and his associates). Description of these initiatives is beyond the scope of the current case.

Conclusion

This chapter has presented an actual example of a company dealing with a compound change. It shows how a rapidly growing company has successfully made the transformation from entrepreneurship to an entrepreneurially oriented, professionally managed firm and positioned itself as the number one player in its market space.

It is incontestable that Countrywide Financial Corporation can be classified as a company that has proactively dealt with environmental change: Countrywide was attempting to achieve industry dominance based upon a concept of how the environment would evolve over time.

We have emphasized one key aspect of this transformation, stra-tegic planning, which has greatly benefited the company as a vehicle of organizational change. One of the broader implications of this case is the success of the strategic planning process. "Strategic planning" is one of the most misunderstood and maligned managerial tools. Entire books have been written to explain why it cannot work.[5] Most organizations have attempted it and many claim to have accomplished it, but relatively few companies actually manage to achieve success through the strategic planning process. Nonetheless, the experience of Countrywide Financial Corporation illustrates how one organiza-tion's committed efforts to embed planning into its culture and embrace planning as a corporate priority have succeeded in creating a bridge between its entrepreneurial roots and the professional man-agement required to sustain its growth.

[5] See Mintzberg, H., 1994, *The Rise and Fall of Strategic Planning*, New York, Free Press.

5 | Leading change at Starbucks Coffee Company

Starbucks Coffee is one of the truly great organizational success stories of the past two decades. "Starbucks" has become a worldwide brand, for many synonymous with lattes and cappuccino. Starbucks has become an icon of corporate success. Today, the company has more than 8,000 stores; it has more stores in California than all its major competitors combined.

If one looks closely at Starbucks, however, its success is not about its coffee; it is about the strategic and organizational changes that the company made to differentiate itself from its competition. These were led by Howard Schultz and his close associates, Orin Smith and Howard Behar. Together they formed the core leadership molecule (see chapter 3) that has created the phenomenon that is Starbucks.

Starbucks has accomplished this with a commodity product that has been around for quite some time: coffee. The company has led a strategic change not only inside the company but within the entire industry in which it operates. It is an amazing example of the role of leadership and management as a key ingredient in organizational success.

Howard Schultz, the founder and leader of Starbucks, had a strategic vision not only to build a national retail brand but also to "recreate the paradigm," and transform coffee from a commodity product to a "truly exquisite product" with brand equity. This is exactly what he has accomplished with Starbucks.

This chapter examines how Schultz and the management team accomplished this industry transformation through a variety of strategic and organizational changes that were required over time, while

This case has been adapted from Flamholtz and Randle, *Growing Pains*, 22–7, and Flamholtz, E. G., and Y. Randle, with a foreword by Howard Schultz, 1998, *Changing the Game: Organizational Transformations of the First, Second, and Third Kinds*, Oxford, Oxford University Press, 91–7.

simultaneously building Starbucks as a great international brand. Our primary focus will be on the changes required to build Starbucks, and achieve the scale required to become the dominant player in its arena. We examine the development of Starbucks from two different, but related, perspectives. First we look at a chronology of key events in the company's history, and then we carry out an analysis in terms of the Pyramid of Organizational Development™ framework described in chapter 2. Both perspectives are intended to provide insights into the process of strategic and organizational change and development at Starbucks. The key issue is: how did Starbucks become what it is today – the leading brand and purveyor of specialty coffee on a worldwide basis?

The company's origin

The original "Starbucks Coffee Company" began as a "local roaster" of coffee. It opened its first store near Seattle's Pike Place Market in 1971. Another was located in a shopping center across from the University of Washington's campus in 1972. The original Starbucks stores did not sell coffee drinks. They sold fresh-roasted coffee beans, imported teas, and spices. Sometimes, however, the individual behind the counter would brew a pot and serve free samples in Dixie Cups.

Starbucks' founders were three individuals who shared a passion for gourmet coffee: Jerry Baldwin, Zev Siegl, and Gordon Bowker. By the end of the 1970s they had four retail stores, a mail order unit, and a wholesale company. Their sales were $2 million per year. Siegl sold out in 1980, while Baldwin and Bowker continued to own the firm.

Unlike many entrepreneurs, who do not know what they do not know, Baldwin and Bowker realized they needed someone with greater business experience to help run what they had grown into a serious enterprise. They became acquainted with Howard Schultz, and invited him to run Starbucks.

Schultz, who is now Chairman and CEO of Starbucks Corporation, joined Starbucks as Director of Retail Operations and Marketing in 1982. He had grown up in Brooklyn and had begun his career in the marketing department at Xerox. At the age of twenty-six he headed the American division of Hammerplast, a Swedish housewares firm, before he joined Starbucks.

A journey to Italy and the seeds of the transformation

Schultz had been with Starbucks for approximately one year when he visited Milan to attend a trade show. While walking the streets of Milan and going back and forth from his hotel to the trade show, he marveled at the ubiquity of the Italian coffee bars. After a few days, he began to be drawn into them himself, because, in his words, "it was so romantic."

In describing his experience, Schultz states: "I saw the same faces and the camaraderie. The coffee bar was an extension of peoples' homes and was *truly* part of the fabric of the Italian culture. It struck me right across the head – this is something dynamic and unusual."

What struck Schultz was part irony and part insight. Starbucks *was* in the coffee business, but: "I thought we had missed it completely, because we had not given people the romance of the beverage and the personal interaction of creating an environment outside their homes where they could enjoy the beverage in a personal, unique way." That notion was what Schultz took back to the United States.

The founders of Starbucks, who had been doing very well for a local company, viewed Schultz's insight with little interest and a lack of enthusiasm. It took him a year and a half to convince them to allow him to test his idea.

He went back to Italy to do more research, and when he came back he was more convinced than ever that he was on to something. In April 1984 they tested the idea, by opening up a small coffee bar inside a new Starbucks store.

Key events and phases in Starbucks' development

We now examine the development of Starbucks based upon a chronology of key events, and then do an analysis in terms of the Pyramid of Organizational Development™ framework.

Creating the vision for Starbucks' transformation

Overnight a transformation took place. The store changed. The customer count became higher. The beverage became a treat while, more than that, the relationship with the customer changed. Starbucks' people were able to develop closer relationships with customers because of the instant gratification and romance that people received from the beverage served in this environment.

In an instant, Starbucks had transformed its business from a purveyor of whole bean coffee to something very different. While whole bean coffee remained the core business, Schultz had changed the game. It was the juxtaposition of two simple elements to create a more complex and, in some ways, more wonderful thing, just as the combination of hydrogen and oxygen creates water.

In spite of the "experiment's" success, the original owners of Starbucks balked at adapting their company to the vision Schultz articulated: an American version of the Italian coffee bar.

1985: founding Il Giornale

Schultz decided to create his own company, and left Starbucks. He called his company Il Giornale, after the Italian daily newspaper. It was founded in 1985.

Within a year of this challenge to Starbucks, one of the founders of Starbucks acquired another company, Peet's Coffee, in Berkeley. After the acquisition the debt to equity ratio of Starbucks was six to one, a very high level – reflecting the fact that the founder was averse to issuing equity, which meant a dilution of ownership.

1987: acquiring Starbucks

In August 1987 Schultz went back to Starbucks with a buyout offer and a vision to take the concept well beyond the boundaries of Seattle. The high debt burden on the owners of Starbucks made them receptive to Schultz's offer. Il Giornale acquired the assets of Starbucks, and changed its name to Starbucks Corporation.

1989–91: building the leadership team

Schultz is the first to say that he alone did not build Starbucks. He states: "I was very fortunate to hire wonderful, gifted people to balance out the weaknesses and the strengths that I had as a business person." Schultz also says, "We've made each other better, like a basketball team. They've allowed me to do what I do well."

Schultz was joined by Dave Olsen (known as "Mr. Coffee" at Starbucks). Olsen, who was Senior Vice-president of Coffee for Starbucks, had opened his own espresso bar in Seattle's university district in the mid-1970s. He was always a "coffee guy," and his search for the perfect espresso led him to Starbucks. Together, Olsen and Starbucks formulated the original Starbucks "espresso roast." Although Olsen's title was Senior Vice-president of Coffee, his role was to be the keeper of the "coffee flame." His personal passion for coffee, and his quest for the perfect coffee, have helped reinforce the overall corporate coffee culture. He was the company's conscience.

Understanding the need to create a strong leadership team, Schultz added several key people, including Howard Behar and Orin Smith.

Behar joined Starbucks in 1989 to help build its retail operations. When Behar joined the company, Starbucks had thirty retail stores. He brought with him years of experience from other, larger, organizations, as well as a passionate commitment to building a different kind of organization. Behar is a "right-brained" creative type, who also has an appreciation for the role that process can play in building a company such as Starbucks. He is a high-energy, very creative type of person – perfectly suited to manage Starbucks' hyper-growth retail strategy.

Smith joined Starbucks as CFO in 1990. He brought not only a strong financial background but a lower-key, more deliberate decision-making and managerial style. This provided a counterbalance to the two Hs, who tended to be passionate, with a strong orientation for immediate action. Schultz has stated, "Orin had a great gift to be able to tolerate my recklessness." Smith was seen as solid and dependable. Together, Schultz, Behar, and Smith (or H_2O) combined to form a true leadership molecule, as described in chapter 3.

1989–91: a crisis of confidence

The period from 1989 to 1991 was also a period of crisis for Starbucks. The term "crisis" refers to a turning point, for better or worse. The company was building its management team, and it was spending a great deal of money to prepare for anticipated but uncertain future growth. As a result Starbucks was losing money, and there was great pressure on Schultz from the board to change the strategy.

When asked if there was an untold secret to the Starbucks story, Schultz said, "Starbucks lost over $3 million during the three-year period from 1989 to 1991." He noted that there was tremendous pressure on him from investors and the board of directors to change the strategy and the vision. They believed that Starbucks was hiring "too far ahead of the growth curve"; that the infrastructure investment was too great for a company as small as Starbucks; that company-owned stores were too expensive; and that the concept wasn't going to work outside Seattle.

George Bernard Shaw has stated, "The reasonable man adapts himself to the world. The unreasonable man does not. Therefore, all progress is made by the unreasonable man." Given the loss of money, what should Schultz and, in turn, Starbucks do? A "reasonable man" might have changed the strategy, and stopped hiring the kinds of people that Starbucks was recruiting. Maybe the company should have started franchising as a way to create capital. Maybe management should have looked at Starbucks as a regional company.

Schultz was not a reasonable man. His vision was to build a national company. He stated:

We could not have gotten where we are today if we had not had the commitment to build a national company with a national brand from the beginning. If you're going to build a 100-story building, you've got to build a foundation for 100-stories; but people were getting very nervous.

Schultz had to raise more money continually. He had to keep saying: "It's going to work, and we will turn profitable." It was a very tough time, a very vulnerable time. His board of directors thought he was being very unreasonable – until Starbucks became highly successful.

A significant key to Starbucks' long-term success was Schultz's leadership, and his ability to keep the investors and board in line on this issue and prevent them from cutting back on the company's investments, including investments in people. Schultz has said that he had to state repeatedly: "It's going to work! Stay with the plan."

1994–7: building the organizational infrastructure

During the period from about 1991 through 1994, Starbucks' own success became the source of its next set of problems and challenges. The company had begun to experience a number of the classic symptoms of "organizational growing pains."[1]

It was then that Smith, CFO of Starbucks, looking for some help with the issues facing the company, came across a book by Flamholtz

---

[1] See Flamholtz and Randle, *Growing Pains*, especially chap. 3.

and Randle, dealing with growing pains and the need to transition to a professionally managed organization. He contacted Flamholtz and invited him to come to visit Starbucks in Seattle to meet with him, Schultz and Behar, and see if the "chemistry was right" to work together. This initiated a three-year-plus process of organizational development, designed to deal with the current growing pains and help prepare to take Starbucks to the next level of success. Starbucks applied the Pyramid of Organizational Development™ framework as part of its strategic planning/organizational development process.[2]

Deconstructing Starbucks' success

It is the Pyramid of Organizational Development™ framework that provides the second perspective from which we want to examine and explain Starbucks' success. Specifically, we use the strategic lens provided in chapter 2 to analyze and deconstruct the Starbucks success story. Our objective in doing this is to gain insights into the nature of the process by which Schultz and the senior management team at Starbucks undertook the task of building this great company.

Starbucks and the Pyramid of Organizational Development™

Prior to 1994 Starbucks did not explicitly use the pyramid in designing an organization capable of supporting the transformation process.[3] Schultz had a vision for the development of the business, and he set about growing a company that would fulfill his vision. We can use the pyramid, however, as a lens to examine what Starbucks did and did not do well in building the company – i.e., in designing a firm to play its chosen game effectively.

The business foundation

Shultz's initial vision was not only to build a national retail brand; it was also to "recreate the paradigm," and transform coffee from a commodity product into a "truly exquisite product" with brand

---

[2] See Schultz, H., and D. Jones-Yang, 1997, *Pour Your Heart into It: How Starbucks Built a Company One Cup at a Time*, New York, Hyperion.

[3] As discussed below, it was from 1994 onwards that Starbucks formally used the Pyramid of Organizational Development™ as part of its strategic planning process.

equity. Another aspect of Schultz's vision concerned his concept of the kind of organization he wanted to build. He had a strong commitment to company-owned stores.

In 1994, as described below, Starbucks began to engage in a more systematic strategic planning process, which led to the formulation of an explicit business foundation consistent with that described in chapter 2. As an outcome of this planning process, Starbucks articulated the strategic mission "To become the leading brand of specialty coffee in the United States by the year 2000." This was to be measured by achieving a total of 2,000 stores and $2 billion by 2000. Stated differently, Starbucks set out in 1994 to grow to 2,000 stores and $2 billion in revenues in just six years.

This was a colossal challenge. At the time that this strategic mission was established Starbucks had no more than about 175 stores, and had never opened more than thirty-five new stores in a given year.

This growth target was intended as a strategic objective, and not as an end in itself. The concern at the time was to build Starbucks to a critical mass, such that it could defend itself and its concept from other competitors. The company was not too concerned with other competitors of similar size, such as Coffee Bean and Tea Leaf, Diedrich's Coffee, or Gloria Jeans; the strategic concern was with potential giant competitors such as Nestlé or McDonald's. Smaller competitors would not have the infrastructure and resources required to copy Starbucks' concept and roll it out to the market and create a dominant position; but a large company such as McDonald's would be able to.

Starbucks' strategic mission was all about protecting the company from this type of long-term threat. This meant that the company needed to attain a size that made it relatively invulnerable if a competitor tried to preempt the market. The internal debate was not over this concept but over the size that Starbucks would need to achieve in order to avoid this competitive threat.

The initial discussion was whether 1,000 stores would be sufficient. The senior leadership team was divided on the question. The planning facilitator then asked, "How many stores would Starbucks need to have to be relatively invulnerable to this threat?" The answer was 2,000 – a huge number. Nevertheless, the team agreed that this would be the goal, and the strategic mission formulated was to reach $2 billion in revenues and 2,000 stores by the end of fiscal 2000 (i.e., September 30, 2000).

This, in turn, had vast implications for all the functional areas of Starbucks, such as roasting, human resources, real estate, etc. They had to work backwards from the goal of 2,000 stores and determine what had to be done over the next six years to reach that goal. For example, if the company was to get to 2,000 stores it was going to have to develop the capability of opening more than 300 stores per year at some point. In addition, the company did not have the roasting capacity to support 2,000 stores.

In any event, by the end of fiscal 2000 Starbucks had revenues of more than $2.2 billion. It had achieved its strategic objective. Today, Starbucks has revised its mission statement to a worldwide rather than exclusively a US focus: "Establish Starbucks as the premier purveyor of the finest coffee in the world while maintaining our uncompromising principles as we grow."[4]

Markets and products

The foundation of Starbucks was its vision of the market and the product. Schultz envisioned a large, national company. He knew that, although the core of his company's product was coffee, the real "product" was the store itself. It was what Starbucks conceptualized as "a third place to be" (or, more simply, "the third place"). As stated in the 1995 *Annual Report* of Starbucks Corporation:

Ever since diners and pubs and plazas and town halls we've needed places to gather outside of home, outside of work, rather [a third place to go]. Coffee … community … camaraderie … connection … It seems we all just need the warmth.

Schultz also understood that service was an integral part of the "delivery" of his product, and that the person Starbucks calls a "barista" (the person who tends the coffee bar) was critical. His concept that it was the "experience" of the customer that was the real product, and not just the coffee per se, was brilliant.

Resources and operational systems

Once the market and product for Starbucks was identified and designed, the next steps in building the organization involved the

---

[4] As stated on its corporate website: www.starbucks.com.

acquisition of resources and the development of operational systems. As already discussed, Schultz spent considerable time identifying investors. In this regard, it was fair to state: "No bucks, no Starbucks!" The financial resources were used to hire people capable of building Starbucks as a national company. In contrast to many entrepreneurships, in which there is a relatively strong senior team but no strong people at the next level down, one of the reasons for Starbucks' success and its ability to manage its rapid growth was a relatively strong team of functional specialists in areas such as real estate and retail operations. This, in turn, reduced the severity of the usual growing pains.

Management systems

Prior to 1994 the company had done an excellent job of developing five of the levels of the Pyramid of Organizational Development™ – i.e., everything except management systems. Until that year there was planning and strategy, but there was no formal strategic planning process. There was training for customer service personnel but no management development. In addition, there was an incentive system for people, but not a well-developed "performance management system."

Beginning in 1994, when sales stood at about $175 million, Starbucks began to develop the management systems that were required to facilitate its continued successful development. The key structure that was developed during the period from 1994 through 1996 was the company's strategic planning system. As with other companies described in this book, Starbucks embraced the planning process and platform for strategy developed by Flamholtz and his associates at Management Systems.

A key to the development of this system was the decision of Behar, SVP of Retail Operations, to (in his words) "do it right." Behar had the entire retail system engage in a systematic planning process for the first time. This process then led to other divisions at Starbucks engaging in the same process, and finally to the process being applied in all the supporting functional areas, such as human resources, roasting, real estate, etc.

Culture

The final building blocks of successful organizations are culture and culture management. Corporate culture was something that was very

- Provide a great work environment and treat each
  other with respect and dignity
- Apply the highest standards of excellence to the
  purchasing, roasting, and fresh delivery of our coffee
- Develop enthusiastically satisfied customers all of the time
- Contribute positively to our communities and our environment
- Recognize that profitability is essential to our future success
- Embrace diversity as an essential component in the way
  we do business

Exhibit 5.1 Starbucks Corporation's six "guiding principles"

important to Schultz. Unlike many other companies at a comparable stage of development, there was an explicit statement of Starbucks' culture (its so-called "guiding principles").

Initially Schultz articulated a set of five "guiding principles," which was intended to serve as the basis of Starbucks' culture. Subsequently, a sixth guiding principle was added to the initial five. All six guiding principles are shown in exhibit 5.1.

Schultz believed that the kind of organization that Starbucks was, and, in turn, the way that it did business, would become a source of sustainable competitive advantage. In his words, "[T]he values of the company and the guiding principles became a unique sustainable competitive advantage." In effect, Schultz understood the role of culture as a building block of organizational success, but he did not know of the concept of "corporate culture" per se as a management tool. Instead, it was an intuitive insight for him.

This set of principles addresses the product, the treatment of people, the treatment of customers, the company's role in relation to the environment, and profitability. One critical feature of Starbucks' culture concerned the treatment of people. Schultz wanted everyone in the company to have a stake in Starbucks' success; in effect, he wanted everyone at Starbucks to be and behave like owners.

Schultz's beliefs

The company's initial culture was a manifestation of Schultz's personal beliefs. From 1987 to 1994 what energized Starbucks, according to Schultz, were the twin pillars of (1) the commitment to the quality of its coffee, and (2) the quality of its values. They were synchronized and, in Schultz's word, "seamless." As he states:

That's what attracted people to the company. That's what sustained us, and that's what gave us our stake in the ground and we were able to measure our decision against that. Why don't we franchise? Because it wasn't part of our value system. Why don't we sell flavored coffee? Because it is a bastardization of the product. Why do we give everyone health benefits? Why do we give everyone ownership? Because these things are central to our value system and the way we treat people.

As in any true entrepreneurship, Howard Schultz is the embodiment of the company. A great deal of what characterized Starbucks is derived from his own background and values. His commitment to Starbucks' treatment of people, all of whom are called "partners," was derived from how he saw his own father treated in the business world. In fact, it was the *reverse* of what his own father experienced.

Overall development of the pyramid

In a sense, the development of Starbucks Corporation's Pyramid of Organizational Development™ was very typical of most companies. It had very well-developed markets and products, somewhat developed resources and operational systems, relatively underdeveloped management systems, and a well-defined culture.

Results of building Starbucks

By 1998 Starbucks had grown to more than $1.3 billion in net revenues and had 1,886 stores, including 1,688 company-owned stores. In addition, the company's stock price increased from $13.50 in the first quarter of the 1993 fiscal year to a high of $58 during the fourth quarter of fiscal 1998. By 2000 Starbucks had over $2.2 billion in revenues and over 2,000 stores, more than achieving the targets it had set for itself six years previously.

Another six years later, in 2006, Starbucks had about 6,000 company-owned stores and some 3,000 licensed locations. The company had grown in revenues to more than $6.4 billion. The company has also announced that the total number of stores it envisions as being possible is about 30,000. This would mean that Starbucks has the potential to become a $30 billion company.

Conclusion

How did Starbucks become what it is today – the leading brand and purveyor of specialty coffee on a worldwide basis? Why did Schultz see opportunity where others did not? Why did he see the possibility of transforming coffee from a commodity into something very different after visiting Milan, which has been visited by countless others for many, many years?

Typically, after an entrepreneur such as Schultz has had a brilliant insight, others can recognize the concept and think that it was "obvious." It was not obvious. If it was so obvious, why did Schultz have difficulty convincing the original founders of Starbucks about the merits of the idea? Why did it take a year and a half to convince investors to provide the $1 million? Why did he have to struggle to keep the support of his board of directors?

One of the keys to Starbucks' ultimate success was Schultz's vision and leadership. He saw the possibilities to create a changed paradigm of the industry. "Starbucks" has become a worldwide brand and synonymous with lattes and cappuccino. Starbucks has become an icon of corporate success. Its success was not about its coffee, however; it was about the strategic and organizational changes that the company made to differentiate itself from its competition. These were led by Schultz and his close associates, Smith and Behar. Together they formed the core leadership molecule that has created the phenomenon that is Starbucks.

6 Strategic marketing through HR interventions: a case study of Indian Oil Corporation

Introduction

Indian Oil Corporation (IOC) is India's first and only Fortune 200 company.[1] IOC is India's largest and most prominent commercial undertaking, with over $41 billion in turnover, and it accounts for about 42 percent of India's refining capacity. It is the nineteenth largest petroleum company in the world and has been adjudged as the number one petroleum trading company amongst all the national oil companies in the Asia-Pacific region.

In spite of its size and economic strength, IOC was not immune to the winds of economic change. The dynamics of the external environment forced IOC's leaders to become acutely aware of the necessity to change *their* way of conducting business. The future success – and, indeed, the very survival – of IOC was in doubt.

IOC needed to change its business paradigm and transform itself from a mere distributor of petroleum products into a strategic marketing organization. The challenge was to bring about a rapid and thoroughgoing change in the way business was being conducted.

This chapter examines how this Asian behemoth with 30,000 employees and a "chaltha hai" (anything goes) culture transformed itself into a professional strategic marketing organization.[2] Even though strategic change efforts were targeted throughout the entire organization, we focus in this chapter on the Marketing Division of the organization. Although this is a functional subunit of the company it is

This chapter was co-authored with Dr. N. G. Kannan, Director (Marketing), member of the board, Indian Oil Corporation, and Ms. Rangapriya Kannan-Narasimhan.

[1] IOC was ranked as no. 153 in the "Fortune 500" list of companies in the rankings published in 2006.

[2] We thank Mr. D. K. Sharma, Lieutenant Colonel C. S. Shankar and Mrs. Purnima Kulkarni for their assistance with this chapter.

a key component of operations. In addition, it is the Marketing Division that bears the brunt of competition and grapples with the strategic problem of retaining market share and industry leadership.

One significant aspect of this case is the unique strategy adopted by IOC's Marketing Division. It was a strategy based upon culture, rather than products and markets or marketing. The mantra was: *"Focus on people, and they will focus on business."* The underlying notion was to channel marketing strategies through human resource (HR) initiatives and cultural change efforts. In stark contrast to organizations that utilize marketing strategies to improve marketing performance, IOC utilized human resource strategies to improve marketing performance!

The beginning of Indian Oil Corporation

Indian Oil Corporation was formed in 1964 as a result of the Indian government's initiatives to establish a self-reliant oil industry. Until 1958 India's oil production had been heavily dependent on foreign countries and was dominated by multinational companies such as Shell, Caltex, Esso and Stanvac. Recognizing the inherent perils of leaving the nation's petroleum sector vulnerable to foreign domination, Pandit Jawaharlal Nehru – India's first Prime Minister – stated in 1956:

A country that does not produce its own oil is in a weak position. From the point of view of defense, the absence of oil is a fatal weakness.

In response to the Prime Minister's call, Indian Refineries Ltd. was set up in the petroleum sector, in August 1958, under 100 percent government ownership. Once the refining process had been set up, the next step was to ensure that petroleum products could be distributed to the different parts of the country. To address this need, Indian Oil Company Ltd., another wholly government-owned company, was formed on June 30, 1959. Its primary task was to distribute petroleum products to consumers, irrespective of logistical constraints, unyielding terrain, or other bottlenecks.

Although the establishment of these two companies was a step in the right direction, the Indian oil industry was still largely in the hands of the multinational companies. The 1962 Indo-China war clearly drove home the point about the necessity for an *Indian* oil company like never before. It was imperative to establish an Indian oil company that could emerge subsequently as the leader in the Indian market.

This was the backdrop against which a new era dawned on the petroleum horizon of India on September 1, 1964, when Indian Oil Refineries Ltd. and Indian Oil Company Ltd. were amalgamated to form Indian Oil Corporation Ltd. The objective of the merger was to synchronize oil refining activities perfectly with the marketing functions. The aim was to achieve vertical integration coupled with economies of scale.

The growth phase

With initial impetus from the government of India (GOI), the growth of IOC was phenomenal. Starting with a meager turnover of Rs. 78 crore ($120 million) in 1964/5, the company's turnover reached over Rs. 1,800,000 crore ($41 billion) in 2005/6. As India's flagship oil company, IOC accounts for 56 percent of the petroleum products market share among public sector unit (PSU) companies and operates ten of India's eighteen refineries, with an output of 1 million barrels per day (bpd). In addition, IOC owns and operates the country's largest network of cross-country crude oil and product pipelines, of nearly 9,000 km, and has a countrywide network of over 33,000 sales points.

IOC's cooking gas (sold under the brand name Indane) reaches out to nearly 43 million households in over 2,100 markets through the country's largest network of 4,500 distributors. IOC's lubricants (under the brand name Servo) have a 45 percent market share and are sold through more than 15,000 company retail outlets, besides a countrywide network of bazaar traders. IOC's ISO-9002 certified aviation service has a market share of 67 percent and meets the fuel and lubricants needs of most of the domestic and international airlines, defense services and private aircraft operators. It is important to note, however, that IOC's impressive growth prior to 1998 (when the Indian downstream sector was deregulated) can largely be attributed to the non-competitive external environment in India and the protection offered by the GOI to the oil industry.

Pre-1991 external environment

Until 1991 the government imposed rigid restrictions on private investments in the oil industry (as with many other sectors), had heavy licensing requirements and discouraged foreign direct investment in the petroleum sector. Being a government-owned company, IOC was able to secure crude oil at extremely low prices and its entire inventory at low, government-determined prices.

In addition, the organization was a virtual monopoly in the industry, supplying basic customer necessities such as kerosene (used as a cooking fuel by India's lowest income class) and liquefied petroleum gas (LPG – cooking fuel for most of India's middle class). As we have seen, it had a leading market share for its higher-end products, such as lubricants and fuel (for both cars and aircraft). Prior to the introduction of deregulation, IOC's closest competitor, Hindustan Petroleum Corporation (HPC), had approximately a quarter of its refining capacity and a half of its market share. The demand for all petroleum products was high and supply was restricted by production constraints (due to government licensing regulations and the lack of private players in the industry). It was a seller's market, and IOC was unquestionably the 900 pound gorilla in the petroleum industry.

The organizational (internal) situation

The internal environment at IOC was equally enviable. As a progressive employer, concerned with employee welfare (which was typical of many prestigious Indian organizations in that era), IOC offered an excellent package of benefits. At the very basic level, employees were provided with subsidized housing in refinery townships and other locations, total medical care, and a host of facilities such as conveyance, leave travel assistance, school facilities for their children, home computers, and holiday homes at subsidized rates in most parts of the country. Above a certain level in the hierarchy other perquisites, such as telephones and car and air travel for the entire family, were added to employee benefits. The defined benefit pension plans and other retirement benefits provided by the organization were also very generous. Even retired employees were eligible to receive subsidized medical care and holiday homes at subsidized rates. At IOC, employee benefits were so liberal that the employees felt: "You ask for it, you get it!" In addition, the organization believed in (and still believes in) employee loyalty through lifetime employment. IOC has an internal labor market, and officers of the company are recruited at the lowest level and moved up the ranks. Moreover, staff cadre employees also have numerous opportunities to move to the officers' cadre and then move up to higher ranks in the organization.

Guaranteed lifetime employment combined with excellent employee benefits and a non-competitive external economic environment bred a laid-back attitude, however, and a sloppy work culture within the organization. The customer did not figure in the scheme of things. It was not uncommon for consumers to wait for six months, occasionally as much as two years, to get a gas connection for kitchen use – a basic necessity. Similarly, service at retail pump outlets was generally up to basic minimum levels only. Customers had to wait in line for long periods of time to fill gas and the quality of the fuel was left to the hands of the onsite dealers and pump attendants. Employees were not pro-vided with adequate incentives to perform. Due to the internal labor market within the organization, promotion up to a certain level was virtually guaranteed. The prevalent attitude then was "If you work hard you will get promoted in three years; if you don't it will take only five." An atmosphere of "laissez-faire leadership" prevailed.

IOC was typical of other public sector companies in that decade – overstaffed, and with underworked employees and unions that discouraged employees to work beyond minimum requirements. Despite the lack of a professional work culture, however, the organ-ization continued to make huge profits on account of the favorable economic environment.

Winds of economic change

The organization's smooth journey was rocked by the winds of eco-nomic change in 1991. The changes brought in by the GOI, culmin-ating in the deregulation introduced in 1998, were unprecedented. The troika of globalization, liberalization, and privatization that were meant to drive India's economic development spelt potential disaster for IOC (in addition to other Indian organizations that had been protected until then by GOI policies). Specifically with regard to hydrocarbons, the liberalization/globalization/privatization policies attracted private players and multinational companies (MNCs) to participate in the petroleum sector – both in the upstream and downstream segments.[3] With private sector and MNC participation in the Indian oil scene, challenges were multiplying by the day.

---

[3] "Downstream" refers to petroleum refining and marketing and "upstream" refers to oil exploration and drilling.

Changes in market conditions

The market shifted from being supply-driven to being customer-driven. The competitive pressures from MNCs and private Indian companies increased enormously. The deregulation brought a whole range of players into the petroleum sector, which had been the preserve of four public sector oil companies for the last four decades: IOC, HPC, BPC (Bharat Petroleum Corporation) and IBP (Indo Burma Petroleum). International and private players entered each and every segment of the downstream marketing arena. This included multinational corporations such as Shell, Exxon, Caltex, Gulf Oil, Pennzoil, Elf, and Mobil; domestic corporations such as Reliance Industries Ltd. and Essar Oil Ltd.; and other public sector organizations such as Mangalore Refinery and Petrochemicals Ltd. and Numaligarh Refinery Ltd. IOC's competitors were not only targeting the retail customers through their retail marketing network but were also selling products directly to bulk customers (commercial, industrial, and defense, and other core sectors such as coal, steel, power, state transport, etc.). The average customer by now was more aware of product quality and service and, most importantly, had the choice to switch brands.

Results of changing to a competitive environment

The competitive nature of the market was reflected in the negative sales performance of the company between 1999 and 2002. For the first time since its inception IOC began to lose revenues, leading to operating loss situations in some quarters. The net result of this change in the competitive environment was that IOC's virtual monopoly ended and the threat of market share erosion and sinking margins hung like the sword of Damocles over the company.

Loss of talent

In addition, the new entrants were poaching high-quality talent from IOC. MNCs and private companies were able to offer compensation packages that ranged from twice to eight times IOC's compensation package. Additionally, these organizations also offered the possibility of future career opportunities abroad, such as in the United States and

Europe. For bright aspiring employees this was a fantastic opportunity to leave a system that treated its best people only *marginally better* than its worst. IOC was losing its most talented individuals to competitors.

Government restrictions

A further corporate problem was that the private players and MNCs were not hindered by the legacy networks and onerous bureaucratic procedures that were mandatory for oil public sector units. For example, a private competitor could set up refineries and other infrastructural facilities such as retail outlets anywhere in the country according to market demands, but Indian PSUs faced many restrictions. IOC, like other Indian PSUs, needed to secure numerous government approvals and clearances to set up infrastructure and retail outlets, which entailed dealing with burdensome administrative procedures and much government red tape.

The pressure of rising international oil prices complicated matters and resulted in a loss of revenues. Because of policy restrictions, the government did not allow oil companies to revise their selling prices, even though the purchase price of crude oil had shot up substantially in international markets. This resulted in a situation in which IOC (and other oil companies) had to sell about 80 percent of their total sales volume below cost, thereby leading to non-recovery of margins and revenue losses.

The net result was that IOC's situation was similar to that of a novice swimmer, thrown into rough waters with limbs tied to a heavy stone and a mandate to reach the shore! It was not, to say the least, an enviable position.

The need for fundamental strategic and organizational change

Given these changes in the external environment, IOC's leadership became acutely aware of the need for fundamental strategic and organizational change. It was clear to senior leaders that they had to change *their* way of conducting business in order to adapt to the new realities of the changed environment.

The IOC leadership believed it was necessary to change the business paradigm and transform the company from a mere distributor of petroleum products to a strategic marketing organization. They also perceived that fundamental strategic changes were required in the organization structure, systems, and procedures, and also in the key area of human resource management. Most importantly, IOC leadership felt that the need for a radical cultural transformation was imperative. This meant that its employees' mindset about how to conduct business needed to be altered dramatically – and this, too, within a short span of time.

The message that had to be sent to employees was: "The way in which we are currently doing business is passé. Being responsive to market demands will be the critical factor for survival." The overall challenge was to bring about a rapid transformation in the way business was being conducted in the organization. IOC's very survival was in question.

Leading the changes (1991–2003)

The top management at IOC took numerous steps to meet the challenges. An important step was the formal redefinition of the organization's *raison d'être*, in the context of the sweeping changes taking place in the Indian nation itself.

Changing the corporate strategic vision

All the stakeholders of the organization were involved in the vision exercise. At a conclave of board directors, senior executives, union and officer collectives, and various internal representatives, a retreat was held to deliberate on the need for a renewed vision. The week-long deliberations threw up several ideas, and the common consensus emerged that IOC should now focus on becoming an Indian transnational company operating in every segment of the hydrocarbon value chain.

IOC redefined its vision statement 1999 in the changed national context.[4] The statement that emerged was:

To be a major diversified, transnational, integrated energy company, with national leadership and a strong environment conscience, playing a national role in oil security and public distribution.

---

[4] IOC's mission statement was redefined at the same time.

It is important to note here that, despite aiming to have national leadership in the energy sector, IOC continued to emphasize its social responsibilities with regard to oil security and public distribution.

To lead the strategic change, one of the first strategies the company adopted was to restructure the entire organization.

Organizational restructuring (1995/6)

The restructuring exercise started in the fiscal year 1995/6 (ending March 31). One of India's premier management institutes, the Indian Institute of Management (Calcutta), was involved in the process. Previously IOC's Marketing Division had been organized on a geographic basis: north, east, west, and south. This had led to inefficiencies, such as delayed communication, delayed customer care decisions, and a duplication of efforts. As the company's leaders appreciated the inadequacies of the existing structure, the Marketing Division was restructured, resulting in the creation of fifteen state offices. The objective of the organizational restructuring exercise was to get closer to customers and fulfill their needs within the shortest possible turnaround time. The fifteen state offices were created to take care of the business lines. This was in addition to the four regional offices, which managed the support services required for business in the northern, eastern, western, and southern regions.

The state offices were the front-line offices, with exclusively sales-oriented functions. The sole responsibility of these offices was to concentrate on customer-related activities in the four core business lines: retail sales, consumer direct sales, LPG business, and lubricant sales. Moreover, customer-related service functions, such as finance, engineering, systems, and legal, were also created at the state offices. Operating and manufacturing units such as product terminals/depots, LPG bottling plants, etc. were under the control of the state offices. Additionally, retail sales units, such as divisional units for fuel sales and area offices for LPG sales, were also placed under the control of the state offices. Thus, the operating and manufacturing units of the organization were placed under the sales function (the state offices), thereby allowing the entire process to be driven by sales and marketing and not the other way around. The regional offices were entrusted with the responsibility of providing major services and resources, such as logistics, HR, accounting and finance, corporate communications, safety, quality, and maintenance, for the smooth functioning of the sales offices. The restructuring exercise was intended to reflect the shift in the organization's business paradigm from being a distributor to a strategic marketing organization.

Leading the changes (2003–6)

This section describes the further changes made within the organization itself to meet the environmental challenges. As noted above, the bulk of the responsibility for quick change fell primarily on the shoulders of the leadership of IOC's Marketing Division, as a result of its key strategic role in adapting to the competitive environment. Our discussion therefore focuses upon the changes in this key organizational unit.

Leadership of change

One of the key factors that influenced the change process significantly was the change in leadership. The board entrusted the responsibility to one of its functional directors, Dr. N. G. Kannan. Dr. Kannan, who was then the Director (HR), was to take on the marketing challenges to turn the organization around. That is, the head of HR was asked to take over the reins of marketing!

This was not surprising, given that Dr. Kannan had an MBA in marketing management and a doctorate in human resource management. In addition, he had about thirty-four years of experience within IOC and had held numerous field leadership positions, and at the same time had also worked in the organization's Training and HR Departments. His background in marketing and human resources, along with his organizational experience and exposure, helped him to have a keen appreciation of both the marketing challenges and the HR issues within the organization. He strongly believed that the only way to effect strategic marketing changes was through strategic human resource management. All IOC had to do was focus on human resources. This would automatically lead to people focusing on business – hence the mantra "Focus on people, and they will focus on business." This new paradigmatic shift initiated by him was well supported by the Chairman and other members of the board. IOC was discovering a new highway to growth.

Organizational changes

The organizational changes brought about between 2003 and 2006 can be classified into:

- changes in structure (organizational restructuring);
- changes in field leadership positions;
- strategic HR initiatives; and
- strategic marketing initiatives.

Organizational restructuring (2003)

Another restructuring exercise was carried out this year. This was intended to give more thrust, exclusivity, and focus to sales (based on the then market situation). Divisional offices (which were focusing on fuel sales) were further bifurcated into *retail divisional offices*, to focus exclusively on retail sales, and *consumer divisional offices*, for direct sales to bulk customers. As with the state offices, the divisional offices also coordinated closely with the operating units to meet the demands and needs of customers.

Identifying leaders for leadership positions

Along with the restructuring of the organization, another critical task was to identify key talent for the leadership positions within the organization. The objective was to place the right kind of people in strategic leadership positions within the organization. Once these leaders were identified and placed, the next step was to empower and energize them to ensure strong organizational performance. Each of the offices (state offices, manufacturing units, and divisional units) needed leaders. The next challenge was to identify leaders within the organization who would drive marketing efforts and subsequent organizational performance.

Although it seemed like an easy and a common-sense solution to place leaders in strategic positions, in practice it was easier said than done. The first challenge was to identify leaders. For identifying potential leaders a two-phased strategy was adopted. In phase I the management team at IOC's Marketing Division elected to follow Vilfredo Pareto's 80:20 rule. The decision was to focus on 20 percent of the outstanding top performers, who would be able to handle

80 percent of the organizational load. Regardless of their formal position in the organizational hierarchy, top performers were identified across the organization to fill these leadership positions. Performers from each grade and level, including those from the lowest levels, were identified and entrusted with leadership positions. This was very different from the earlier model, in which employees had been positioned in leadership roles based on their position in the formal organizational hierarchy and seniority, irrespective of their competence and performance.

The new guiding philosophy was that if the leadership positions are managed efficiently and effectively, then everything else will follow. The leaders chosen were to act as "champions of change." The mandate for these change leaders was to enable, empower, and energize their followers to perform. In phase II employees with high potential were targeted, and the organization's focus then was on developing these as high performers and future leaders.

The change leaders selected in phase I were empowered by providing them with the necessary resources and the requisite decision-making authority for ensuring good performance. They were also exposed to competency-building workshops, soft skills training to hone their people-handling aspects, and customer relationship management and orientation for achieving customer excellence. The key message that permeated throughout the organization was that they could not afford to demotivate or disempower even a single leader, even by chance. Doing so would be tantamount to demotivating the entire team under that leader's command. This astute piece of forethought bore significant results for the organization, as will become clear in the next section of this chapter.

As indicated previously, IOC started as a rationing company, moved to being a distribution company, and was now struggling to emerge as a professional strategic marketing company. During this process, the demands on the workforce, especially the sales force, in terms of the competencies and skill sets required have changed. Targeted human resource interventions were required to equip the workforce with new competencies.

It is important to remember that the Marketing Division's top management's philosophy was "Focus on people, and they will focus on business." Given this philosophy, the organization adopted a unique approach for achieving marketing excellence: "Achieving marketing excellence through strategic HR initiatives." These initiatives were a powerful tool for reorienting the marketing efforts and for aligning HR with the company's marketing efforts.

Strategic HR initiatives

Two consulting firms (Hewitt Associates and Ernst & Young) were engaged to do a gap analysis on employee competencies and employee engagement. One of the two studies measured what the employees were able to do and the other measured what they were willing to do. Based on the feedback from both the studies, the management team at Marketing Division designed a plan to align human resource capabilities with the business requirements. A number of initiatives were taken.

(1) Identify top performers – i.e., stars – and identify people with high potential to develop them into stars.
(2) Career tracking. This referred to monitoring the career progression of top performers to focus on, develop and retain star employees.
(3) Competency-building workshops. The competencies required for different product lines and sales were different. Depending on product lines handled and individual job responsibilities, competencies were built throughout the organization.
(4) Empowerment through assignment. Through this exercise top performers were given prestigious assignments. For example, certain positions in the organization, such as divisional heads, had more clout than others. Thus, although two employees could be of the same grade levels, top performers were assigned more prestigious positions.
(5) Leadership mirroring exercise. This exercise was aimed at evaluating leaders in leadership positions throughout the organization and providing them 360 degree feedback for improving their leadership abilities.
(6) Introduction of Employee Satisfaction Index and Customer Satisfaction Index to measure employee and customer satisfaction on a regular basis and take immediate corrective action based on their feedback.

In addition to introducing HR interventions on a systemic level, numerous ad hoc initiatives were introduced. The Training Department of the organization was a partner for these change initiatives. An example of one such initiative was the "Instrument of Appreciation." Employees who contributed to the organization beyond their job descriptions were awarded an "Instrument of Appreciation Certificate." Awardees of this certificate entered the hallowed "Hall of Fame" within the organization. Furthermore, the Appreciation Certificate became a part of the employee's file and was considered during promotion and bonus decisions. As opposed to an "informal pat on the back," this instrument held significant importance for employees because it translated into high visibility and tangible benefits.

Another initiative that was highly appreciated by the employees was rewarding top performers in the presence of their families. Top performers were explicitly identified for the first time within the company and rewarded at state level, regional level, and headquarters level. The reward functions were held in the presence of families at a holiday resort to enable employees' families to share in the employee's success. The families of employees took deep pride in their family member's recognition. This led to families of employees encouraging the employees to contribute their best to the organization.

Another exercise carried out by the Training Department was the "Petro Quiz," in which all employees were eligible to participate.[5] The quiz was held at different levels to screen talent within the organization, and was concluded at national level. The final-round participants and the winners of the competition had the opportunity to interact with the top management. This resulted in two important benefits to the organization.

Firstly, employees increased their knowledge base in order to participate in the quiz and win. This created more awareness within the organization. Secondly, given that IOC has eight levels of management tiers (grades A through H, starting with A), officers from the lowest grade rarely had the opportunity to interact more than about two or three levels beyond their immediate supervisor. With the introduction of the quiz, final-round participants and winners were

---

[5] The "Instrument of Appreciation" and "Petro Quiz" details are based on interviews with Lieutenant Colonel C. S. Shankar (Chief Training and Development Manager, IOC).

catapulted into high visibility (which affected their subsequent job posting into high-profile and leadership positions) and interacted with the board of directors and other senior management personnel. Participants at other levels, such as quarter-final and semi-final levels, had the opportunity to interact with the senior management teams at the state and regional levels. Thus, an A-grade officer from a remote part of the country had the opportunity to be visible and successful. This motivated employees tremendously and created increased awareness levels within the organization.

As a result of these efforts, the organization was restructured, leaders were identified, and HR interventions were introduced to ensure a future pipeline of leaders and to have the employees with the necessary awareness and competencies to perform. The next step was to design and implement strategies for market share growth and market leadership.

For practitioners and researchers in management, it is important to note that researchers in management have consistently highlighted the importance of organizations having their infrastructure in place before attempting to grow their market share.[6] Most organizations play "catch-up" with infrastructure once they have increased their market share, however. More often than not their attempts come to naught, because their infrastructure is not adequate for the organization's stage of growth. In the case of IOC, the organization's infrastructure and, more importantly, its front-line leaders and employees were prepared meticulously and were ready to handle the challenges. The next logical step was to win the war on market share and leadership.

Marketing initiatives
One of the important steps taken by the Marketing Division was to designate customer service themes for each year. The three years 2004, 2005, and 2006 were called "Customer Care Year," "Customer Delight Year," and "Customer Service Excellence Year" respectively.

On January 1, 2004, amidst the festivity in IOC retail outlets throughout the country, the concept of "Customer Ambassadors" was launched. A customer outreach team comprising IOC employees drawn from a wide range of functional groups such as LPG, HR,

---

[6] Based on Flamholtz and Randle, *Growing Pains*.

Lubricants, Pricing, Aviation, Training, Consumer, Finance, etc., irrespective of ranks and positions, participated in this program. This program was launched as a motivational exercise to support and supplement the regular field force and to bring a sense of ownership to the employees. These dedicated "Customer Ambassador" teams not only monitored the levels of customer service in the retail outlets but also surveyed customers on their satisfaction levels and received feedback. The objective was to receive structured customer feedback through independent sources, which would in turn be used to formulate new initiatives to enhance the service standards of the retail outlets.

The exercise had a significant impact on two counts. The obvious advantage was the "Hawthorne effect." The mere fact that employees from retail outlets were being monitored by teams led to increased motivational levels. Hitherto unheard-of retail outlets in remote parts of the country were receiving attention from officers of the company. This led to better "on the spot" customer service. An additional benefit, which was not immediately apparent, lay in sensitizing the staff to the needs of the line. Employees from staff functions who were not used to dealing with customers were put through an "experiential exposure." This enabled these employees to get insights into customer behavior. By sensitizing staff to the needs of the customer and the organization, IOC was able to get the staff employees out of the piles of paper and see the organization in action. The company's leaders understood that the organization could not succeed without sensitizing people at all levels. Thus, the organization was able to better align the support functions with the line functions. The approach was people-centric and not system-centric.

To take the concept of customer care even further, 2005 was observed as the "Customer Delight Year." A comprehensive feedback mechanism was designed to elicit responses and measure the happiness levels of customers. Additionally, different functions within the organization were instructed to prepare a formal schedule for customer-centric activities. All business lines created monthly schedules with the objective of delighting customers. These business lines were evaluated against certain parameters on customer service. This initiative improved the overall customer satisfaction index significantly and created awareness at field levels to go for customer-related activities. Intensive on-the-job training of the forecourt personnel, retail outlet managers, and dealers was unleashed to bring in bench-marked levels of service throughout the country.

2006 was designated as "Customer Service Excellence Year." A program campaign called "Sambandh" (meaning "relationship") was launched to bring together all the stakeholders, with the aim of achieving extraordinary results in marketing. "Sambandh" had two themes: (1) theme one was that the organization "cares" for its stakeholders, and (2) theme two was "Let our passions fly."[7]

To ensure that all employees shared this collective dream, structured programs were conducted at each and every location, with a missionary type of zeal. Two-person teams, consisting of one executive and one non-executive, were coached on the various facets of this initiative, so that the euphoria of "Customer Service Excellence Year" could be visibly reflected in every activity across the organization.

The "Sambandh" program was carried out at different levels, namely at the level of individuals, family members, dealers, etc., but also at local unit level, state level, and national level. Employees' families were also involved in the "Sambandh" program, so as to create awareness among them and so that they could spread the news by "word of mouth" regarding IOC's activities. The objective was to help forge a very strong relationship between stakeholders and to ensure that these stakeholders would have a strong urge to perform to maintain the leadership position of IOC through the achievement of customer excellence.

By specifically designating each of these years with particular goals, the leadership was able to communicate exactly the focus of that year and what was expected of the employees. These messages from top management had the additional advantage of providing local managers and union leaders with a platform from which to communicate the change efforts and objectives clearly to employees without diluting the content of the message. The concept of customer service was reinforced by bombarding employees with these messages, and this had a cascading effect throughout the organization. Every single employee understood how his or her actions contributed to the organization's performance overall. For example, for the first time a

---

[7] This latter theme aimed to kindle fire in the belly of the stakeholders, and was particularly applicable to employees.

pump attendant at an IOC retail outlet was able to understand the importance of providing excellent service to a truck driver, who in turn would come in for repeat sales and bring in more customers. Once the year's goals had been clarified and memorized by employees, they were able to forge ahead to meet the expectations for that year.

Two of the major sources of revenue for IOC, as with any other organization, were retail sales and direct sales. We first focus on the initiatives taken in the retail sales sector, and then discuss the marketing initiatives in the direct sales area.

Retail sales

Even as early as the mid-1990s IOC had revolutionized the Indian petroleum retail segment with its unique "Retail Visual Identity" programs. These programs were all about boosting visibility by upgrading retail outlets and modernizing and automating them. As competitors caught up with this idea, IOC's retail branding had to be stepped up several levels beyond what the competition was offering. The XTRACARE retail outlet template was launched in 2005. This was the culmination of planning in retail design, product and service upgrades, capability training, automation, loyalty programs, and retail site management techniques, all of which were benchmarked to global standards. All IOC's XTRACARE outlets were benchmarked to international standards of quality and quantity, housekeeping, maintenance, and customer service, certified by the world-renowned agency M/s Bureau Veritas (BV).

Furthermore, IOC introduced fortnightly random sampling, with specific importance given to RON (Research Octane Number) testing, which is truly the definitive test for quality and quantity. In another pioneering move, third-party certification – by BV – is also being implemented, for the first time, on a range of parameters, including hygiene, service, the efficiency of the forecourt (pump island), housekeeping, maintenance, allied services, and customer satisfaction. The maintenance of various pieces of equipment at the XTRACARE outlets is being carried out by regular original equipment manufacturers under a unique "Equipment Quality Outsourcing" system.

A vital differentiator in the IOC XTRACARE outlets has been the importance given to the front-line pump attendants at the gas stations. The gas stations' attendants represent the organization to the customer, and hence special emphasis was given to training these attendants. The front-line pump attendants were trained in three levels of competencies: customer service, personal hygiene/grooming, and customer complaint redressals. Additionally, the XTRACARE dealers underwent a state-of-the-art training system from the "Retail Site Business Management" module, a unique training template culled out of "best global practices" in retail sales management.

As part of the program, high-performing pump attendants are rewarded with extremely attractive compensation packages. High-performing dealers who continue to sustain the high levels of XTRACARE are eligible for a wide range of monetary incentives for every kiloliter sold, and also get lump sum cash rewards for every year. This is in addition to the regular commissions and promotional benefits that are offered to the dealers. This resulted in boosting the brand equity value of IOC to $5.6 billion for the fiscal year 2004/5, a significant improvement from the previous year's figure of $3.75 billion. IOC was ranked as number one in India among all companies (including MNCS operating in India) in terms of brand equity.

Direct sales

One of IOC's primary strengths in the area of marketing and customer satisfaction is its excellent infrastructure. Having been in business for over fifty years, IOC has a vast infrastructural network of refineries, cross-country pipelines, and supply points, etc., which are well spread out across the Indian subcontinent. This offers an unparalleled and inimitable advantage to this organization: IOC has a logistics advantage that provides its direct customers with an enhanced level of confidence with regard to timely supplies of quality products at competitive prices. By leveraging this advantage, IOC has been able to retain its current businesses, despite competition from the new entrants, through the signing of strategic medium- and long-term agreements with customers.

Moreover, IOC has a unique "Key Account Management" concept for high-volume customers, to ensure total customer satisfaction through single window services. In the Key Account Management concept a single IOC representative is responsible for specific customers. The IOC representative assigned to a given customer will cater to all the customer's needs and give him or her assistance. Earlier, customers had to deal individually with different departments.

This led to gross inefficiencies, such as communication gaps between departments and between the customer and the organization, delayed customer service, and lower customer satisfaction levels. As a result of the Key Account Management exercise, the overall customer satisfaction index score at IOC increased to 9.0 (on a scale of 0 to 10), as compared to the baseline average of 7.0. This single initiative for bulk customers earned tremendous goodwill for the company and resulted in customers becoming increasingly loyal to IOC. It was not surprising, therefore, that IOC's market share showed a positive turnaround, even while the heat from the competition was picking up!

Barriers to the change process

Although the company had identified numerous strategies to engineer the turnaround, it encountered numerous problems during the change process, as is typical with any large organization. Two of the primary challenges were (1) effectively communicating the need for change, and (2) changing the mindset of the trade unions, which were capable of derailing the entire process.

IOC is a very large organization, with over 500 work locations. In addition, it has over 20,000 dealers and distributors, who represent IOC to the customers. Even more so than usual, therefore, the communication of important policies, decisions, new work values, and other important issues became a major problem in itself. It was particularly difficult to communicate the need for "change" in the organization down the line without distorting the content of the message. Compounding the problem was the lack of an adequate communication infrastructure in India in terms of Internet access or a reliable telephone service. Some of IOC's employees were in remote and inaccessible areas of the country, and it was necessary to communicate the new face of the organization to each and every one of them.

The second challenge was changing the mindset of the leaders and members of the trade unions who were required to understand the organization's imperatives and respond to the situational demands. It was far from easy to bring in a quick change of mindset for employees, however, especially with workmen who had over thirty years of tenure and were embedded in a particular organizational culture.

They had a certain way of doing things and it had worked very well for them for a long time.

The solution to these issues was found by interacting with collectives on a frequent basis and by taking them into the company's total confidence. Trade union leaders were taken into complete confidence, and were made aware of the survival issues that the company was facing. Additionally, their assistance was enlisted to communicate the absolute necessity for change to the union members. Having the buy-in from union leaders and the informal communication through them helped the process to a great extent. Furthermore, several workshop sessions were conducted to create awareness and educate the employees. The Training Department completely revamped the training content for these training programs.

The leaders of the collectives addressed such workshops to ensure a better appreciation of the issues on the part of their members. Changing the mindset of trade union members continues to be a major challenge, however, and many of them still do not have a complete picture of the deregulated scenario and the fierce competition the company is facing.

Similar procedures were used to create awareness among the company's large network of more than 20,000 dealers and distributors. By creating champions among them, through panels such as a chairman's panel and gold circle, platinum circle, and star distributors, IOC created superstars among the dealers and distributors. These dealers and distributors in turn acted as role models for other channel partners. Special communication bulletins were also issued for the channel partners.

Results of the change efforts

Despite the bottlenecks, IOC was extremely successful in its change efforts. The results of the strategic organizational changes in the Marketing Division led to outstanding performance by the company as a whole.

2004 closed with sales of 46.2 million metric tons (mmt) of petroleum products and record growth of approximately 875 thousand metric tons (tmt) – i.e., 1.9 percent – over the previous year. For the first time since 1999/2000 the division closed the year with positive growth. Therefore, 2003/4 can be aptly described as the "turnaround year" (see exhibit 6.1).

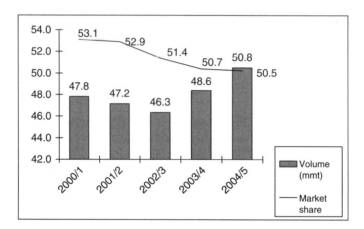

Exhibit 6.1 Indian Oil Corporation: growth, 2000 to 2005
Notes: The sales trend has been reversed even though the market share trend remains the same. The breakdown of the 2004/5 volume figure of 50.8 mmt includes the Marketing Division's sales of 48.1 mmt and the export sales of 1.9 mmt, plus Assam Oil Division's sales of 0.8 mmt.

IOC's blazing advance in the face of relentless competition is a testimony to the commitment and professional competence of the company's Marketing Division. The added impetus provided by the multifarious activities of the Customer Care Year resulted in IOC selling over 48.1 mmt of fuels and lubes, besides exporting 1.9 mmt during 2004/5. The landmark achievement has been arresting the trend of reducing market share experienced since 2000/1.

All these have led IOC's Marketing Division to emerge with flying colors against its competitors' performance since 2003. This has been possible only with the complete organizational focus of seizing every opportunity for selling that single extra liter of product. The quick turnaround would not have been achievable without the focused implementation of the strategic change process, with encouragement from all divisions of the company, the passionate involvement of employees, excellent support by the collectives and the reseller network, and the continued patronage of customers.

The company's efforts to be a strategic marketing company and a professional organization have received recognition from outside agencies as well, through several prestigious awards. The laurels that were conferred on the company by outside agencies during this period include an "Excellence in Marketing" award, an "Excellence in Communication" award, a "Best Corporate Citizen" award, and a "Best Employer to Work for" award.

Continuing changes required

As noted in chapter 1, change is a process rather than an event. Although IOC has been extraordinarily successful thus far in its turnaround and in meeting the challenges, the war is still far from being won. As in any deregulated market, the company with the biggest market share is the most vulnerable. Although the initiatives discussed above continue within the organization and yield the desired benefits, there remains vast scope for improvement.

IOC's present challenge is to continue to remain the least-cost supplier. To address this issue, the organization is now looking at every step in its supply chain so as to optimize the process. An optimization group has been set up, tasked with looking at the supply chain all the way from crude procurement to the ultimate sale in the supply outlet.

Another continuing challenge is to ensure that everyone in the organization – every stakeholder, including the dealers and distributors of IOC – understands the revised role and mission of the organization and reorients himself or herself to facing the impending challenges. This was the biggest challenge then, and it continues to be a challenge. Once this has been established, the whole organization will respond effectively to any situation, as there is no dearth of capabilities in the company.

Conclusion

IOC's case study provides a sterling example of how an organization can change itself radically through its people. The philosophy followed in the Marketing Division ("Focus on people, and they will focus on business") has yielded extraordinary results for the company as a whole. IOC transformed itself from a sluggish, inert giant into a proactive, agile strategic marketing organization that was able to exceed expectations in meeting marketing challenges. This case study has important implications for management theory and practice.

It is significant to note that the organization's transformation occurred through HR strategic initiatives, through cultural change, and through galvanizing people into action. Often cultural change initiatives and HR interventions are seen as "soft and mushy," "nice to have" but not a must-have. IOC's case example disproves this notion and demonstrates that strategic change through HR interventions and organizational culture impacts the bottom line rapidly and significantly.

A second point to note is that managers are aware that most organizations have been successful in designing innovative change strategies, but that they have failed during the implementation stage. IOC's case study provides a live example of how leading strategic change through people can lead to successful implementation of change strategies. It is hoped that this case study will serve as a guideline for leaders of organizations who wish to lead strategic change successfully in the future.

7 | *The evolution of Stan Tashman and Associates*

This chapter describes the transformation of Stan Tashman and Associates (a privately owned family-run business) from an entrepreneurial manufacturers' representative agency in the hardware and home improvement industry to an innovative, "best in class," professionally managed sales and service business as a response to changing environmental (industry) conditions. The chapter also describes how, after completing the initial transformation of the company, the management team successfully guided the company through a period of rapid growth in response to changing industry dynamics. Specifically, the company quadrupled in size between 2004 and 2006 (increasing from 130 to 570 employees) while maintaining satisfied customers and retaining key cultural values (including a commitment to operating with integrity, valuing people, and providing excellent service).

The case gives us insight into the process of leading strategic and organizational change in response to changes in the environment. Specifically, the organizational changes were driven by current and expected industry consolidation. First we describe the history and development of Stan Tashman and Associates, and then we examine the process of change undertaken by the company.

Company background

The company was founded in southern California in 1961 when Stan Tashman agreed to represent his first manufacturer, Oxwall Tool Company. As a manufacturer's representative, or agent, it was Tashman's job to persuade retail businesses – such as hardware, drug, auto, discount, and variety stores and chains – to stock the manufacturer's products.

Over the next fifteen years Tashman built a solid foundation for his business by representing increasing numbers of manufacturers and developing relationships with new retail accounts. By 1976 he was representing product lines in the hardware, housewares, and home improvement industries to retailers in the western United States. He realized that it was time to move the business office out of his home and to hire people who could help him grow the business.

That year Tashman hired his first employees ("associates") – a salesman and a secretary – and opened an office in downtown Los Angeles. He continued to add employees and moved the office to leased space in Santa Monica in 1980. In 1987 Tashman purchased a building in Santa Monica, where the company's corporate head-quarters are still located.

When the founder's son, Rich Tashman, graduated from San Diego State University in 1981 with a degree in business, he accepted his father's offer to work full-time in the business. (During his college years, Rich had been exposed to the merchandising side of the business by working part-time to keep store shelves stocked at Builders Emporium and Handyman Stores with products represented by Stan Tashman and Associates.) Rich started out as a salesman calling on accounts in California. He focused initially on mid-sized retail accounts, and later on larger accounts. He did well and enjoyed the process of closing a sale. When Rich joined the company the total number of employees was seven; by 1990 the company had grown to twenty-seven employees.

The company gained a reputation as one of the most respected and recognized agencies on the West Coast. Many of the manufacturers that Stan Tashman and Associates represented during the 1980s and 1990s regularly named the firm as "Sales Agency of the Year" or "Top Producer of the Year."

Manufacturers expressed appreciation for the creativity and effectiveness of Stan Tashman and Associates' staff in helping stimulate significant growth in product sales. For example, a sales manager from one manufacturer wrote a letter acknowledging that the Tashman agency was really a "business partner." He continued, "Their knowledge of our customers and level of professionalism have proven to be a successful formula year after year."

The "mutual respect, trust, and confidence"[1] between father and son contributed to a solid partnership that helped spur further growth

---

[1] Quote from "History" document prepared by Stan Tashman and Associates, Inc. © 2005.

of the business. One major area of growth was in sales to the home improvement retail industry.

Adding a servicing function

Stan Tashman and Associates started a Service Division in the mid-1970s to help promote the sale of their customers' products at the retail level by setting up and maintaining in-store product displays and providing product training to store employees.

Servicing represented a new dimension of the relationship between Tashman and the manufacturers it represented. A major benefit for manufacturers was that effective servicing could increase product sales. A letter from a customer, Baldwin Hardware, illustrates this impact:

There are many service agencies that provide service to factories, but your company is passionate about what they do and it shows. We have had double digit positive comp[arable] sales in our lock business 2 of the 3 months since you came on board and the momentum is building!

Elmer's Glue acknowledged the Tashman agency's positive impact on sales by awarding them first, second, and third places in their sales contest – for increasing product sales by 25 percent over the prior year. Jacuzzi also recognized Tashman, for increasing sales by 76 percent. Stan Tashman commented about the level of account-ability required to be effective in servicing:

It's simply a whole different environment today than when I opened my doors 40 years ago. There are no smoke and mirrors in the service business – you either provide the service or you'll be out of business."[2]

Servicing also gave Stan Tashman and Associates an opportunity to provide valuable support to retailers.

Impact of industry structural change: "Big Box" retailers

In the 1980s consolidation and the rapid expansion of the Home Depot and other "Big Box" retailers brought major changes to the home improvement retail business model. The Home Depot opened its

---

[2] Quoted in "Training to Be the Best," *Agency Sales, the Marketing Magazine for Manufacturers' Agencies and Their Principals*, March 2001, 11.

first store on the West Coast in 1983, and by the end of the 1980s it had approximately thirty stores there, with plans to add more.

With a dwindling number of potential retail partners, agencies such as Stan Tashman and Associates needed to adjust to the changing business environment. Stan and Rich Tashman took the lead in responding to the opportunity to demonstrate to the Home Depot how their rep agency could contribute value as a business partner. Success in building a reputation for excellence with the Home Depot enabled Stan Tashman and Associates to grow more rapidly in the 1990s than in previous decades.

A major source of this growth was a significant increase in the proportion of Tashman's revenue that came from servicing "Big Box" retailers – such as the Home Depot and Home Base. Both accounts preferred to outsource responsibilities for stocking products, maintaining inventory, setting up and taking down displays, setting up new stores, etc. to service companies.

As the servicing side of the business grew over the next few years, Rich Tashman began to provide oversight for this component of the business.

Expanding the management team

Stan Tashman was proud of Rich's dedication to the business, his positive relationships with customers and employees, and his effectiveness in taking on management responsibilities.

In 1999 Stan made a decision that he felt would position the company well for the future. At a company dinner in August (attended by most of the company's employees) he surprised Rich by handing him the gavel and naming him President. The assembled employees rose to their feet and cheered the announcement. Stan assumed the role of Chairman and CFO, and Rich became responsible for the overall management of the business.

In August 2000 Ty Olson, an industry veteran, joined the Tashman management team to provide leadership in sales. The company benefited from Ty's expertise and talent in sales, his detailed knowledge of the retail flooring industry, and his contacts with manufacturers throughout the country. In 2002 Olson's successful contributions to the business were rewarded by an invitation from Stan and Rich Tashman to become a part-owner of the firm.

The complementary skills and mutual support among the three executives created an effective leadership team. Stan contributed his financial expertise and a passion for satisfying customers. Rich was able to articulate and communicate a vision that motivated employees and to apply his skills in management and organizational leadership to developing infrastructure and improving operations. Ty contributed merchandising expertise, an in-depth understanding of the needs of retail customers, and a talent for identifying potential problems and offering solutions to customers. In effect, these three executives now comprised the "leadership molecule," as described in chapter 3.

Another strength of the management team was that the three held similar values regarding customer service, relationship building, and the development of employees. While Rich took the lead in culture management activities, all three executives actively contributed to promoting, modeling, and reinforcing the company's cultural values.

This executive management team was called upon to play a critical role in helping the company successfully make another transition as the industry experienced further changes.

Further change in industry dynamics

The cumulative impact of changes in the business environment through the 1990s can be seen in the growth of the servicing component of Tashman's workforce. By 2001 the company had ninety-five employees, consisting of eight regional managers, seventy service people, ten administrative staff members, and seven sales people.

In 2003 Tashman's senior management became aware that one of their key customers, the Home Depot, was initiating a major change in the way it interacted with agencies that provided in-store merchandising services. Based on a study by a process improvement team, the Home Depot announced a plan to institute a new "partnership model" for in-store service merchandising.

This model was designed to improve the effectiveness, efficiency, and consistency of servicing functions at the Home Depot stores through working with a more limited number of vendors, defining rep responsibilities clearly, and adding technology to improve communication and measure rep performance.

The executive team was determined that Stan Tashman and Associates would maintain a relationship with the Home Depot by becoming one of the servicing agencies selected through this process. They realized, however, that they needed to make changes in their business strategy and enhance their infrastructure in order to be able to respond to this strategic challenge successfully.

Planning organizational response to industry changes

Rich Tashman had been exposed to the thinking and ideas of Eric Flamholtz, who was a professor at the Anderson Graduate School of Management at UCLA, an author, and a strategic consultant to a number of businesses. The Tashman senior management team decided to hire Flamholtz and his firm, Management Systems Consulting Corporation, to help them prepare and plan for the future.

Management Systems began with a familiarization that was based on interviews, surveys, and a review of company records. The consultants provided feedback on how well Stan Tashman and Associates had developed at each level of the Pyramid of Organizational Development™ (described in chapter 2).

Strengths and opportunities for improvement

Key findings from the familiarization that helped highlight company strengths and opportunities for improvement included the following.

- Tashman is strong in terms of markets and products/services. Managers and staff maintain excellent relationships with manufacturers and retail customers. The company has solid expertise in a number of product categories.
- Tashman has a number of strengths in resources and operational systems – especially in the areas of finance and people. Tashman has made significant investments in technology, but has an opportunity for the further development of systems that will help the company achieve optimal benefits from technology, such as increased efficiency and timely reporting.
- With respect to management systems, the executive team is a strength. The company has opportunities to improve in terms of developing more formal systems for strategic planning and management development. Performance management systems are good, but could be enhanced.

- Culture is a real strength. The company is known in the industry for excellence in customer service and integrity. Executive management gives priority to ensuring that new employees understand the core values and uses company meetings to help reinforce the culture.

With respect to the company's reputation for providing excellent service to the Home Depot and other customers, the consulting team highlighted the following strengths.

- The company provides excellent training to employees, both at the time they are hired and on a regular basis thereafter.
- Employees are motivated to do a good job because they respect the owners' integrity and recognize that executive management values the employees.

Next, the consulting team met with senior managers of the company to help them develop a written strategic plan that would address opportunities for improvement and prepare the company to compete under the new business model being implemented by the Home Depot.

The plan that was produced in this process provided a road map, which the company immediately began to put into action. Some areas of focus that were highlighted in the plan included the following:

- exploring acquisition as a way to grow;
- upgrading internal education and training programs;
- recruiting employees to support rapid growth;
- focusing more on the retention of employees; and
- adapting the organizational structure to accommodate business changes.

Raising performance to a new level

In 2004 the Home Depot made the announcement that Tashman had been anticipating, letting rep agencies know that it intended to take the service business "in house" and hire the service companies directly. This would significantly reduce the number of agencies handling the merchandising in each of its six regions to cover its ten product departments. Following this change, manufacturers whose products were sold through the Home Depot would no longer pay commissions to rep agencies, and the Home Depot would directly compensate the agencies selected to service each department.

At the time of the announcement, Tashman estimated that there were approximately thirty-five rep agencies servicing the Home Depot stores in the west/northwest areas of the United States.

The planning efforts in 2003 had helped Tashman's executive management clarify how they would respond to this announcement. They knew that it would take more than a good reputation with the Home Depot to come out a "winner." They had to demonstrate that they would be able to hire and train enough new people to more than double the number of employees dedicated to store services. In addition, they needed to develop enhanced operational systems that would meet the Home Depot's expectations for effective communication and measurement, and the quality execution of assigned tasks and projects.

A decision was made to seek an acquisition that would enable Tashman to add experienced staff quickly. In September 2004 Tashman acquired the Home Depot business of P. J. Boren, Inc., a well-respected northwest rep agency with employees who had experience in servicing the Home Depot stores. This move enabled Tashman to add fifty experienced staff and gain better connections and coverage in the northwestern states.

In November 2004 Tashman emerged from the competition as one of the winners. The Home Depot reduced the number of agencies servicing their stores in the west/northwest to six. Tashman was given a three-year contract to handle all servicing responsibilities for the Home Depot's Flooring and Home Organization Department in 400 stores in the western United States.

Being selected was only the first step, however. The executive team of Stan Tashman and Associates knew that they needed to take decisive action and raise the company's performance to a whole new level in order to ensure that the Home Depot would continue to be a satisfied customer. They needed to simultaneously manage exponential growth, maintain and enhance the quality of their services, streamline operations for efficiency, and maintain financial strength.

The team focused its efforts on three key areas: people, technology, and accountability for performance.

Investing in people

The acquisition of P. J. Boren helped Tashman staff the Home Depot stores in the northwest. To cover the remaining states in the Home Depot's west region, Tashman needed to recruit and train an additional 200 Service Reps and managers. The new staff members had to be in place by February 2005 to ensure that Tashman would be ready to cover all 400 stores of the Home Depot at the start of the contract. The management team met this deadline, and began to implement the contract.

During the first year of the contract with the Home Depot, the scope of work was expanded further, and yet more employees were needed to implement Tashman's "best in class" service.

To help accomplish this rapid growth in staff, Tashman increased staffing for recruitment and training and formalized a career ladder within the Service Division. Individuals who performed well as reps had the opportunity to be promoted into Manager-in-Training or District Manager positions.

Tashman was looking for these characteristics in new hires: maturity, professionalism, good skills in dealing with people, the ability to work in an organized fashion and pay attention to detail, the ability to multi-task and function effectively within the discipline of an electronic tracking system, and dedication to providing excellent service. New hires received intensive training from the District Manager regarding products, policies, and processes. They also attended group training sessions, which included an orientation to the company's culture and values.

To assist in the training of new employees, in 2006 Tashman produced a training CD that helped orient new Service Reps to their responsibilities, provided consistent coverage of training topics, and assisted managers with the training process. With the use of the CD by new employees, managers were able to devote more of their time with new employees to emphasizing and reinforcing key principles of effective servicing. (The CD was also used as an interview/selection tool – to help screen prospects and ensure that they understood the role.) In addition to developing the CD, the company also posted the same training information, along with helpful reference and technical information, on the company's internal website for easy access by new and experienced employees alike.

Although the number of employees had grown significantly, Tashman executives still wanted to make sure that each employee felt connected to the values of the founders and recognized that management appreciated each individual's contribution to the company's success. They used a variety of methods to communicate these values, including the following:

- providing each employee with a formal annual statement of the monetary value of the benefits he or she was receiving from the company;
- communicating changes in benefits with easy to understand materials;
- offering regular training sessions to employees at each level of the career path;
- having owners attend culture training sessions and communicate with employees about the "state of the company" – sharing information and answering questions;
- using rewards and incentives to recognize performance (including plaques, gift certificates, and cash bonuses); and
- sending a quarterly newsletter to each employee (which always included a President's message).

Investing in technology and systems

Tashman executives realized that they needed to enhance technology in order to be able to meet the Home Depot's requirements, keep overhead expenses under control, and obtain timely information about how well the company was doing in fulfilling its contracted responsibilities.

The Home Depot partnered with a software company, Enfotrust, to develop a custom software package that works with hand-held devices (PDAs – personal digital assistants) to track the work being done by Service staff in each store. The system requires Service Reps and District Managers to "log" the time they spend in the store on specific work tasks. It also captures pictures of completed product displays. Each rep synchronizes data from the PDA daily via telephone modem to a main server.

Reports regarding variances and other areas of concern reflected in the data are available by the next morning for District Managers to review. In addition, proprietary reports developed by Tashman's technology staff help managers provide appropriate oversight of Service Reps.

Because the Tashman executive team felt that it was important to be able to communicate with reps while they were working in the stores, they decided to purchase a BlackBerry wireless communication device for every rep. The comprehensive distribution of BlackBerry devices in January 2005 made it possible for reps, managers, and the corporate office to be in contact via e-mail or phone throughout the working day. The decision to provide BlackBerry devices to all in-store staff distinguished Tashman from competitors, who limited BlackBerry devices to staff at the level of manager and above.

Tashman IT staff have developed applications for the BlackBerry device that simplify and/or automate administrative tasks for field and corporate staff. For example, weekly timesheets are now filled in daily by staff on the BlackBerry and e-mailed at the end of the week to a central company mailbox, where they are processed by the Payroll Administrator. This electronic system is much more efficient than the previous paper-based process.

When the Home Depot makes a special request for information, Tashman's IT staff can e-mail a survey to the reps via the BlackBerry device. As soon as a rep replies, the response is added electronically to a database on the company server. Corporate staff use reports from the database to provide the Home Depot with the requested information. This capability has greatly enhanced Stan Tashman and Associates' ability to be responsive to the customer.

Tashman's IT staff continue to develop the capability to move additional processes from paper to computer. One application is an electronic routing guide to ensure the completion of all activities to set up a new hire. Another is a new "Document Box" system, which provides the capability to scan and convert incoming paper documents (e.g., project reports, surveys, and human resources files) into electronic documents for easy access and storage.

Working to meet and exceed customer expectations

The third area of focus for management was accountability for meeting the customer's performance expectations. Tashman hoped to go beyond the minimum requirements and challenged employees to strive to exceed expectations whenever possible.

One tool that the Home Depot uses to assess the performance of servicing contractors is a monthly report regarding key metrics. Tashman management works hard to ensure that there are "no surprises" in this report by proactively monitoring data from the field.

One key measurement of performance is the number of hours that staff are logged in and working in the stores during a month. Tashman ensures continual coverage of every store by deploying its Managers-in-Training as additional skilled rep staff to assist when the regularly assigned staff person is absent or additional help is needed. Tasks that are regularly performed for every product in the department include keeping shelves and other merchandising displays well stocked and orderly, making sure that all products have appropriate signage, and confirming that the correct pricing is displayed for each product. Tashman staff also are responsible for maintaining flooring samples in the showroom (i.e., design center area). Workers follow Tashman's "daily service guidelines," which are stored in their hand-held device, as well as in the "service updates" they receive daily through their BlackBerry.

Another key area of performance is the execution of a variety of "special projects" that the Home Depot assigns each month. Tashman's systems enable management to stay informed about the status of special projects, so that they can initiate corrective action if any store is lagging on a project.

Tashman places great importance on frequent communication between its field-deployed staff and the Home Depot staff at the store level and district level. Tashman District and Regional Managers meet regularly with store and district managers. Olson and Rich Tashman take the lead for the management team in maintaining contact with the Home Depot regional staff. The company is vigilant in ensuring that the Home Depot staff are informed promptly about any potential problems – and offered suggestions about how problems can be resolved and prevented in the future.

Tashman management also communicates regularly with the 100 manufacturers whose products are sold through the Home Depot's Flooring and Home Organization Department. Manufacturers appreciate the efforts that Tashman management makes to keep them informed.

Tashman staff are expected to be knowledgeable about the products they support. Periodic meetings and training sessions with manufacturers' staff help Tashman Service Reps keep current on each product.

Growing reset business

In addition to the servicing work Tashman does for the Home Depot, the company deploys Reset Teams – separate staff who assist the Home Depot with capital projects, the opening of new stores, and major resets for stores in the west region. Staffing for this component of the business has grown significantly since 2004.

Preparing for the future

Between 2004 and 2006 the number of employees at Stan Tashman and Associates grew from 130 to 570. Tashman's senior management team know that they must continue to stay alert and prepared for new growth opportunities and further changes in the marketplace.

They are committed to maintaining their record of performance as a valued supplier to the Home Depot and to increasing their business with the Home Depot as opportunities arise. They continue to field a separate sales team that represents manufacturers to independent retailers. In addition, Tashman continues to monitor other companies in the retail environment in order to be well positioned to take advantage of strategic opportunities as they arise.

8 | Leading strategic and organizational change at IndyMac Bank

Introduction

In 2003 IndyMac Bank, a public company, was ranked nineteenth in volume among mortgage originators in the United States. While this position reflected a substantial rate of growth in assets, revenues, and employees over a ten-year span, executive management realized that the company could be vulnerable to both smaller and larger competitors at its current size. This chapter describes how senior management implemented a planning process that enabled executive management to revise the business vision and a culture management process that enhanced competitive effectiveness. It also shows how IndyMac Bank completed the transformation from an entrepreneurship type of company to an entrepreneurially oriented, professionally managed organization.

Company overview

IndyMac Bancorp, Inc., is the holding company for IndyMac Bank F.S.B. (known as Indymac Bank®). In 2006 IndyMac Bank was the largest savings and loan in Los Angeles and the seventh largest mortgage originator in the United States. The company is listed on the New York Stock Exchange (NYSE) as IMB. Through its hybrid thrift/ mortgage bank business model, IndyMac is in the business of providing cost-efficient financing for the acquisition, development, and improvement of single-family homes. IndyMac also provides financing secured by single-family homes and other banking products to facilitate consumers' personal financial goals.

This chapter was co-authored with Shalini Lal.

Early beginnings

Founded in 1985 as a real estate investment trust (REIT) known as IndyMac Mortgage Holdings, Inc., IndyMac began as a conduit for Countrywide Mortgage Investments, Inc. Countrywide Mortgage Conduit was primarily a passive investor in residential mortgage loans and mortgage-backed securities, specializing in the purchase of Alt-A mortgages (i.e., mortgages for borrowers who have difficulty documenting their income, such as self-employed people).

Development 1993–2003

In 1993, when Michael Perry assumed leadership as CEO, Countrywide Mortgage Conduit was a relatively minor and unprofitable subsidiary of Countrywide Credit Industries,[1] with four employees and $714 million in assets. The impact of initial efforts to transition the company to an operating mortgage banker business model was reflected in year-end results: assets had doubled to $1.4 billion, mortgage production rose to $3.4 billion, and the company generated profits of $2.4 million.

By the end of 1995 the company had reached $2 billion in assets and $50 million in net income. The company was renamed CWM Mortgage Holdings, Inc., and its principal operating subsidiary was named Independent National Mortgage Corporation.

Competitive advantage in technology

A key contributor to the initial growth and development of IndyMac between 1993 and 2003 was a strategy of investing in technology and taking advantage of the Internet. The company developed a proprietary electronic Internet-based loan-processing platform, called e-MITS® (Electronic Mortgage Information Transaction System) in 1997, which provided several competitive advantages: (1) the system was able to perform automated underwriting and risk-based pricing, making it possible to provide a customer with an approval decision and rate lock within minutes; (2) it automated the delivery of loan

---

[1] Countrywide Credit Industries has changed its name to Countrywide Financial Corporation on the NYSE.

documents over the Internet to closing agents; (3) it enabled IndyMac to respond quickly and efficiently to customers across the country without having a branch system; and (4) e-MITS helped IndyMac maintain lower costs in originating mortgage loans than many of its competitors.

In 1998 IndyMac began a pilot program that allowed its largest customer group – small to medium-sized mortgage brokers and mortgage bankers – to use e-MITS to process loans funded by Indy-Mac. The program was successful, and in 1999 IndyMac began to move all its third-party lending customers toward using e-MITS. IndyMac also adapted e-MITS to be used in its direct-to-consumer mortgage lending channel, called LoanWorks.

Growing the management team

Another challenge related to growth for Perry, as CEO, was to build his management team. Closely related to this effort was a larger change in corporate culture that Perry wanted to implement, to make IndyMac a "meritocracy."

The new culture placed an emphasis on accountability and rewarding people for performance. Performance would be evaluated based on assigned targets. The new mantra was: "Don't ask for permission, ask for forgiveness." One step in creating more accountability was putting the whole senior management team on renewable contracts. Decisions about renewal were to be based on key criteria, which included performance.

When asked nowadays about this change process, Perry often says that it was changing people that was, in the end, the most difficult part. He also believes that most issues can be traced back to people issues. When something is not going well, he often reviews the organizational chart and tries to understand whether the problem is an accountability issue or a restructuring issue.

The next phase of development: 1997

In 1997 the company became self-managed (by purchasing its management contract from Countrywide) and changed its name to INMC Mortgage Holdings, Inc. At this time, the company was still structured as a REIT.

Following separation from Countrywide, the IndyMac management team adopted the following business definition:

IndyMac operates in the secondary mortgage market as a mortgage conduit linking the originator of a mortgage loan with the ultimate investor in that loan.

Business results in 1997 were once again positive. Net profits (prior to a non-recurring charge for separating from Countrywide) totaled $100 million. At the end of the year the company had $6.5 billion in assets and a workforce of 814 people. The next May the company changed its name once more, to IndyMac Mortgage Holdings, Inc.

Managing through a crisis

During the first nine months of 1998 the company achieved record results. Total assets grew to $7.4 billion and the workforce expanded by 83 percent, to 1,492, by the end of September.

A global liquidity crisis disrupted US financial markets in the fourth quarter of 1998, however, and threatened IndyMac's very existence. In early October the company's stock price dropped 61 percent in just three trading days. Caution in the financial markets severely reduced IndyMac's access to the capital that it needed to fund new mortgages.

Company management took immediate action to keep the company in good standing with its lenders, while at the same time working to improve liquidity and modify operations to reflect the new market environment. By the end of the fourth quarter IndyMac's assets had declined to $5.7 billion and the workforce had fallen to 1,202. IndyMac had survived the crisis, however, with its value-added business units intact.

In 1999 the management team began to address some serious strategic questions. Should the company remain a REIT? How could the company diversify its financing sources to help ensure greater stability during market fluctuations?

The company decided that its status as a REIT was no longer an asset, and formally terminated it in January 2000. Instead, the company opted to expand in the area of consumer financial services and to organize as a bank (a depository institution). One reason the banking option was chosen is that it would allow IndyMac to attract consumer deposits and Federal Home Loan Bank (FHLB) advances, which would improve the stability of the company's funding. IndyMac had reached an agreement in 1999 to acquire a southern-California-based bank, SGV Bancorp, and become a consumer depository institution. Once the proposed purchase and the conversion to a bank had received approval from the Federal Office of Thrift Supervision, in 2000, the acquisition was completed. Over the next year the company adapted to operating as a federally regulated depository institution.

IndyMac's organizational structure

Under the leadership of Perry, IndyMac Bank has evolved into a sophisticated enterprise. By 2003 it consisted of three major segments: IndyMac Mortgage Bank, IndyMac Customer Bank, and the Investment Portfolio Group, with responsibilities as described below.

IndyMac Mortgage Bank

This segment is focused on providing consumer mortgage products through relationships with mortgage and real estate professionals. It also provides commercial loans to homebuilders for the purpose of constructing new, single-family residences.

IndyMac Customer Bank

This provides the platform for the mortgage and deposit products and services insured by the Federal Deposit Insurance Corporation that IndyMac offers directly to consumers.

Investment Portfolio Group

This segment invests in single-family residential mortgages and mortgage-backed securities. It services a large portfolio of single-family mortgage loans.

The next phase of development: 2003

Perry was committed to the continuing development of IndyMac. He saw tremendous potential for future growth, but was concerned about the company's market position. IndyMac's position as nineteenth in size among mortgage originators was thought to be an unsustainable strategic position over the long run. At this size, the company was vulnerable both to the lower costs of smaller organizations and to the advantages of scale of larger competitors.

Perry was willing to be critical of what he had created and/or to hire consultants to do an assessment of the business in order to take the organization to the next level of success. In July 2003 he invited the authors' firm, Management Systems Consulting Corporation, to assist him in taking the company to the next level of success. The intent was to develop the management systems at IndyMac further, as well as to establish a plan for the next phase of the company's strategic development.

Organizational strengths and areas for improvement

Management Systems began its work by administering its Organizational Effectiveness Survey© to gain an understanding of the strengths and opportunities for improvement in the company. This survey, which is a validated instrument, contains sixty-five questions that assess the extent to which the organization has developed at all six levels of the Pyramid of Organizational Development™ (see chapter 2), plus another area called "financial results management." This is based upon the notion that an organization must effectively manage all six levels of the pyramid, as well as its financial results, in order to achieve long-term success and profitability.

The results indicated that the respondents (all members of the IndyMac organization) believed that the company had certain areas of considerable strength, but several opportunities to improve as well. Specifically, IndyMac had shown considerable strength in its markets, products and services, and financial results. The survey indicated that IndyMac had specific strengths with respect to its ability to understand its competition and maintain advantages over them in specific market segments, and in being able to understand the needs of its customers. In addition, the organization had strengths in being able to secure sufficient financial resources to continue to grow and be an effective organization.

At the same time, the survey indicated potential for improvement in areas related to culture and operational and management systems. Of particular concern were the areas of management development and the development of human resources, which received some of the lowest scores. The survey also brought to attention the fact that formal planning had not yet become established as a way of doing business and that people tended to spend time on "firefighting" and resolving crises. The survey also suggested that the culture at IndyMac did not support the discussion of some sensitive issues and that there were problems related to trust among different parts of the organization.

Evolution of strategic planning systems

Prior to the survey, Perry was already convinced that there was a need to take the process of strategic planning at IndyMac to the next level.[2] The survey confirmed this, and indicated that there was a clear need to develop strategic planning systems so as to embed the process of planning within the organization, and to ensure that the various parts of the organization were working together on common objectives. The next step of the development process, therefore, was to begin a comprehensive process of strategic planning at all levels of IndyMac.

Strategic planning was introduced through two levels. The process began with strategic planning at the corporate level for the company as a whole. This provided the context for the development of strategic plans for the three major groups comprising IndyMac – IndyMac Mortgage Bank, IndyMac Customer Bank, and the Investment Portfolio Group. Group strategic plans were developed, followed closely by strategic planning at the level of each of the subunits or divisions comprising each group. This planning process began at the end of July 2003 and lasted until the end of the year. Approximately twenty different planning meetings were held at the strategic corporate, group and/or unit level.

Corporate strategic planning

The corporate planning process began at IndyMac with a presentation of the planning framework to be used, as well as a discussion of the platform for strategy (see chapter 2). It also included a facilitated discussion of the various challenges that the company would face in the process of industry consolidation. This was particularly relevant to the issue of IndyMac's size and market position. The purpose was to provide the senior executive team with a strategic lens to view the

---

[2] The company already had a strategic planning process and a Vice-president of Strategic Planning.

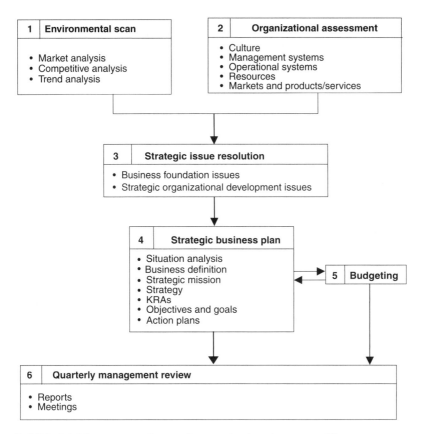

Exhibit 8.1 Management Systems' strategic planning process[SM]
Note: This exhibit is effectively an alternative version of exhibit 4.1, with just a few small differences.

bank and plan for its future. The approach used for strategic planning is shown schematically in exhibit 8.1.

The next step was to do an environmental scan and an organizational assessment.[3] Using the results of these analyses, the team would

---

[3] This is similar to the classic notion of a "SWOT" analysis, where "SW" refers to organizational strengths and weaknesses and "OT" refers to external opportunities and threats. The process used here – "environmental scan" and "organizational assessment" – can be viewed as the next level of sophistication beyond the classic SWOT analysis, because both are more specific in their focus and because the Pyramid of Organizational Development™ provides the lens for the organizational assessment.

develop a "business foundation." Once the foundation has been developed the strategic plan is developed for the six key areas of the pyramid and financial results. This was the process followed at IndyMac, as described below.

Environmental scan: external analysis

There were detailed discussions of the primary competitors of Indy-Mac and their relative strengths and weaknesses from the perspective of the customer. A detailed analysis of the competition was followed by a discussion of the strengths that IndyMac could leverage relative to the competition.

Similarly, participants conducted a detailed analysis of the trends within the environment that might have significance for the organization. For each of the trends, the opportunities presented to IndyMac and the threats to the organization were examined.

Through small group exercises, the participants worked simultaneously on identifying the components of the scan (i.e., competitive analysis, trend analysis, and market analysis) and identifying the three to five key aspects in each area that IndyMac needed to focus on as part of the planning process.

Organizational assessment

Internal analysis focused on a market analysis (i.e., an analysis of the specific segments the organization was operating in) and a discussion of which specific segments IndyMac would gain from competing in.

In addition, the corporate strategic planning meetings began with a review of the results from two surveys: (1) Management Systems' Organizational Effectiveness Survey©, and (2) Management Systems' Growing Pains Survey©.[4] Both surveys were completed by sixty key employees.

The results of the Growing Pains Survey© indicated the presence of several growing pains within the organization. There were strong indications that there were significant issues to be resolved at IndyMac, as

---

[4] These are proprietary instruments that have been developed and validated by Management Systems Consulting Corporation.

well as significant pressures on the resources of the organization. Other areas of concern were a lack of awareness of the roles of others within the organization and an understanding of how these various roles were linked together.

The presence of "growing pains" signaled that IndyMac needed to be able to transition to the next stage of development, based on the size and complexity of the business. If these growing pains were not addressed, they could potentially become barriers to the achievement of goals for growth and financial results.

A key conclusion was as follows: "It appears that people are feeling that there are not enough hours in the day and that they spend the majority of their time 'putting out fires.'" These issues might be the result of underdeveloped systems for strategic planning and management development. Also, it was argued that the finding of "people not being aware of what others are doing" might have been a direct result of the "'crisis' mode that many people seem to be operating in."

The Organizational Effectiveness Survey© identified opportunities for improvement that might be contributing to these growing pains. In particular, the operational and the management systems of the organization needed strengthening. Comparisons with other organizations within Management Systems' database indicated that there were significant areas for improvement relative to other organizations of similar complexity.

Given the above backdrop, the strategic planning meetings were used to define the business that IndyMac was in, and what the strategic mission of the organization should be. The team also discussed specific financial targets for the year, along with detailed discussions of the market segments that the organization should be involved in.

The new IndyMac business foundation

After reviewing the survey results, the group moved on to developing the business foundation for IndyMac. The business foundation is the platform on which the strategic plan is built and consists of a business definition or concept, strategic mission statement, and core strategy.

After much debate on whether the organization's customers were the intermediaries or the final customer, the group finally agreed on the following business definition:

IndyMac Bank is in the business of designing, manufacturing, and distributing cost-efficient financing for the acquisition, development, and improvement of single-family homes. IndyMac also provides financing secured by single-family homes to facilitate consumers' personal financial goals and strategically invests in single-family mortgage-related assets.

After developing the business definition, the group moved on to the strategic mission statement. A strategic mission is a broad, measurable, time-dated statement of what the organization wants to or needs to become by the end of the planning period. Key areas of discussion with regard to the mission focused on IndyMac being a low-cost provider of mortgage financing. The group discussed the fact that it was operating in a commodity market, and that the winning strategy in such a market is to be a low-cost provider. Concerns were expressed about the implications for customer service – i.e., would customer service suffer if IndyMac focused on being low-cost?

The group agreed that driving down costs and making that the top priority did not mean that service had to suffer. It also emphasized the importance of risk management to the group's continued success. Finally, the group agreed that it did not want to include any revenue targets in the mission. Instead, the focus needed to be on being a "low-cost provider."

The group eventually settled on the following wording for IndyMac's corporate strategic mission:

By year-end 2008 IndyMac, operating with the highest level of ethics, in compliance with all relevant regulations and laws and with a customer-friendly orientation, will be a top eight lender in the United States of America by being a low-cost provider of single-family permanent and construction lending financing, and the best manager of the risks related to such lending programs.

The third and final component of the business foundation is the core strategy. The core strategy defines where you play "the game" and how you play "the game." It is the overall concept of how the firm or business unit will compete in its chosen market(s), and describes how the company will achieve its mission.

In discussing the core strategy, the group talked about the fact that it should continue to focus on getting to the consumer through intermediaries and affinity relationships. The group also discussed the fact that it needed to standardize and optimize the mortgage process in order to make it easier for the consumer.

The group eventually agreed the core strategy as captured below:

We and our partners will re-engineer the mortgage process with a focus on speed, the customer experience, and self-service options. We will also build a strong customer-friendly culture and state-of-the-art capabilities in risk-based lending, trading, and investing.

After agreeing on the business foundation, the group began to develop the set of objectives for the plan. In order to do this, the group used Management Systems' strategic planning terminology.[5] Key result areas are areas of the business where performance has a critical impact on the achievement of the mission. They are categories, not actions. Under each KRA there are several objectives, which are overall definitions of what needs to be achieved within that KRA during the planning period. Objectives describe broad outcomes that the company needs to achieve. Under each objective there are specific goals that need to be achieved in the next twelve to eighteen months. These goals follow the SMART goal definition.

The process also builds in quarterly reviews. Each meeting would include time for IndyMac senior management to gauge progress against the objectives in the plan, as well as time to discuss emerging strategic issues and determine their impact (if any) on the plan.

Cascading the plan: subunit planning

Once the corporate planning process was complete it provided the context for the development of the plans for IndyMac's business units. Nineteen subgroups met to discuss the roll-out of the corporate strategic plan.

Each subunit repeated the same steps that were discussed at the corporate strategic planning meetings. The environmental scan and organizational assessment were debated, followed by discussion of strategic issues. This was followed by the articulation of a business definition (wherever appropriate). The process once again culminated in the setting of SMART goals for each of the business units.

---

[5] This is part of the "Management Systems Strategic Planning Method," developed by the authors at Management Systems Consulting Corporation.

Expanded core strategy

In the 2003 *Annual Report* the company published its business definition, strategic mission, and core strategy. For the purposes of this publication, the core strategy was restated as follows to help explain the company's hybrid thrift/mortgage bank model.

We will gain share without compromising our profitability goals by executing a hybrid thrift model where we:

(1) Leverage our mortgage lending infrastructure through the expansion of our marketing and sales efforts and geographic presence, and create specialty niche mortgage lending businesses
(2) Balance earnings and enhance franchise value by:
    (a) Establishing a southern California retail branch franchise
    (b) Building our investment portfolio
(3) Support the above with a platform of internal capabilities and best practices by:
    (a) Investing in a strong team and state-of-the-art capabilities in manufacturing mortgages, risk-based lending, trading and investing
    (b) Enhancing our performance culture to out-execute the competition.

Planning as a way of life

The strategic planning process at IndyMac has become institutionalized (i.e., it has become part of the way the company does business). It has become a way of life at IndyMac.

Strengthening the culture at IndyMac: next steps

Perry, CEO of IndyMac, was well aware that the company's product (mortgages) is a commodity product. Accordingly, the company needed to look at other levels of the Pyramid of Organizational Development™ for sustainable competitive advantages.

As part of the process of continuing to strengthen and improve IndyMac, Perry decided in the summer of 2005 to reexamine the stated cultural values of the company to make sure that they were still relevant and gave appropriate emphasis to the values of "meritocracy."

As explained in chapter 2, corporate culture can be a source of competitive advantage for a company. Perry felt this was particularly true for IndyMac, since labor costs (i.e., human resources) made up two-thirds of the budget.

The original set of stated values for the company had been inspired by General Electric's (GE's) values twelve years earlier. The syllogism for senior management had been as follows: GE is a great company; IndyMac wants to become a great company. If it works for GE, then it will probably work for IndyMac.

During the twelve-year period since those values had been established, IndyMac had grown and changed a great deal. Perry decided that it would be prudent to reexamine the company's values and to make any revisions that seemed appropriate.

The task to review and possibly rework the values was taken on by Executive Vice-president Grove Nichols. Nichols was an inspired choice. Since he had been with IndyMac and Perry for several years, he understood the company and its culture as well as anyone else, and he understood Perry's leadership style and his way of thinking.

Nichols believed that a reevaluation of the values was important for IndyMac at this time. He believed that culture and values helped hold the company together. He knew that, in order to be able to deliver superior returns to the shareholder and superior service to the customer, IndyMac needed to be able to tap into the creativity and energy of its people.

At the start of the project, Nichols wondered how well the current values helped employees know what was important and made them want to contribute their creativity and energy. He knew that a fundamental aspect of IndyMac's culture was its focus on meritocracy. The company had an opportunity to strengthen its ability to evaluate individuals and teams solely on the basis of their performance, without regards to politics.

The next step

As a result, Nichols and Perry developed a new draft set of values that they thought would capture what was unique to IndyMac and would be able to support their meritocracy foundation. This set of values is shown in exhibit 8.2.

Fairness
Customers entrust IndyMac with their business. Employees entrust the company with their careers. Investors entrust IndyMac with their capital. We must treat them all fairly and deliver them value in return.

   (a) For *customers* (superior service, adding value, fair loan pricing and terms).
   (b) For *employees* (living culture of "meritocracy" – people get what they deserve based on their performance).
   (c) For *shareholders* (superior financial performance and reporting with transparency and integrity).

Accountability
IndyMac people thrive on objective measurement, take responsibility for what they do and hold others accountable.

Adaptability
Competition and technology bring constant change. IndyMac people react to change positively, overcome obstacles, and adapt quickly.

Speed
Speed is important in responding to our customers – although not at the expense of quality and accuracy.

Candor
We are always truthful and ethical with our customers, employees, shareholders and regulators and face the truth candidly, no matter how difficult it may be to do so.

Teamwork
Our people interact and work effectively in a variety of team situations, keeping group performance targets and the company as a whole in mind at all times.

Diversity
Our meritocracy system – built on fairness and lack of discrimination – leads to cultural and ethnic diversity in our workforce, which we view as an important source of strength.

Compassion
Employees who have demonstrated their commitment and dedication to IndyMac deserve our support in times of need. Also, we support local, national, and global causes through charitable acts of giving, while not losing sight of our ultimate responsibility to perform for our shareholders.

Opportunity
We are entrepreneurial and fast, and we aggressively seek to capture business opportunities that emerge. Our culture and our success also present career and financial opportunities for our people that they could not easily find elsewhere.

Exhibit 8.2 IndyMac's values

Testing acceptance of the proposed values

After preparation of this draft of values, it was then taken to the Executive Committee (consisting of twenty-eight people), who further refined the set of values. At this point, Nichols consulted with Flamholtz (a consultant to IndyMac). Flamholtz suggested that it was important to test whether there would be "buy-in" to this set of values by the organization. This is consistent with his approach to culture management as a vehicle of organizational change.[6]

Based upon this, a survey was distributed to people at IndyMac. Respondents were asked to comment on (1) how important they thought these values were to their culture and overall success, and (2) how well these values were actually practiced at IndyMac. The survey was anonymous, but it did gather demographic information in order to enable data analysis.

The response to the survey was phenomenal, with the team receiving 4,252 responses in just one week – almost an 80 percent response rate in just five business days. A snapshot of the results is shown in exhibit 8.3.

Culture survey results

The results indicated that all the values were deemed to be important, with six of ten receiving favorable ratings greater than 90 percent. Only one value, fairness to employees, received a favorability rating for actual performance of less than 50 percent.

This was, naturally, a cause for concern. Further analysis revealed that this item received somewhat higher ratings from relatively new employees (those with the lowest tenure), and that the rating dropped as employees acquired more tenure, only to rise again as tenure increased. In addition, data analysis revealed that the "hot spots" for this issue were Corporate Support Units (especially IT and HR) rather than profit centers or the company as a whole. In Corporate Support Units, performance targets are less concrete. This ambiguity in performance goals might have contributed to a perception of a lack of "fairness."

---

[6] See Flamholtz, E. G., 2001, "Corporate culture and the bottom line," *European Management Journal*, 19, 3, 268–75.

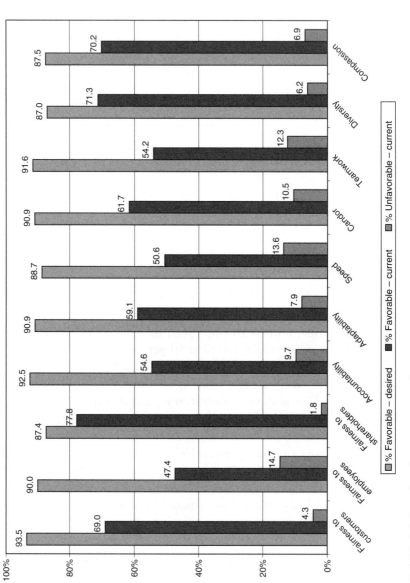

Exhibit 8.3 Sample culture survey results

Another area for concern were lower "actual" ratings for the values of speed, accountability and teamwork.

Further analysis of the data

These responses were then compared to the benchmarks available from previous cultural analysis work done by Management Systems. From this further analysis, IndyMac realized that the responses the company received were not atypical. In fact, the responses for accountability and teamwork actually compared favorably with other companies in the data set.

Of the set of values, four values received strong favorability ratings for actually being practiced in the current culture. These were fairness to customers, fairness to shareholders, diversity and compassion.

Using the data

After the survey, IndyMac set specific goals to make its culture more productive and to work toward having "the best workforce possible." For example, changes to the recruitment function helped make it fit better with the culture of IndyMac. Other areas to be strengthened and aligned with the cultural values included training for managers and supervisors and employee award programs.

Communication and culture building

Since culture is, largely, the shared values of an organization, it requires frequent communication to keep the understanding of culture strong. One key communication initiative at IndyMac is the month-end meeting, which is broadcast live on IndyMac TV. At these meetings the whole organization is included in a discussion of the achievements of the month. At the main office in Pasadena, many employees can physically attend the meeting. At all other locations, however, employees get a chance to submit questions they would like to have addressed at the upcoming month-end meeting.

Quarterly performance reviews involve the publication of a communiqué from Perry, giving a recap of the quarter. This explains the financial performance of the firm and announces the earnings of the quarter.

Thus, communication has begun to play an increasingly important role in the setting of the culture at IndyMac.

Conclusion

Under the leadership of Michael Perry, IndyMac has implemented a number of strategic and organizational changes. Results show that the company has made great progress over the past few years.

Perhaps the most significant accomplishment is that IndyMac improved its market position in mortgage origination by growing from nineteenth in 2003 to seventh in 2006. It grew from a company with revenues of $708 million in 2003 to annual revenues of $1.47 billion in 2006.

To a great extent these results were facilitated by the underlying changes in the organization. Three years of strategic planning at the corporate and the subunit level have allowed the organization to examine its internal and external environment, clarify its business foundation, and set strategic goals that are monitored on a quarterly basis. While the Organizational Effectiveness Survey© of July 2003 revealed growing pains and significant operational and managerial opportunities for improvement, a similar survey in 2005 revealed significant improvements in almost all areas.

The strategic planning process provided a forum to identify and prepare solutions to these issues. The very process of setting these goals also necessitated that key organizational members discuss and debate issues of organizational significance. This very act may have brought about a shared understanding of the organization's goals, as well as their role within it.

IndyMac has also made significant progress in culture management. It has "fine-tuned" its culture statement. It has also identified some areas where culture as practiced on a day-to-day basis could be improved and has taken action steps to improve it.

At a more subtle level, the very act of participating in definitions of business, culture, etc. may have provided organizational members with a sense of ownership toward the organization. The recent move toward regular organization-wide communications to discuss progress along important organizational objectives is another key move in this direction.

9 | *Leading strategic and organizational change at Infogix*

Introduction

By 1998 Infogix had grown to be a $20 million company with offices in North America and western Europe. The company had completed a decade of sustained growth. During that period the company's founder and leader, Madhavan Nayar, had experimented with a number of conventional and unconventional management ideas.

In 1999 Nayar attended a Forbes Presidents' conference, where he heard one of the authors of this book (Flamholtz) make a presentation about a framework for building successful organizations. The approach made sense to Nayar, and later that year he invited Flamholtz to work with the company and apply the approach described in this book (see chapter 2).

This chapter presents a case study of a company that was simultaneously involved in two different but related types of change: strategic and organizational. The company needed to make the transition from entrepreneurship to professional management, while simultaneously defining a new market space.

The company is Infogix (formerly named Unitech Systems).[1] This case also shows that the changes were supported by a combination of new organizational systems, including strategic planning, "performance optimization" (a version of performance management), and culture management. It shows how these tools were used at Infogix to help make the transition from entrepreneurship to an entrepreneurially oriented professionally managed firm, while simultaneously helping to define a new market space.

This chapter was co-authored with Madhavan Nayar.

[1] The company changed its name to Infogix from Unitech Systems in 2005.

Background

Infogix, Inc., provides Information Integrity® software solutions that help major corporations ensure the accuracy, consistency, and reliability of their operational, financial, and management information. It is a pioneer of the information integrity space. Today, with nearly 200 team members and offices in major cities across North America and Europe, Infogix is a world leader in its market space. The organization has both an innovative set of software products and a range of professional services. Its customers include industry-leading organizations such as Citibank, American Express, Verizon, Target and Wal-Mart. Over 400 of the Global 2000 use Infogix's products and services. The "Excellence in Information Integrity" award, which Infogix has sponsored since 1995, recognizes organizations that have demonstrated exceptional progress toward achieving information integrity. Some of the past winners of this award include Sprint, Bank of Nova Scotia and TSYS (Total System Services, Inc.).

This section summarizes the key events and phases in the company's history. This is intended as context for the case discussion.

Phase 1: Infogix as a new venture

The company which today is known as Infogix was founded as Unitech Systems by Nayar in 1982. It began as a one-man consulting firm.

Nayar, who holds degrees from universities in India and the Illinois Institute of Technology, pioneered the concept of "information integrity" software solutions at a time when few had realized the need for specifically designed systems that helped customer organizations ensure the validity and accuracy of information.

Nayar has described the need for information integrity as follows:

For us to effectively harness the benefits of the information revolution, and avoid the costs of widespread information pollution, we need to recognize and treat information as a shared, universal resource. We need to develop the science, technology, products and services to measure, monitor and manage its integrity, much like the environmental science, technology and industry emerged in the wake of the industrial revolution to answer our need for clean air, pure water, reliable power and safe food.

In 1982 Infogix developed its first software product, U/ACR, for, and in partnership with, the Blue Cross Blue Shield of Illinois. Over the next two decades, the company successfully developed a number of other products through similar strategic customer partnerships.

Phase 2: Infogix's growth and development

Through 1992 the company grew rapidly, reaching $12 million in revenue and an average annual growth rate of 65 percent for the first ten years.

During this period Infogix evolved from a one-person consultancy into a company employing approximately eighty people, with a President, Executive Vice-president and Chief Operating Officer, and several Vice-presidents, with Directors, Managers and employees below them. At the beginning of 1992 the company was reorganized into six Operating Groups, each headed by a Group Leader, and the position of Executive Vice-president and Chief Operating Officer was eliminated. Throughout this stage Infogix adopted a series of conventional business practices for a growing entrepreneurial company. This included the way the company was structured as well as the way people were compensated.

The company sold its products through sales representatives, who were paid a base salary, commissions and various incentives, such as bonuses for selling new products, "Salesperson of the Month/Quarter/ Year" awards, and "100% Club" trips to exotic destinations for those who met their quotas.

Beginning in 1993 the company initiated a series of changes, many of which, in retrospect, may have impeded its continued rapid growth, but contributed to organizational learning. That year the company decided to decentralize sales management by hiring Area Sales Managers in North America and establishing a separate International Sales Group. By the end of the year, however, no Area Sales Managers had been hired, and there was no revenue growth. Also in 1993 the senior leaders of the company learned about the management philosophy of W. Edwards Deming, and after several months of study and deliberation decided to adopt and implement it. The decision was implemented by holding a weekend retreat for influential team members from different groups in the company and then a two-day off-site meeting for everyone. The Deming philosophy was adopted on April 1, 1994.

Phase 3: impact of the Deming philosophy

The adoption and implementation of the Deming philosophy is often difficult, if not impossible, in most organizations, particularly in the West. It requires the reorientation and alignment of many of the principles, policies, and practices of running a business. It requires the optimization of the entire organizational system rather than each component; the understanding of the variation and fluctuation of performance across the system and over time; the use of data to understand performance and make decisions; and the recognition that each individual is different from every other. In order to benefit from Deming's philosophy, an organization must be prepared to abandon conventional practices, adopt a holistic approach, and look for long-term results.

The implications of the Deming philosophy were radical and extensive. Quotas and other numerical objectives linked to incentives and compensation were discontinued. Formal performance evaluations and salary adjustments tied to performance evaluation were also eliminated. All processes within the company were to be mapped, defined, and improved. The reaction of most of the team members of the company was skeptical, if not negative. Many of the "star" salespeople left the company, and over the next eighteen months almost 95 percent of the sales force turned over. Company-wide, employee turnover exceeded 50 percent in 1994. An employee survey revealed that employee morale was far below the industry average.

In 1994 it was also decided to organize the company into four geographic divisions: three (east, west, and central) in North America, and one international. The senior executives (Group Leaders) in charge of Sales, Marketing and Finance were assigned the responsibility for the three North American divisions. The international group already had a Group Leader. Additionally, each division was organized into Business Units. Business Units were established in Dallas, San Francisco, Atlanta, Cleveland, Boston, Philadelphia, Chicago, and Paris. Each Business Unit was headed by a Business Unit Leader and included three Sales Executives and one Application Consultant, with each Sales Executive assigned 100 accounts in two or three industries.

All the changes during the year resulted in a great deal of uncertainty and anxiety throughout the company, especially among the Group Leaders. In February 1995, while Nayar was in Europe for a speaking engagement, all the Group Leaders met to discuss their concerns, and they decided to present a list of issues and recommendations to him upon his return. The issues concerned primarily Nayar's leadership style. One of the recommendations was for him to play the role of a non-executive "Chairman" and for the Group Leaders to run the company. The recommendation was not accepted, and shortly thereafter two of the Group Leaders resigned from the company.

In early 1995 the three divisions in North America were reorganized into two geographic locations: east and west. The Product Development function was distributed among the three Group Leaders responsible for East, West and International Divisions. For the third year in a row there was no revenue growth in 1995.

There were relatively few changes and modest revenue growth in 1996. At the end of the year it was decided to combine the two North American divisions into one and designate a single Group Leader for North America.

In April 1997, to help revive the company, "Project Oxygen" was launched. It consisted of establishing industry-focused Customer Teams in the Business Units (now renamed Customer Units). Each Customer Team consisted of a Sales Executive, a Solution Consultant and an Account Representative. Each Customer Team was responsible for a handful of major accounts in a specific industry group (banking and finance, insurance and healthcare, communications and utilities, distribution and manufacturing). All other existing customer accounts were assigned to the Customer Teams based on geographic proximity. Also, the Business Unit Leader was renamed the Customer Unit Leader.

Project Oxygen was a significant effort, which required the hiring of over fifty new people in the field and training all of them for three weeks in the Home Office in Naperville, Illinois. Some of the Customer Unit Leaders were new, however, and there was much confusion about how the "team" concept was deployed and practiced. Some teams performed exceptionally well, while some others were dysfunctional and had to be rebuilt or disbanded.

In 1998 it was decided to align the Customer Unit Leaders along industry lines as well. This meant that all the teams in a given industry group (for example, banking and finance) would be supported by a Customer Unit Leader for that market sector. This was a major change for the teams and the Unit Leaders. Most teams no longer had a local leader they could go to, and the Unit Leaders had to travel and oversee the activities of teams based in several locations.

By 1998 Infogix was a $20 million company, and had offices in North America and western Europe.

Phase 4: the catalyst for strategic change

The impetus for comprehensive change can be dated to March 1999, when Nayar attended the Forbes Presidents' Conference and heard Flamholtz's presentation about building successful organizations. The framework for the approach made sense to Nayar, and it was in late 1999 that he invited Flamholtz to work with the company and apply the approach.

Organizational transformation at Infogix

The organizational development process began with a series of interviews with selected Group Leaders and Unit Leaders during the summer of 1999, to provide Flamholtz with an understanding of the company and its development issues. The next step was a strategic planning retreat, attended by all leaders in early December. The retreat was to introduce the whole of Infogix's leadership team to the Pyramid framework and take the company to the next level of planning capability.

Planning has always been a part of Infogix's culture. The company has long had a well-established strategic planning function, and the leaders of the Operating Groups have prided themselves on their strategic capabilities. The growth and diversification experienced during the 1990s demanded a new scale of planning altogether, however. Management needed to address not only new industry segments and larger operating units but increased organizational complexity as well. The strong entrepreneurial spirit and autonomy that had long been part of Infogix's culture now presented a management challenge. While it had at one time helped to create a vibrant, nimble operating environment, it had also resulted in counterproductive organizational "silos" that resisted cooperation.

Although Infogix already had a formal strategy and planning process, the key was to improve the existing planning system and ensure that it became a way of life. The strategic planning process was intended as a tool for the alignment of the various units of the company.

The role of strategic planning in transformation to professional management

At the retreat, a management planning simulation revealed the areas that needed to be strengthened internally. The group discovered that its planning was too grandiose to be feasible, choosing instead to adopt the approach to strategic planning described in this book. There are two major components to this approach to strategic planning: (1) a conceptual framework that serves as a platform for strategy, and (2) the strategic planning method per se.

Infogix adopted the Pyramid of Organizational Development™ framework, described in chapter 2, as the platform for the development of its strategic plan. This template was used to assess the strengths and areas for further development at the company.

Based upon this analysis, it was clear that Infogix was relatively strong at the bottom four levels of the pyramid, but needed further development at the top two levels, which include management systems and culture management. It also required some redefinition or fine-tuning of the business foundation to fit the founder's vision.

Although there are many approaches to planning, Infogix chose to adopt the method developed by Flamholtz and his associates. This methodology had been used previously with such diverse companies as Starbucks, PacifiCare, American Century Investors, Simon Property Group, and Navistar International, as well as with many other companies, including entrepreneurial companies such as Bell-Carter Foods and Royce Medical.[2]

Changing the strategic direction

The first step in changing the strategic direction of the company was to develop a new business foundation. This consists of three

[2] See Flamholtz and Randle, *Growing Pains.*

components: (1) a business definition, (2) a strategic vision, and (3) a core strategy (at Infogix, the term "strategic vision" has been used in preference to "strategic mission," as used in chapter 2).

By the end of the initial planning workshop the leadership team had defined the company's business as that of "helping Global 2000 organizations improve the quality of their information through information integrity systems."

This meant that the organization was going to evolve from one that was currently focused upon selected tools for the automated balancing of accounts and statements into a total information integrity solutions business. This meant, in turn, that Infogix was going to create a new market space: the "information integrity space." An intermediate step was for Infogix to evolve from its current product portfolio to a business with automated controls, services, and processes for information integrity. This was to happen in three stages:

stage I: pre-1999, automated balancing/manual;
stage II: 1999, automated controls + services + processes; and
stage III: 2003 Infogix becomes true information integrity business.

By the end of these stages, Infogix was to transform from a business focused upon selected controls to a genuine information integrity business, with a full set of products and services – to be defined in the planning process.

Building upon the new business foundation

Once the new business definition and strategic vision for the organization had been established, there was a need to complete the plan to the level of developing goals and assigning priorities and roles. Another related key challenge now was to make planning a way of life.

A "secret" key to this was to hold a series of quarterly planning meetings. At some organizations, planning is episodic: it occurs and then stops. The plan is there but it is not reviewed on a regular basis or updated. At Infogix, planning was carried out on an ongoing basis.

Quarterly planning retreats facilitated by Flamholtz and members of his consulting firm would become an opportunity for the organization to reflect on the progress through the quarter and to set goals for the next quarter.

Developing priority objectives

Although there are many objectives in any strategic plan, a well-thought-out set of priority objectives (key objectives that receive the most management focus) was another of the "secret ingredients" that proved important in making planning work at Infogix. These objectives are derived from the strategic vision and related key result areas.

The role of performance optimization in transformation to professional management

Another strategic innovation at Infogix was the creation of a unique "performance optimization system" (shown in exhibit 9.1), which combined with the planning system to create an overall "strategic management system." In order to strengthen the levels of account-ability and enhance the execution of the strategic plan, a performance optimization process was introduced. "Performance optimization" is a term coined at Infogix to refer to an innovative alternative to the conventional notion of performance management, as discussed below.

The conventional model of performance management typically links the planning system and the measurement of results with the evaluation and reward systems within the organization. One thing that is very different about the concept of performance optimization at Infogix, compared with the conventional concept of performance management, is that the former does *not* link performance directly to rewards. This is for philosophical reasons (examined below), and suggests an important difference in the culture at Infogix vis-à-vis many companies.

Nayar, the company leader, believes strongly that rewards ought to be based upon *company performance* rather than individual performance. The overall objectives of Infogix's rewards philosophy are to:

(1) attract top industry talent compatible with the unique character-istics of the Infogix environment;
(2) retain team members in a long-term developmental relationship;
(3) foster an environment that promotes teamwork through colla-boration and cooperation;

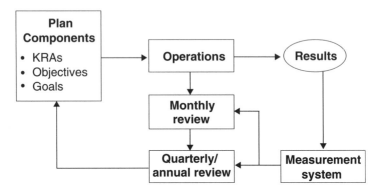

Exhibit 9.1 The performance optimization system

(4) foster an environment for personal and professional development;

(5) maintain equity across the company;

(6) compensate Leadership Group members based on overall company performance; and

(7) manage fixed costs by providing higher variable pay.

The term "performance optimization," as used at Infogix, is therefore intentionally different from the more conventional term "performance management." The latter term would include rewards as a key component of the system, while performance optimization deliberately does not include rewards, for the reasons outlined above.

The use of measurement in planning and performance optimization

One of the key factors that ultimately contributed to the success of Infogix's strategic innovation with planning and performance optimization was the development of detailed measurements for objectives. As one CPA (certified public accountant) once told one of the authors, "What gets measured gets counted!" This means that the things that get measured are the ones that are most important in influencing people's behavior in organizations.

At Infogix a great deal of time and care was put into the development of measurements of goals. In part, this is because Infogix is a highly analytical and process-oriented organization. The company takes great care to be precise with its use of terminology and the need for operational definitions.

The net result is that Infogix has created a detailed set of measurements for every objective and goal. These measurements are critical to making the plan operational and specific. They are a significant source of strength in its performance optimization system.

The role of culture in transformation to professional management

While it was relatively easy to introduce the model to the core team at the quarterly planning retreats, several internal issues would require resolution for the model really to work effectively. There were elements of Infogix's special culture that made it difficult to integrate the model into the organization. These were to come up many times before they could finally be resolved.

Infogix had an organizational philosophy that was different from most companies; the unfamiliarity with many of the elements of the Deming philosophy necessitated a greater degree of communication than might have been required in many other companies. Discussions at the planning meeting revealed that the Deming philosophy had, in fact, often been misunderstood, resulting in the misinterpretation of company values, practices, and policies. The lack of a formal statement articulating the desired organizational culture further exacerbated the problem.

There were similar difficulties in terms of understanding the accountabilities and responsibilities within self-managed work teams. There were several situations in which team members could take advantage of the system to suit their needs. This had several important implications for Infogix's competitive position within the industry, with more recent entrants threatening Infogix's industry leadership.

Results of the transformation to professional management at Infogix

The transition from entrepreneurship to professional management at Infogix remains a "work in progress," as does the strategic planning/performance optimization system. Nevertheless, significant benefits (both tangible and intangible) have been realized.

First, there is a clarity and focus to the vision of the company that did not exist to the same extent in the past. People understand that Infogix is in the information integrity business. This broader concept has replaced the more narrow focus upon specific information integrity products, such as automated balancing and controls. People now also understand that its long-term vision is to help create and, ideally, to dominate the information integrity space. This provides a 'big picture" context for short-term decisions and actions. One of the company's "growing pains" was that a relatively large number of people did not understand "where the company was headed." This is no longer the case.

Another benefit of the planning/performance optimization process is greater focus on priority objectives. It is always the case in a business that there are almost literally countless things to deal with. The Infogix plan provides focus upon the priority objectives. People understand what the priorities are and where the emphasis must be for the company to achieve its longer-range vision.

A third benefit concerns the productivity and accountability of people. The specificity of the measurements has increased the extent to which people are accountable for specific results rather than just vague responsibilities. The plan provides a tool that can be used to monitor the overall performance of the company, as well as that in specific business units, on a systematic basis.

Another benefit is that, as a result of the strategic innovations described above, there has been a cultural change at Infogix. One dimension of this is that planning and performance review has become a way of life: it is part of the "Infogix way." This, in turn, has led to other significant aspects of cultural shift at the company. Specifically, at the commencement of this process the organization was operating in "silos," and there was a considerable degree of internal conflict. One of the by-products of this process is "team building." By continually discussing the issues and working to resolve them, the leadership team tends to come together with a common mindset and focus. During this type of process there is always some turmoil, as certain leaders are seen not to have bought in to the company's plans or remain committed to their own agendas. Over time these people tend to leave or change, with the result that the company develops a more cohesive leadership team. This was the case at Infogix, and there was significant turnover. Today the company has a core team of capable senior leaders who operate as a true team.

One of the ultimate tests of a company is its financial performance. Venture-capital-funded firms are generally characterized by an emphasis on financial performance, short-term results, and exit strategies that yield the maximum return to the venture capitalists. Infogix has followed a different path. It has been focused upon building a strong business for the long term; it has been focused upon building the products and the infrastructure for the business, even if this took a great deal of time and investment.

Like other information technology companies, Infogix has had to deal with the collapse of IT investment since the boom that led up to "Y2K." Infogix is a privately held company, and financial information is proprietary. Nevertheless, we can say that the company is strong financially and has become stronger over the past five years, in contrast to some of the larger companies in this space, such as Compaq, Hewlett Packard, and Sun Microsystems.

A successful transformation

This case has described how one company, Infogix, has made the transition from an entrepreneurship to professional management. It also describes how strategic planning and the innovative system of "performance optimization" have produced changes in the company's vision as well as changes in its operations and culture.

Unfortunately, there is no "magic pill" or "silver bullet" for complex strategic and organizational changes of this type. As a result, the transformation has taken time. All the indications, however, are that the transition has been successful.

10 | Leading strategic and organizational change: the transformation of structure at Pardee Homes

Introduction

This chapter examines the transformation to professional management at Pardee Homes. Its particular emphasis is upon the transition from one type of organizational structure (functional) to another (matrix) as part of the overall transformation.

The focus upon structure is of particular significance, because the experience of Pardee Homes highlights the critical but often neglected role of structure as a key variable in determining organizational growth and success. Typically, the academic literature on organizational structure treats it in a descriptive way rather than as a driver or limitation of organizational success.[1]

Company description and history

Pardee Homes is a multi-regional real estate development company with a focus on developing master-planned communities and building single-family and multi-family homes. It is headquartered in Los Angeles, and has regional offices in southern California (Corona, Irvine, San Diego, and Valencia), northern California (Pleasanton and Sacramento), and Nevada (Las Vegas). In 2006 Pardee Homes achieved revenues of about $2.0 billion from the construction and sale of more than 3,000 units (homes) by approximately 700 employees.

This chapter was jointly authored with Michael McGee, President and CEO, Pardee Homes.

[1] For example, see one of the classic treatises on structure: Galbraith, J. R., 1995, *Designing Organizations*, San Francisco, Jossey-Bass, 12–13. Galbraith states: "Strategy is the company's formula for winning. [...] The structure of the organization determines the placement of power and authority in the organization."

The company was founded in 1921 by George Pardee, Sr., as a builder of custom homes. In 1969 the company was acquired by Weyerhaeuser, a global leader in the forest products industry, and became the largest subsidiary of Weyerhaeuser Real Estate Company (WRECO).

In 2003 Pardee Homes celebrated fifty years of homebuilding in Nevada, and in 2004 it celebrated fifty years of building in San Diego. The company is ranked among the top five builders by volume in most of its markets. Pardee was named "America's Best Builder 2003" by *Builder* magazine, and has received numerous awards for its master-planned communities and innovative home designs.

A recognized leader in "green" building practices, Pardee Homes was the United States' first builder to make a commitment to build 100 percent of its homes with the energy-saving features that meet the US Department of Energy's criteria of the Energy Star® program.

Development of professional management systems

In 1992, when the organizational transformation process began at Pardee, the company was led by David Landon, President, and Vance Meyer, Executive Vice-president and Chief Operating Officer.[2] Prior to this Pardee had been a family business; and it had reportedly been operated on the requirement that all three brothers who were owners had to reach consensus before significant business decisions were made.

Landon and Meyer were committed to preserving the values and strategic approaches that had made Pardee such a successful company. That year Landon attended a seminar delivered by Flamholtz at UCLA, on the subject of "growing pains." Landon recognized that Pardee was experiencing "growing pains" and asked for Flamholtz's help in developing more professional management systems for the company.

Organizational assessment

The first step was a preliminary organizational assessment. This initial assessment of the organization revealed a number of points.

- There was a lack of long-range organizational planning.
- The current functional organization structure was approaching its limits as an effective structure.

[2] Previously, the company had gone through various management changes, and had been family-managed by three brothers: George, Jr., Hoyt, and Doug Pardee.

- Landon and his EVP/COO, Meyer, were functioning as "super project managers," responsible for coordinating the work of the entire organization.
- The structure was fostering a "relay race" approach to building homes rather than a "basketball team" approach: *a sequential handoff rather than "continuous interaction" process that lacked accountability and follow-through.*
- There was no system for developing new Project Managers other than "sink or swim."

Proposed organizational changes

After conducting a preliminary assessment of the organization, Flamholtz pointed out that most of the company's operational and strategic decisions were being made by Landon and Meyer – following the tradition of the Pardee brothers. Pardee's business had expanded, however, and the decision-making load had increased. Both Landon and Meyer were close to becoming bottlenecks. In addition, they were personally under a great deal of stress from the amount of responsibility. It appeared that Pardee was reaching a point at which the capacity to grow would be limited unless the company transitioned to a different structure.

Based upon the initial assessment, Flamholtz recommended:

(1) enhancing the management team, by creating an executive committee and offering a management development program to grow managers;
(2) developing a formal, longer-range planning/organizational development process; and
(3) transitioning from a functional structure to a divisional structure by developing decentralized regions to oversee the day-to-day planning and operations in key geographic areas.

Executive committee
The executive committee would serve several purposes:

- giving Landon and Meyer a forum for involving a select group of senior leaders in strategic planning and leadership; and
- beginning to prepare the next generation of leadership, by giving functional leaders (department heads) an opportunity to consider

issues from a broader corporate perspective and by sharing unwritten strategies and guidelines for decision making that Landon and Meyer had learned from the Pardee brothers.

Planning and organizational development
This recommendation also included a longer-range planning process, focused not just on strategic planning per se but on the overall organizational development of Pardee, to help it transition from entrepreneurship to professional management. Pardee had always undertaken planning on a project basis, as well as planning for land acquisitions, but not for overall organizational development, including the development of organizational infrastructure.

Decentralizing organizational structure
Flamholtz further recommended that the bottlenecks and pressure created by the current system of organization be overcome by transitioning from Pardee's functional structure to a more decentralized divisional structure.

Pardee's response to recommendations

Landon agreed with the first two recommendations, but not with the proposed structural change, believing that a divisional structure would put Pardee at risk. It was his experience that all organizations that had tried this approach had experienced difficulties, and even failed.

The recommendation to form an executive committee was accepted. The executive committee included Landon, Meyer, and six other senior executives.

The recommendation for strategic planning and organizational development was also accepted. In addition, Flamholtz's "strategic lens" (the Pyramid of Organizational Development™ – discussed in chapter 2) and the related strategic planning methodology were adopted as the basis for Pardee's planning process.[3]

Four times a year the executive committee spent a day (off-site) on strategic planning. At other times, the committee met to consider specific business issues. The company adopted the mantra of "continuous improvement" in all aspects of its business.

[3] See Flamholtz and Randle, *Growing Pains*.

The structure issue was put on hold, however. Landon's reluctance to adopt structural change moved other organizational development issues to the forefront. The effect of the delay was to allow Flamholtz to learn about Pardee and see if a different and intermediate structural solution could be implemented.

Pardee's growth and transition, 1992–6

Between 1992 and 1996 Flamholtz and his firm, Management Systems, helped the executive committee implement a program of strategic organizational development, which included management development for senior and middle managers and the facilitation of strategic planning.

During this period some initial steps were taken to deal with the structural issue by proposing a redefinition of the role of the Project Manager and the formation of regional project management teams.

Selected results of this process

Several changes occurred at Pardee, including some specific results or outcomes of the organizational development process.

(1) Pardee changed its business concept and the name of the firm from "Pardee Construction" to "Pardee Homes," both to reflect and project a different understanding, image, and focus of its business.
(2) Pardee developed its management systems, including
   • planning systems;
   • management development;
   • organizational structure;
   • performance management systems; and
   • culture management.

Pardee's growth and transition, 1996–2000

During the next period of growth at Pardee, the development of the company continued both in terms of operational measures and organizational changes. At this stage, in 1996, Pardee had revenues of $403 million, a headcount of 358, and the number of units sold ("closings") was 1,669.

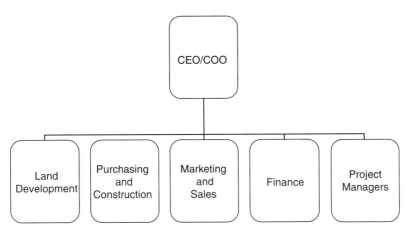

Exhibit 10.1 Pardee Homes' functional/silo structure (simplified version)
Note: The "Project Manager" role was something of a misnomer. The role primarily involved dealing with land entitlement and legal issues rather than managing a land development project per se, as occurred later.

Pardee's structure in 1996

Pardee was still organized in 1996 in a classic functional structure, as shown in exhibit 10.1. The business was conducted in such a way that the process was akin to a "relay race," with projects moving from one organizational function to another, as shown in exhibit 10.2. The process was similar to the flow of "product" in a manufacturing process. The functional areas, or "departments," as they were termed, operated as virtual "silos." Each did its own thing, and did it well, but with limited interaction and coordination, follow-up, or follow-through with other areas.

Although there were nominally Project Managers, the job title was misleading. Their real role was to deal with the complex entitlement issues that all real estate development involved and this, in turn, meant that their skills singularly emphasized dealing with the political entities that controlled discretionary governmental approvals.

The true project managers were Landon and Meyer, and they functioned as the only real "general managers," overseeing budget and schedule coordination responsibility on all Pardee's projects. The burden on Landon and Meyer as "super project managers" (a term that was coined by Flamholtz and adopted by Pardee to describe this

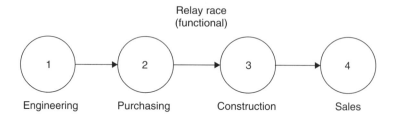

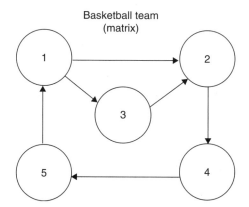

Exhibit 10.2 Alternative team concepts

role) was an overwhelming obstacle to growth in volume and breadth of product offering, as well as in geography.

At this point, Landon and the executive committee recognized that the effectiveness of the current organizational structure built around a group of strong department heads and Landon and Meyer as "super project managers" had reached its limits. Pardee had to make a decision about keeping its current structure or transitioning to a new structural concept.

Structured around regional teams

In 1996 Landon, Meyer, and the executive committee oversaw the launch of a more formal system of regional cross-functional teams. The intent was to move from a loosely coordinated system to a more formal assignment of responsibility and accountability. Cross-functional teams of professionals would be created that would focus on the projects in a regional area and be responsive to the differences in local government needs, and the needs of customer segments. The characteristics of this initial team system included the following elements.

(1) The teams were led by Project Managers, who had previously spent most of their time on "entitlement" issues (i.e., working closely with local governments to obtain approvals to develop a property), while also coordinating project time schedules.
(2) Team members were specialists from the functional departments that played a role in project planning and development, including Architecture, Construction, Engineering, Finance, Marketing, Purchasing, and Sales. A few of the team members were located in the regions, but most were based at the corporate office in Los Angeles. Often an individual was a member on more than one team.
(3) Teams were charged with keeping projects on budget and on schedule.
(4) Each team participated in a three-session training program, conducted by Management Systems. In addition to team building, the training program focused on skills related to effective meetings, interpersonal communication, and business decision making. Each team adopted a list of team norms (i.e., agreements about the responsibilities of team members and how team members would interact).

Examples of agreements reached regarding team norms included:

• there should be no surprises at team meetings (in between meetings, team members should use e-mail or voicemail to notify other team members about any problem that might impact them);
• keep Project Manager informed about any issue or problem that might have an impact on a project's "bottom line"; and
• when a problem arises, "work on solutions" rather than "search for the guilty."

The concept of a matrix organization structure was introduced. The idea was to move from a functional structure of a "relay race type" to one that was more of a "basketball team type" (as shown in exhibit 10.2). A basketball team moves up and down the court together as a team rather than functioning in a relay race fashion.

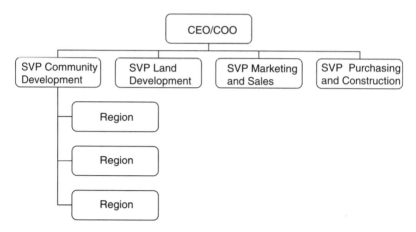

Exhibit 10.3 Pardee Homes' matrix structure (simplified version)

Pardee's matrix structure is shown in exhibit 10.3. In this structure, team members had a solid direct reporting ("solid line") relationship to one of the functional department heads at corporate level, and an indirect relationship ("dotted line") to one or more of the regional team's Project Managers. Department heads were to be responsible for the quality of the expertise and technical support that their team members brought to the team. Project Managers were to be responsible for orchestrating the efforts of the various functions to keep a project "on track." Project Managers were also encouraged to communicate with functional department heads if there were concerns about a team member's participation in and contribution to the team.

The catalyst for change: Pardee 2000

The primary catalyst for change was a leadership transition that took place at the senior management level. A secondary catalyst was Weyerhaeuser's interest in having the leadership team propose strategies for more rapid growth.

In 1999 Pardee had revenues of $615 million. The headcount was 432 people and the company closed (sold) 1,969 homes that year. The next year Landon and Meyer retired. Two of the members of the executive committee were selected to replace them. Michael McGee was named President and CEO of Pardee, and Hal Struck was named Executive Vice-president and COO.

Over the next few years changes at the parent company, plus a favorable housing market, were to afford the new Pardee management team an opportunity to strategically explore opportunities for growth and geographical expansion.

Leadership of change

McGee, along with Struck and other senior managers, led the changes that followed the management succession in 2000. McGee had an appreciation of the values of both entrepreneurial thinking and professional management systems. He was committed to building on the valuable legacy from Landon and Meyer, while also having his own vision about how Pardee would evolve.

Prior to being hired by Pardee, McGee had held an investment analysis position at another WRECO subsidiary and a planning position at WRECO, and then he had managed an East Coast division at another of the WRECO homebuilders. These earlier experiences gave him insight into Pardee's parent company, and multiple housing markets, that proved to be of great value in his new role.

Also, his own experience as a Project Manager at Pardee and his central role in developing the regional team restructuring gave him an in-depth understanding of the development process and an appreciation of the ongoing challenges involved in the tension between Pardee's centralized departments and regionally focused teams.

The change process and initiatives, 2000–4

There were several critical components of the change process. The first was a change in leadership style and a clarification of cultural principles. The second was a series of initiatives to make structural changes that would support strategic growth.

Expanding the senior leadership team

McGee and Struck chose to continue to operate with an executive committee, but expanded it from eight to thirteen members. The new committee included four members from the first (1992) executive committee, including McGee and Struck. The nine senior managers added to the executive committee reflected a mix, including some who had worked at Pardee for many years and others who were relatively new. A broader range of ages, tenure, and professional disciplines were now participating in executive decision making and corporate policy setting.

McGee communicated his desire and expectation that executive committee members would be actively involved in strategic planning and corporate oversight, would work together collaboratively and support each other, and would be committed to more aggressive continuous improvement.

Quarterly strategic planning/organizational development meetings provided time for the group to spend a day off-site, thinking about the "big picture" for Pardee. An annual executive seminar provided time for a mix of learning opportunities and team building.

By expanding the executive committee, McGee brought new voices into the decision-making process, demonstrated a willingness to receive input from a variety of perspectives, challenged a new generation of management to think strategically, and created a strong foundation for guiding Pardee's future growth.

Culture management and leadership style

As part of their vision for the transition, McGee and Struck resolved to implement a more participative style of leadership. They wanted to empower department heads, regional leaders, and team members to be more proactive in addressing opportunities and challenges. In addition to expanding executive committee membership, the tactics to move in this direction included seeking broader input before decisions were made, giving recognition to managers and staff who took the lead on specific issues, and increasing communication throughout the organization about company performance and management initiatives.

Some of the specific strategies that they used to demonstrate this change in leadership style and management cultural values included the following:

Semi-annual Pardee Progress Meetings

Expanding on a process of annual meetings in the regions that began under Landon and Meyer, McGee and Struck instituted the "Pardee

Progress Meetings." These involved a half-day meeting in every region at least twice a year. These meetings provided a forum for providing updates on overall company performance, introducing new corporate initiatives, and inviting feedback from regional staff via candid question and answer sessions. In addition to presentations by McGee and Struck, most meetings included a brief update on progress in each region (presented by the VPs of Community Development) and featured other managers to share information on key initiatives.

The format and frequency of these meetings demonstrate changes in management style at the top by including more managers, from multiple levels, as presenters, and by sharing more information with staff about company performance against goals together with future expectations.

Field visits with front-line staff

McGee and Struck made sure that they scheduled time to meet with workers in various departments during their visits to regional areas. For example, they might conduct "skip level" breakfasts and lunches at which they would meet with the Construction Superintendents or Customer Service staff. They used these meetings to listen to concerns and suggestions from the people who were on the "front line" of community development. These meetings helped demonstrate that the company's leaders respected and valued staff at all levels of the company and that they were willing to *listen* to staff as they committed resources on a timely basis to corrective actions designed to improve the effectiveness and quality of work processes. In addition, these meetings helped McGee and Struck keep abreast of the progress of existing initiatives throughout the organization and gain personal exposure to high-potential employees who could accelerate plans for growth.

Company newsletters

McGee initiated the inclusion of the "President's message" as a regular editorial feature of *Inside Pardee*, the company's newsletter. This provided him with an additional forum for the dissemination of information, the reiteration of critical goals and objectives, and the opportunity to introduce new initiatives or comment on market trends.

Annual team seminar

McGee expanded on a tradition that he had begun when he headed Project Management. Once a year all the team members are invited to a resort location for three days of meetings, followed by a weekend at which family members join in the fun. The meeting content is varied, but generally includes a mix of team presentations, skill building, and strategic thinking, as well as team-building activities. Senior executives usually participate on the last day of the seminar at least, often sitting as a panel to receive team recommendations.

Goal-oriented incentive compensation

Prior to the transition, Pardee executives felt that they had little control over their incentive compensation. McGee revised the system of incentive compensation, with support from WRECO, to ensure that a component of the bonus was determined based on how well individual executives accomplished annual goals that were set with McGee and Struck. This change was very positively received by executives, and resulted in more dedication to the completion of individual goals.

Changing the structure at Pardee

The evolution of Pardee's structure continued during the period from 2000 to 2004. During this period it was recognized explicitly that Pardee's structure had become a "matrix structure," as already shown in exhibit 10.3.

Regionalization of project teams

Before his promotion to President, McGee had been the department head responsible for all the Project Managers who led regional teams. He provided oversight and guidance for Project Managers individually and as a group. He was an advocate of relocating project team members from the corporate office, so that they could be housed with the Project Manager and other team members in regional offices. This process was begun prior to the leadership transition, but was accelerated after McGee became President.

Positions in regional offices were filled in two ways. In many instances, the current holder of the position agreed to make the physical office move. In other instances, department heads filled vacant positions by hiring candidates who already lived in the region.

Physical co-location of team members produced tangible benefits – including improved communication among team members on a daily basis (not just in formal team meetings), more awareness of local trends and requirements, closer focus on customer requirements, more timely recognition of (and response to) schedule delays, and enhanced team spirit. It also facilitated improved opportunities to fill new positions created by growth by sourcing better-qualified candidates who were typically more experienced in the local market areas.

Changes in department head roles

The relocation of functional staff from the central office to regional offices made it necessary for department (functional group) heads to change their approach to interacting with and overseeing the technical work of department staff.

For example, two of the departments that were most heavily impacted were Land Development (Engineering) and Purchasing. Both functions went from having all their staff located close to each other in the central office to having most staff located in the regional offices. The department head's role in Pardee's matrix organization was to ensure that functional staff provided expert technical support to their team and that their work performance met Pardee standards for quality and conformed with company policies. Therefore, new approaches were needed for orienting new hires, reviewing individual work output, establishing policies and procedures, conducting staff meetings, and helping to resolve difficult technical issues. Some of the common changes made by managers included the following.

- More frequent visits by department heads to regional offices to review work product, discuss challenges, and keep current on specific regional issues.
- More work on documenting formal policies and procedures.
- Staff meetings conducted in various locations.
- More use of upgraded telephone and video conference facilities.
- The creation of at least one subordinate manager to help with more detailed oversight of a portion of regionally based staff. This had

the added benefit of exposing potential succession candidates to increasing levels of responsibility.

Changes in team leader roles

By 2004 all the regional team leaders who had successfully transitioned to effective managers within the matrix structure had been promoted to Vice-president of Community Development, a title that was intended to reflect their leadership role as Pardee's local representatives, as well as their expanded responsibility for bringing team recommendations to senior management for approval. They were referred to informally as "regional managers." It is important to note, however, that, of the eight original Project Managers whose role it had been – remember – to function almost solely as entitlement experts, only three survived the redefinition of their role to include the expanded responsibilities for the coordination of budgets, schedules, and personnel.

Development of supporting systems

Flamholtz's approach to structural design is that it is multifaceted. First, strategy drives structure; this means that structure follows from the organization's strategy. A second precept is that structure does not exit in a vacuum; this means that there are certain "supporting systems" that have to be developed to support an overall structural design.[4]

Typically the supporting systems that must be developed as part of an overall structural design include the organization's culture (which specifies how people will work together), the compensation system, and the planning system.

Articulation of cultural principles

In 2003 the executive committee began work on a statement of Pardee's cultural principles. A major purpose of this initiative was to help ensure that shared cultural values would be implemented at headquarters and across all the regions. Vice-presidents of Community

[4] Flamholtz and Randle, *Changing the Game*, chap. 8.

Development were invited to review and discuss an early draft of the principles with the executive committee. It was recognized that these regional leaders would have a critical role in managing culture in their locations.

Team incentive compensation

McGee and other executives felt that it was important to motivate and recognize strong team performance through annual financial incentives. There was common agreement that metrics needed to be set for regional performance that would help set the incentive compensation for all the professional members of a team.

There were a number of procedural challenges to resolve before such an incentive could be implemented – including what portion of an individual's incentive compensation would be determined by the department head (regarding technical performance and individual goals), how teams would give input regarding contributions of individual members to team functioning, and what input the regional office head would have in determining bonuses for individual team members. The procedure also required WRECO's approval, because it was a new approach and required ongoing financial commitment from the parent company.

After a long gestation period, the team incentive system was introduced to team members in 2002 and first paid in 2003.

Enhancing team participation in planning

John Osgood, a former Project Manager who had left Pardee to take a regional leadership role with another builder, was recruited by McGee to become Senior Vice-president of Community Development.

Osgood recognized a need to develop more formal plans at project and regional levels. This effort proceeded in several phases.

(1) The first phase was to have teams develop a formal "project business plan" for every physical property in development that the team was overseeing. This plan documented assumptions regarding the project's budget and schedule, identified key milestones and challenges related to the development process, and presented

detailed goals for the project. These plans were to be updated regularly.

(2) The second phase was to develop regional strategic plans that were future-oriented. Teams were asked to include proposals for future land acquisition and strategic initiatives that would maintain and enhance Pardee's market position and the delivery of its value proposition in each region.[5] Management Systems conducted training workshops for each regional team to help stimulate the ability of team members to think strategically (e.g., about market positioning, competitors, trends impacting the building industry, etc.).

(3) The third phase was to involve the executive committee in making semi-annual visits to each region to hold a regional operations review. In this meeting, the team leaders (and selected team members) would update executives on progress against project business plans and present information about significant local trends.

Structural change: Pardee 2005

As Pardee expanded to include additional regions, McGee began to believe that the current structure at Pardee was again in the process of being outgrown. Initially he discussed this with Flamholtz, who again suggested the concept initially recommended in 1992: the organization of the company into divisions based upon geographical regions.

During 2004 and early 2005 the executive committee held in-depth discussions about the possible need to change the matrix structure so that regional team members had a direct reporting relationship with the Vice-president of Community Development and a dotted-line reporting relationship with a department head.

In 2005 a pilot project was launched in one region to implement this structure change and determine best practices for continuing the rollout in other areas. The new divisional structure is shown in exhibit 10.4.

---

[5] Pardee's "value proposition" is: "We build homes and communities for the way people want to live, creating premium value through a trusting builder relationship."

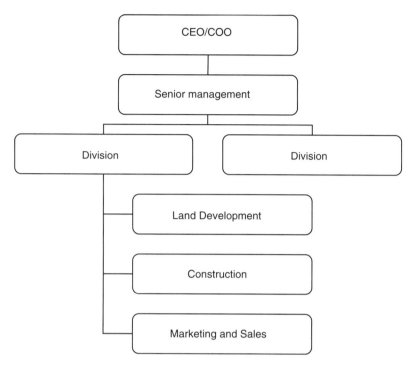

Exhibit 10.4 Pardee Homes' divisional structure, 2005 (simplified version)

Results of change

What have the results of these changes been for Pardee? The number one reason for changing Pardee's organizational structure was to facilitate company growth. The original functional structure at Pardee had reached its limits, and a new structure was required that would allow the company to grow, to grow profitably, and to grow without the difficulties experienced by many of the companies in the same industry that had tried decentralization.

This was accomplished. During the period from 1996 to 2006 Pardee grew from just over $400 million in revenues to around $2.0 billion. During the same period the number of units sold grew from 1,669 to 3,007. Moreover, the company achieved record-setting financial performance, not just in terms of its own performance but also in relation to other similar companies.

In addition to these results, there were certain other non-financial results with significant benefit to the company.

- The changes in management style implemented by McGee and Struck resulted in more engagement and proactive thinking by people at all levels of the organization.
- The transfer of staff to regional offices, the enhanced leadership role of VPs of Community Development, team involvement in planning, and the team incentive program resulted in regional teams taking more responsibility, which has made it possible for Pardee to function in more geographic areas without totally exhausting senior management.
- During this period there was a major transition of senior management. The new top management team (McGee and Struck) was able to build upon the foundation provided by its predecessors and take Pardee to a new level of success. Many companies do not achieve such a smooth transition.

Limitations and lessons

As with any organizational development effort, there were certain difficulties encountered. A primary difficulty was the amount of time it required to make the changes. This effort took several years. One reason was the initial reluctance to move in this direction, which, in turn, was the product of a somewhat risk-averse culture. Although the company embraced large financial risks whenever it purchased land, it was more risk-averse with respect to managerial practices. Things tended to be done the way things had always been done. This was reinforced by the company's history of success. It is difficult to create change in successful organizations with "unproven" ideas. As a result, change took a considerable period of time.

There is, however, another, more positive way to look at this. There was a great deal of patience with the process of organizational development. It has become a way of life at Pardee, which now embraces a culture of continuous improvement.

Conclusion

Pardee Homes is still a "work in progress." Michael McGee and Hal Struck continue to encourage the executive committee to maintain a consistent focus on opportunities for Pardee to improve – in performance, efficiency, and culture. The company has made significant progress, however, and represents a significant case study of the problems and possibilities of transitioning from entrepreneurship to professional management. The experience at Pardee also demonstrates how organizational structure can be a critical variable in a company's success.

11 | *Leading strategic and organizational change at Tata Steel: the role of culture*

Introduction

The Tata Group is one of India's most successful and prestigious business groups. Tata Steel is one of the key components of the group and one of the most important companies in India.

From its founding until the early 1990s Tata Steel was a classic paternalistic employer. This was facilitated by economic conditions that made India a producer's or seller's market. There was an environment of scarcity, and people would be forced to wait until something was produced. This was not an environment conducive to competition or efficiency. It allowed Tata to take care of its employees, but not to be a highly efficient competitive organization.

During the 1990s the winds of change swept into India. Tata Steel was forced to change its way of doing business in order to adapt to the new era of competition. By the early 1990s Tata's technology had become so outdated that the then Managing Director, Dr. Irani, would joke that if they did not change their technology they may as well convert Tata Steel to a museum of steel-making history!

This chapter deals with the initial development and, later, the strategic and organizational changes at Tata Steel in response to this environmental change. The particular focus of this chapter is on the need to transition from a very paternalistic culture (in which employees are cared for like family) to one that is still humanistic but is now more efficient and competitive and focused on the needs of all its stakeholders, including investors. As a result of this process of

This chapter was co-authored with Shalini Lal, who is the lead author, and was prepared with the permission of the Managing Director at Tata Steel, Mr. Muthuraman. It is based upon interviews conducted by Shalini Lal in the Tata Steel headquarters at Jamshedpur.

change, Tata Steel has transformed itself from a company on the brink of obsolescence to the low-cost producer of steel in the world.

The history of Tata Steel

The nineteenth century witnessed the Industrial Revolution in the United Kingdom, and, with this, the role of India as a British colony changed. Until the Industrial Revolution the East India Company had largely been concerned with exporting handicrafts and cottage products by artisans. With the onset of the Industrial Revolution, Manchester's cotton textile industry demanded a cheap supply of raw materials from India. India was also a large market for the products of British industry. The year 1857 marked the transition of rule from the East India Company to the British government, and, in 1877, Queen Victoria became the Empress of India.

The Tata Group was one of the earliest large manufacturing business groups in India.[1] The founder, Jamsetji Nusserwanji ("JN") Tata, was born at the height of British rule in India, in 1839. His father was the first-generation entrepreneur in his family.

At the age of twenty JN Tata entered his father's business. He spent the next fifteen years traveling the world on business, and particularly in expanding his father's business to corners as far afield as China, Japan and England.

JN would habitually set time aside in the evening to contemplate plans for the economic progress of India. He began to believe that the three basic ingredients of economic progress were steel, electric power, and technical education combined with research.[2] A chance voyage with a great thinker of the time, Swami Vivekananda, added to his inspiration for contributing to India's economic self-reliance.

The business concept

A report on the rich iron ore deposits in India motivated JN to believe that it might be possible to start such a venture in his country. For several years he researched the process of steel making, and traveled to Europe and the United States for technical advice.

---

[1] Harris, F. R., 1956, *Jamsetji Nusserwanji Tata: A Chronicle of His Life*, Mumbai, Blackie and Son (India).
[2] Harris, F. R. *Jamsetji Nusserwanji Tata.*

It would also be many years before he received governmental approval. At that time getting approval meant not just the approval of the Viceroy and the executive government in India, it meant approval from the Secretary of State in London. Although his interest in setting up the steel plant began in 1882, the regulations governing the mining and prospecting industry caused several years of delay, and it was only in 1900 that he finally secured approval for building a steel plant. In addition, many years were spent on the scientific survey of raw materials and climatic conditions in India.

In 1907 Tata Iron and Steel Company began operations in Sakchi (the city was renamed as Jamshedpur in 1911). Unfortunately, Jamsetji did not live to see that day; but his legacy was carried forward by his sons.

Growth of Tata Steel

The steel city of Jamshedpur was created as a model industrial town of 300,000: built, developed, and administered by the company. This meant providing electricity, housing, sanitation, water, schooling, crèches, medical and recreational facilities, parks, and even a zoo for all the inhabitants of the township. Across its history of over 100 years, Jamshedpur has consistently ranked as one of India's model cities. Even today it is one of the few cities in India with a twenty-four-hour water and electricity supply.

Over the next few decades Tata Steel grew to be one of the most important companies in the Indian corporate world, with some of the most progressive policies of its times. In 1948, when as a newly independent country India enacted its first set of labor regulations, the work norms adopted by Tata Steel played an important role in influencing the facilities that all employers from then on would be required to provide.

A producer's or seller's market

After its independence from the British Empire, India adopted a socialist model of development. This meant that all industry was regulated by the government. Private companies had to apply to the government for a license to produce goods, and, depending on the extent to which the product they had applied for matched the authorities' priorities at that time, licenses were issued.

At that time India had a rapidly growing population. Furthermore, not all entrepreneurs who were granted licenses ever produced the product they had been licensed to manufacture. As a result, this created an environment of scarcity and a seller's market. Given the economic environment in India, there was little incentive for organizations to become competitive. The idea of being customer-oriented had not as yet taken root; rather, the situation was very much the opposite. As a very senior executive of the Tata organization describes:

At the time when the economy opened we first started talking about the customer. Till that time, the customer was someone to be sort of kept waiting outside for two hours, and if you felt like giving him something – you gave him something. In fact, there was a time when we could actually package material. If you wanted high-silicon sheets, which was a very "in demand" product, you actually told the guy, "Imagine you are a motor manufacturer. You want high-silicon sheets? I tell you: you want high-silicon sheets, fine – but take about five tonnes of these bars with it.[3]

This attitude and situation prevailed in many other domains of the industry as well. For example, if you wanted to purchase a car such as the premier Padmini, made by Fiat, in those days you paid a booking amount and then waited patiently in line for several years before your turn came. Capacity restrictions had ensured that demand far out-stretched supply in many areas of the economy.

Environmental change in the 1990s

Everything began to change in India during the 1990s. This was driven to a large extent by changing technology, which made Tata uncompetitive. This, in turn, forced a series of organizational changes, as described below.

Technological change

As the 1990s commenced Tata Steel realized that it had no option but to change its technology. Although previous attempts to convince the board of the need to invest in new technology had not proved

---

[3] Interview with Mr. Sarangi, General Manager, Personnel, conducted by Shalini Lal.

effective, the strength of the international competition now made this absolutely essential.

The new technology was more productive, however, and it required only one-fourth the labor of previous technology yet had a capacity up to five times greater. There was very little choice but to reduce the numbers of people employed. Back in 1956, however, management had agreed not to retrench employees; instead, management launched a voluntary employment separation scheme, whereby incentives would be offered to employees who chose to take retirement.

Before the 1990s the protected economy and unfavorable labor laws had ensured that layoffs were very rare. Now, however, as the winds of change began, different businesses across the country started to undertake large-scale layoffs, including Tata Steel's primary competitor – the state-owned Steel Authority of India.

Conflict between technological change and employment practices

Until the early 1990s nobody seemed to worry about Tata Steel being overstaffed. This led to a classic case of a paternalistic culture coming about. The Senior Vice-president, Human Resources, of Tata Steel explains the employment tradition as follows: "In Tata Steel the story was: Tata Steel does not hire villagers, it hires whole villages. If you were an employee, you could just write a note and your uncle, brother, or son could get employed."

These practices left the organization not just overstaffed but under skilled as well. In fact, in a rather stagnant economy, it was considered socially responsible to provide employment. In the words of one senior executive:

Until 1990–92, we really did not feel the need to separate employees, even though we were in fact overstaffed. Yet one of the things we used to do, without too much thought, was to keep on recruiting people throughout the company... We never thought this was bad or something. It was a Tata Steel township. Everything was Tata Steel: more employment meant more relationships with people and so on. To provide employment was considered a good thing to do.[4]

---

[4] Interview with Mr. Mahanty, Senior Vice-president, Human Resources, conducted by Shalini Lal.

Mr. Mahanty recalled how, when he had returned from a stint with an international company in 1992/3, he spoke with the Managing Director and told him that, to their horror, at any given point in time Tata Steel did not really know how many people it employed. In counting employees, there was a difference of about 4,000 people in the number counted by Payroll, IT, and the Personnel Division.

Organizational changes in response to changing environment

The changing economy dictated that the company had to begin to control all costs, including labor costs. This led to a process of reconciling the different labor records. Mr. Mahanty recalls Dr. Irani's interest in this. "So I remember, every dialogue after that, Dr. Irani used to ask me, 'So, Niroop, how close are you?' So I told him, 'nearest thousand, nearest hundred...'"[5]

Until that moment, senior management had never thought of reducing staff numbers. Even though Tata Steel had a long history of taking care of its people, it was now necessary to launch the first employee separation scheme. This was not something that the organization really knew how to do. The first employee separation scheme, launched in the late 1980s, had been a disaster. Of the 1,000 employees to whom the scheme was offered, only four or five people actually availed themselves of the scheme.

Since the scheme offered employees almost the equivalent of their current salary until their age of retirement, this was puzzling to the company. Investigations revealed that employees did not really want to break their relationship with the organization. Many of them had been born and brought up in Jamshedpur and they didn't want to move elsewhere. They had relatives, friends, and family in the town. Further, Jamshedpur offered them a quality of life that few towns in India did, and, within Jamshedpur, there were few employment opportunities other than Tata Steel. Employment at Tata Steel had entitled employees and their families to subsidized medical care, cheap housing, and electricity. So, while they would have continued to receive their salaries, most were unwilling to give up the benefits and lifestyle associated with being part of the company.

[5] Interview with Mr. Mahanty, Senior Vice-president Human Resources, conducted by Shalini Lal.

By 1993 it had become clear that one of Tata Steel's melting shops would need to be closed to accommodate the new technology. Given the somewhat disappointing experiences of the past employee separation scheme, the organization decided to ask people what they would like to be offered in case they had to leave before their retirement age. Describing this somewhat unusual step, Mr. Sarangi, who had been entrusted with the task of implementing the organization-wide employee separation scheme, recollects its impact on the employees:

When, in 1993, we had to close down another steel melting shop, we did not repeat our earlier scheme. Instead, we went about asking everybody that, while their job was guaranteed, and while there was still employment security, what would they like to be offered if they were to want to leave the company before their official year of retirement? We conducted an interview with a large number of employees.[6]

Unfortunately, this approach, while appealing, led to some unintended consequences. As Mr. Sarangi states:

This had its own repercussions, because people thought that we were asking them to go. But most people took it very sportingly. They said so many things in so many ways, and what we interpreted all this to mean was that one thing was very clear: that they were talking in terms of not snapping the relationship with the company. They were telling us that, whatever we did, we needed to make sure that the relationship continued.

If the organization wished to be true to its word to the unions in 1956 and true to the Tata Group's philosophy of caring for its employees, managers realized that they needed to make an offer that was generous enough for people to feel comfortable accepting it. One thing became clear: for any employee separation scheme to be effective, it would require the continuation of many of the benefits that employees had become accustomed to.

A culturally positive approach to downsizing

Consistent with its culture, Tata created a humanistic approach to downsizing. It created attractive offers for employees to leave Tata's

---

[6] Interview with Mr. Sarangi, General Manager, Personnel, conducted by Shalini Lal.

employment. Mr. Sarangi explains the logic of the early employee separation schemes as follows: "Given the feedback we received from our survey, we developed a scheme whereby the company undertook to keep paying a pension till the person retired at sixty years of age, which is his due date of retirement."

A formula was worked out so that, for those who were more than forty-five years of age, their pension would entail one and a half times their current basic and dearness allowance. For those younger than forty-five years there were different formulae, ranging from 75 percent to 100 percent of salary. Clearly, the scheme was more attractive for those older than forty-five.

In addition, Tata provided other financial incentives for people to leave its employment. In Mr. Sarangi's words: "We also said that the company will give some money, so that the employee can start some business. Then we said, for the employee and his spouse, the medical facility will continue. So, we found that, when the first steel melting shop closed, people accepted the employee separation scheme offered." Tata Steel had finally discovered the financial incentives it needed to use to encourage people to retire.

There were other reasons as well why the employee separation scheme began looking far more acceptable. Many of the older employees had been recruited not for their skills or education but because of the company's long-standing philanthropic policy of letting employees who had completed twenty-five years of service nominate their wards for employment. As the technology changed, many employees who lacked any formal education realized that they might not be able to fit in the changing environment, and felt that they were too old to learn so many new skills. The change in technology had meant that physical hardiness was no longer sufficient as a qualification; instead, the new technology required that they be able to understand and work with electronic drives and high-tech instruments.[7]

Since 1995 employee separation schemes have been offered on many occasions, about once a quarter. The organization was very careful about not offering the scheme to everyone at a time, but to target selectively those departments that would need to be shut down or

---

[7] Interview with Mr. Sarangi, General Manager, Personnel, conducted by Shalini Lal.

significantly changed so that the rationale for letting people go was always clear.

In order to prevent younger and more trainable people from availing themselves of these schemes, the scheme was modified over time. Before a particular plant was to be closed, the employees the organization did not wish to lose were taken out of the department and placed in a central pool to which this scheme would not be applicable. The general pool would be responsible for implementing many of the organization-wide projects during this time, and, as positions opened up in newer departments that matched their talents, they would be moved to these departments.

The process of identifying the better-qualified and more trainable people in the organization proved tremendous. The act of cross-matching involved department heads regularly reworking their needs for skills and matching positions with people from the pool. Each department tracked the age and skill distribution of its employees with the aim of improving the age/skill profile through the process as it sought to improve its employee profile. Department heads were given the option of offering the employee separation scheme to specific employees within their department whom they wished to replace. To take the place of the departing employee, the department head could select people from the general pool.

Results of the separation schemes

These efforts paid off, and ten years and forty rounds of employee separation schemes later the employee headcount had decreased from about 75,000 to about 40,000. Moreover, by selectively allowing employees to take advantage of the separation scheme, the average age of the departments dropped from about fifty-four to about forty-seven, while the average education and skill levels of the organization improved.

The process of downsizing, while maintaining the trust of employees and improving the skill/education profile of the employees, required tremendous care and patience. In the words of a senior executive at Tata Steel:

What was the other option available to us? The other option was simple. Circulate a scheme, and, whosoever wants, let them go. We would have got the number, but we would have lost good people. At the end of the day – today, probably – we would have been bogged down with older people and the less skilled people. Or we would have landed up in a situation where we would have had to recruit people from outside, having separated people by paying money to one set of people.[8]

The extensive downsizing was not without its mistakes. As a result, Tata Steel appointed Xaviers Labour Research Institute (a leading academic institution in India) to conduct regular interviews with the families of employees who had been separated, to understand the experiences of people who had been separated from the company. These interviews served as a useful link to enable the company to learn what it could do to make the process less painful for the people. In the colorful language of the group chairman, Ratan Tata (in an interview with *Newsweek*), "[W]e don't want to build the success of our company over dead bodies."

Vision and culture changes at Tata Steel

The change that Tata Steel was attempting was far larger and far more wide-ranging than any Indian company had experienced until then. There needed to be a way to emphasize across such a large organization what the change was and what its implications would be.

Like any other company of its time, Tata Steel also had a culture statement that, until then, consisted of a few sentences, to be found either hanging from the walls of the boardroom or, more often than not, only in company publications.[9] What was needed was a new vision for Tata Steel, one that was far more than words in a statement hanging on walls.

Crafting the new cultural vision

To involve the whole organization in the process of building the new vision and culture, a campaign, termed the "Lakshya [Mission] 2007," was launched. The senior team invited everyone from across the organization to participate in the building of the organizational vision.

---

[8] Interview with Mr. Sarangi, General Manager, Personnel, conducted by Shalini Lal.

[9] As discussed in chapter 2, culture involves the core values of a company. It is a key part of the Pyramid of Organizational Development,™ providing focus on what is important to a company and serving as a guide to people's orientation and behavior.

The invitation to offer suggestions for the future of the organization was accepted by a broad cross-section of employees. The company received some 5,000 suggestions from workers, supervisors, and management across the company.

The new core values

A centerpiece of the new culture was the concept of becoming a company that was "EVA- (economic value added) positive." A well-known Indian theatre personality, Alyque Padamsee, was invited to help craft the statement so that it incorporated all that people were saying they wished for in the new company.

The final vision document read as follows:

To seize the opportunities of tomorrow and create a future that will make us an EVA-positive company.

To continue to improve the quality of life of our employees and the employees we serve.

This vision contained both strategic and cultural elements. One aspect was to become a company that was EVA-oriented. The second was to be a company that served its employees and the larger community of which it was a part.

The vision was to be supported by a number of strategic goals and specific strategies the company would adopt. These were pictorially represented as the pillars that would support the vision.

Communicating the new vision/culture

The Managing Director decided that, since the whole organization had together created the cultural vision, it had to be understood by every person in the company. In the first round of what was to be a massive communications campaign, all the General Managers and all the executive directors discussed what the implications of this vision would be. One of the key points that needed to be explained was how the place of the shareholder was going to change in the new model. In the words of Mr. Sarangi,

Tata Steel has historically placed very little emphasis on the shareholder. So we explained that, if there were a queue of people lined up according to their importance, the employee and community were far ahead of the customer and the shareholder was last. We needed everyone to understand that the shareholder was now becoming an important person, and he needed to be moved to the head of the line.

The organization therefore needed to make sure that everyone became conscious of the changing role of the stakeholders.

In the second phase, this message had to be passed on throughout the company. Communication kits, with workbooks and slides, were prepared. The communication packages themselves needed to be translated into the various languages that people throughout the company, spread as it was across the whole of India, would understand.

Explaining the new core values

The core construct of the new culture was the concept of becoming a company that was EVA-positive. This is a complex abstract notion, and it was necessary to explain to everyone in the company in comprehensible terms. Mr. Sarangi shares his recollections about the challenge this posed. "Even we did not understand what was the meaning of 'EVA-positive.' Now, we had to make sure everyone understood this."

To make this construct meaningful to workers across the company required a "story" that people would be able to understand and relate to.[10] A common, small business option in India is the tea stall.

So we told them a story about a chai wallah (tea seller) who has Rs. 200. The story explains how much the seller would make if he makes tea and sells it, and compares this to a lazy friend of his who has the same Rs. 200 and puts it in a bank. We asked them to think about how much more money should the chai wallah make if his business is to be considered successful. That's how we made people understand, and once they understood they started asking questions about what they would need to do in order to make this happen.[11]

In each location of the company, the senior managers first had to ensure that they met with small groups of people, and then take them

[10] One of the key "tools" of culture management is the use of "stories," just as with fables, that send "messages" to people.
[11] Interview with Mr. Sarangi, General Manager, Personnel, conducted by Shalini Lal.

through the communication package. It was six months before every single person had attended such a briefing.

Communicating how each individual fits into the vision

The second set of briefings was through the creation of a one-day workshop about the cultural vision. This workshop included a short motivational film.

In India, cricket is a sport that is understood and loved almost universally, so, in an attempt to make something that everyone could feel inspired by, the corporate film had the Managing Director batting against Shoaib Akhtar (a well-known Pakistani fast-paced bowler), and "hitting a six."[12] The film then tells people that, just as it was possible for the Managing Director to take on such a challenge with hard work and determination, each employee of Tata Steel would need to do the same for the company to achieve its vision.

About 600 managers were selected as emissaries to transmit the new culture across the organization, based on their ability to communicate well and influence others. These 600 managers were provided with the materials and training required, and were then given the task of facilitating these workshops. Each workshop had between twenty and twenty-five participants and began with the film. It was then followed by the chief of that particular department presenting the department's "balanced scorecard."[13] The scorecard would cover the important performance indicators of that department and the staff's progress in these. The second half of the workshop involved organizational members working in small groups to figure out how, within their role, they could contribute to making the vision a reality.

This was a detailed exercise. As stated by Mr. Sarangi:

You know, we prepared a workbook, where people wrote down all the individual activities they performed as part of their roles. We made them write individual activities, and their current understanding of EVA–person–pillar relationship [each pillar was an element of the vision]. They then had to think

---

[12] A "six" means that the batsman hits the ball bowled hard and outside the boundary, scoring six runs.

[13] The "balanced scorecard" is a performance management tool. See Kaplan, R. S., and D. P. Norton, 1992, "The balanced scorecard: measures that drive performance," *Harvard Business Review*, 70(1), 71–9.

about how they are connected with a particular pillar. For example, there was a pillar which says sustainable growth, or lowest-cost producer of steel. We told employees: "Can you please describe that, if the company wants to be the lowest-cost producer of steel, what can you do about it?" Right, so people came out, they scratched their heads and thought hard, and some wondered what they could do. But then some would realize that perhaps they could save costs in some ways: for instance, maybe if they could save grease or recycle it they could save the company money, and so on.

Besides providing an important understanding of how each person related to the individual vision, these workshops became a source of new ideas of changes that could be implemented to make the company more efficient.

Organizational and systems changes at Tata

There were many other changes in the organization. The period from 1992 to 2001 saw a sharp drop in global steel prices, which fell from $310 per tonne in 1992 to only $218 per tonne in 2001.

In order to remain competitive in this business, a highly focused effort on improving all-around efficiencies was necessary. Several programs were launched with this intent, a few of which are described below.

New operational systems

As discussed in chapter 2, operations and related systems can be a driver of change. Tata Steel used this approach, and initiated several new programs. An umbrella structure termed "Aspire" was formed to launch initiatives such as "Total Operational Performance [TOP] Improvement," "Quality Circles," "Six Sigma," "Total Productivity Management," and "Knowledge Management."

One of the interesting features of all the performance improvement initiatives was the extent to which their success was dependent on the wholehearted participation by employees across different levels and departments of the organization. The fact that Tata Steel had taken so much care to ensure that the morale of the workforce did not go down during the downsizing would now prove to be a major "intangible asset." It created the climate for Tata to reap substantial benefits for the organization. Thus, the culture of the company and the positive feelings engendered within Tata Steel were inextricably related to the success of its operational initiatives.[14]

Total Operational Performance Improvement

Tata Steel used the assistance of outside consultants McKinsey & Co. to assist the company in improving operational initiatives. The aim of this initiative was to tap knowledge and creativity at different levels of the organization so that the people closest to a job could generate ideas that could significantly improve operations. These ideas could be performance-focused, people-driven, or comprehensive.

To help coordinate the overall change and facilitate implementation across the organization effort, Tata created what was termed a "TOP center." This was headed by a senior manager with considerable operational experience and familiarity with the TOP methodology. A steering committee, headed by the Deputy Managing Director, Steel, was created to monitor the progress of the initiative. Another technique used was that all the savings resulting from TOP initiatives were subject to audits.

In the three years between 1998 and 2001 thirteen programs of TOP had been launched. Each wave lasted for about eighteen months and comprised the generation of ideas, their evaluation, and the implementation of these ideas.

Quality Circles

The concept of quality circles took a while to gain root in the company. Although the use of quality circles dates back to the 1980s, it was only towards the end of the 1990s that the movement really took off at Tata Steel, with a growth from about 1,000 Quality Circles in 1996 to close to 8,000 in 2002. The Quality Circles were small, with only five team members and one facilitator per circle. A criterion for the continued existence of a Quality Circle at Tata Steel was that the team present at least one completed quality improvement project to the department head every year.

[14] For a discussion of corporate culture as an intangible organizational asset, see Flamholtz, E. G., 2005, "Conceptualizing and measuring human capital of the third kind: corporate culture," *Journal of Human Resource Costing and Accounting*, 9(2), 78–93.

Effective participation in Quality Circles required substantial training and encouragement from the managers. All Quality Circle members were exposed to basic TQM (total quality management) concepts, such as the use of fish-bone diagrams and basic cause–effect analysis.

Quality Circles also participated in several competitions, both at the departmental level and the divisional level. A pre-qualification for any of these competitions was the number of quality improvement projects completed by the Quality Circles. There were different levels (symbolized by "bands") of achievement for the Quality Circles: black (highest recognition), yellow, green, and white bands. Any Quality Circle that received a black band for two or three years was given the opportunity to take on bigger improvement projects across the company.

The overall results of the changes: the Tata miracle

What were the results of the changes in vision, culture, and operations at Tata Steel? Did all this careful planning and effort make a significant difference? The answer, clearly, is "yes."

Transformation to the lowest-cost producer

World Steel Dynamics ranks the major steel plants in the world every year. The "miracle" of Tata Steel is that, through the process of change described above, the company has transformed itself from an overstaffed, technologically obsolete company into a world-class competitor. Since 2001 World Steel Dynamics' annual study of costs, operational efficiencies, and financial management has ranked Tata Steel as the lowest-cost producer of steel in the world.

The new strategic vision for change

Now that Tata has made these changes in its cost structure, it is strategically positioned as a front-rank player. The focus of the company is now switching to becoming a truly global player, with business interests across the world. Tata is planning new steel units not just within India but in many new countries as well. The organization is expected to boost capacity by 200 percent within five years, partly by buying other Asian steel-makers. November 2005 saw the launch of a joint venture with BlueScope Steel of Australia.

The organization also continues its mission of corporate social responsibility: 66 percent of the profits of its highly successful holding company, Tata Sons, continue to go to charity, supporting a number of educational institutes, research institutes, and hospitals all over the country.

Conclusion

This chapter has described how Tata Steel transformed itself from a company on the brink of obsolescence to the lowest-cost producer of steel in the world. We have examined how Tata did this not with a "slash and burn" strategy but with the skillful use of initiatives designed to transition from a very paternalistic culture (in which employees are cared for like family) to one that is still humanistic but is now more efficient and competitive and focused on the needs of all its stakeholders, including investors.

In the words of the Managing Director, Mr. Muthuraman, "A company is not only measured by the returns it gives its shareholders, but also by the returns it provides to the society; that is surely the true measure of any corporation."[15]

We have no illusions that it is impossible for anyone, anywhere, to find fault with Tata, and something that the company did. Nevertheless, this is an important success story about the leading of strategic and organizational change.

---

[15] Quoted in *Business and Economy*, June 2006.

12 | Leading strategic and organizational change at Westfield: transformation to a global enterprise

Introduction

The Westfield Group is an Australian listed public company that owns, develops, renovates, and manages shopping centers in Australia, New Zealand, the United States, and the United Kingdom. It is an example of a company that has transformed itself from an Australian company into a truly global business.

In late 2001 Frank Lowy, Executive Chairman and co-founder of Westfield, and his son Peter Lowy, Joint Group Managing Director, were sitting in the Amstel Hotel in Amsterdam discussing the details of Westfield's bid to acquire Rodamco NV, a Dutch company listed on the Amsterdam Stock Exchange that owned North American real estate assets. As they reflected on the impending deal – an Australian company investing Australian dollars to buy the stock of a European company in euros in order to own shopping mall assets valued in US dollars – they had an epiphany. They realized that Westfield had become a global enterprise and that the commercial real estate industry was about to follow suit. This insight prompted Peter, Frank, and other company leaders to recognize that Westfield needed to begin to think of itself as a global business rather than as a purely Australian business.

This case provides background on the origins of Westfield, and then relates how company leaders managed growth, development, and globalization through multiple phases of expansion and diversification, and describes the lessons learned in each phase. As the case ends, the company is entering a new phase of operating as a global company.

This case is based upon a number of sources, including an interview with Peter Lowy, Joint Group Managing Director of the Westfield Group, on November 6, 2006, and a presentation on the Westfield Executive Development Programme in Sydney by Frank Lowy, Executive Chairman of the Westfield Group, to attendees of the UCLA – Australian Graduate School of Management on October 24, 2006.

Company history and background

John Saunders and Frank Lowy were eastern European Jews who survived the Holocaust and emigrated to Australia in the early 1950s. Their first partnership was a delicatessen in Blacktown, a suburb of Sydney, where they served a mixed population of railway commuters and workers who were overwhelmingly European immigrants. Soon they were able to open an espresso bar in a nearby shop, which became a great success with local Italian-born workers.

Within a few years they began their initial venture in land development, by purchasing and subdividing local farms around Blacktown in order to meet the housing needs of the expanding population. In what would be a characteristic of their approach to business, the partners personally involved themselves in the details of developing and selling their lots.

Success in property development prompted Saunders and Lowy to convert their partnership into a private company, called Westfield Investments. They expanded to developing property into retail shops. In 1958 they sold the delicatessen and focused all their energies on property development.

Pioneers in the shopping center industry: 1956–60

Australia's first two modern shopping centers opened in 1957. Saunders and Lowy, who had already read about the success of shopping centers in the United States, were determined to develop their own. While Frank was overseeing the building of their first shopping center in Blacktown, John traveled to the United States to survey shopping centers there. He met with developers and retailers and visited as many shopping centers as he could fit into his schedule. He noted the importance of car access and parking facilities to success.

Westfield Place in Blacktown opened in the summer of 1959. It had twelve shops, a small department store, and a small supermarket, arranged around an open square, with a car park to the side. The center drew many shoppers, and Frank and John began to receive unsolicited offers for partnerships and joint ventures.

To obtain new sources of capital for expansion, shares in a public company, Westfield Development Corporation Ltd, were floated in

September 1960. The partners decided that the public company would own four Westfield properties. Two business executives with public company experience helped Frank and John form the public company and joined the board of directors.

While Frank and John conferred closely on all business decisions, their roles in the company were becoming more clearly defined. John focused on finding new business opportunities, while Frank focused on the financial and legal aspects of running the company and on assessing the potential for risk and reward in the business opportunities that John had identified. One business partner observed how effectively Frank and John complemented each other: "John was an astute, calculating operator, and while Frank was equally so he was a bit more casual and friendly. Frank would calm John down if he became heated during negotiations. John was a bit impulsive, Frank a natural diplomat. But it's my opinion that one without the other wouldn't have had the same success."[1]

In 1960 Frank had a chance to make his own trip to the United States, to study how shopping centers and motels were run in California. Over the years Frank and John went to the United States periodically, often to attend meetings of the International Council of Shopping Centers, and they frequently came home with new ideas.

As the business continued to expand, the partners' roles evolved. Frank took responsibility for management and administration. John oversaw leasing, marketing, and promotion. John loved to spend his time at the shopping centers. He had an instinctive ability to judge the success of individual shops and he enjoyed exchanging ideas with local center management about ways to draw more traffic. Frank valued detailed financial planning and budgeting. "Frank was not given to rash decisions and his orderly method combined well with John's appetite for expansion and growth."[2]

An example of the detailed, hands-on approach to running the business was the way the two partners would spend Saturday mornings. They would drive to one or more of Westfield's shopping centers to assess crowds (based on numbers of cars parked) and mingle with shoppers to hear their opinions.

[1] Tom North of retailer G.J. Coles, quoted in Margo, J., 2000, *Frank Lowy: Pushing the Limits*, London, HarperCollins, 87.
[2] Margo, *Frank Lowy*, 91.

Growth and expansion: 1961–71

Throughout the 1960s Westfield expanded into other parts of Australia. Besides opening new centers, Westfield invested in redeveloping existing centers where there was an opportunity to enhance revenues and improve profitability. The pace of business growth and the intense involvement of the top executives were remarkable. "From the mid-1960s to the mid-1970s, the company was opening a shopping center a year. To keep up with the exponential increase in work, Frank and John were each putting in twelve to sixteen hours a day. [...] Every detail about every development was decided by them; everyone reported to them."[3]

In 1971, its eleventh year as a public company, Westfield reported its eleventh consecutive profit increase and announced a name change to Westfield Ltd. Further recognition of the business's attractiveness came in the form of an investment in two new Westfield shopping centers by the European company General Shopping SA, a Luxembourg-based investment company and an associate of Credit Suisse.

Expansion and diversification

By 1972 Frank and John were becoming increasingly concerned about how many more shopping centers could be built in Australia before the market would become saturated. A new Labor government that was elected that year changed the strict currency regulations and made it easier for Australian companies to make major investments overseas.[4] While continuing expansion in Australia, therefore, the partners began to look for investment opportunities abroad.

Beginning in 1972 the company began a process of expansion and diversification. This process was not a "grand design"; it occurred as a result of many individual decisions. In retrospect, however, the process can be viewed as being comprised of four different phases, as explained below.

- Phase 1: entry into the US market and continued expansion in Australia, 1972–85.
- Phase 2: diversification outside the real estate industry, 1985–9.

---

[3] Margo, *Frank Lowy*, 102.   [4] Margo, *Frank Lowy*, 123.

- Phase 3: participating in industry consolidation in the United States, 1989–2000.
- Phase 4: becoming a global company, 2001–present.

Phase 1: entry into the US market and continued expansion in Australia, 1972–84

The first phase of Westfield's expansion (1972 to 1984) included diversification outside Australia. The company leaders had visited the United States several times in the 1960s to learn from American shopping centers, and by the mid-1970s they were intent on buying a shopping center there that would give them an opportunity to learn more about doing business in this new country.

In 1977 they agreed to purchase a shopping center in Trumbull, Connecticut. As Peter Lowy states, "This was as far away from Sydney as you could possibly get."[5] The Trumbull center's attractive features included location in an affluent community and underutilized space, which had the potential to be turned into profitable shops.

Westfield's original concept was to come to the United States with a local partner to help with center management. Initially Westfield was planning to have a Canadian firm manage the Trumbull center. As Peter Lowy says, "Whether you consider a Canadian partner local or not, coming from Australia it seemed local to us." When this deal fell through, however, Westfield decided to manage the center on its own.

Frank spent six months in Connecticut during the first year of the center's operation, along with his oldest son, David, who had recently joined Westfield after graduating from college. Frank brought an experienced manager over from Australia to run the center initially. After a year David Lowy became manager of the Trumbull center, while Frank remained in constant contact.

Westfield was able to apply strategies the company had learned in Australia regarding the intensive development of property to enhance the value of its first American project. At the time that Westfield had purchased it, the Trumbull center had two department stores (one of which was in financial trouble) and sixty shops. After Westfield finished developing the center, it had a new department store, another 100 or so shops, and no unutilized space.

---

[5] Interview with Peter Lowy.

After looking at opportunities across the United States, Frank and David found their second project near the first in Connecticut. The Connecticut Post was an open shopping center that had been built in the 1950s, and it had a lot of underutilized space that Westfield could develop. This time, Westfield planned from the beginning to manage the center. As Peter Lowy states: "It took us a couple of years to figure out that we were better off on our own than with a local partner."

Their third project was a center in Los Angeles, which showed great potential for being redeveloped from a flat one-story layout to a three-story enclosed mall with rooftop and underground parking. The original building was taken down and the Westside Pavilion was built in its place. The success of this center with both retailers and customers made Westfield more visible in the United States.

Other critical events during the period 1979–84

During this period, while Westfield was engaged in the process of expansion and diversification, several other critical milestones in the company's development took place.

In 1979 Westfield underwent a financial restructuring of the overall company into two companies – a property trust (equivalent to a US REIT) and a management holding company. This greatly enhanced shareholder value.

In 1984 John Saunders notified Frank Lowy that he wanted to sell his shares. Although the timing was a surprise to Frank, he acted with characteristic speed to seize the opportunity. (Saunders continued to play a role in management until 1987 and to serve as a director until 1990.)

In 1985 Westfield celebrated its twenty-fifth anniversary as a public company. A letter of congratulations from the head of the Sydney stock exchange observed:

Over the 25-year period to 1985, Westfield has outperformed all other listed shares available to the public in 1960. An initial investment of £500 [equivalent to A$1,000] in Westfield's first public issue would today be worth over A$1.8 million if all dividends, capital repayments and proceeds from the sale of rights and property trust units had immediately been reinvested into additional Westfield shares. Even after allowing for inflation (up 430%) this initial investment would have increased 300-fold in real value – a remarkable achievement over a 25-year period.[6]

It is estimated that this initial investment would be worth about A$180 million in today's market.

Lesson from Phase 1

Peter Lowy summarizes how the process used in Phase 1 to approach expansion in a new country became a Westfield strategy:

I think the lesson from phase 1 is that, unless someone extremely senior in the organization can dedicate the time and resources to a modest investment to understand the market, you run the risk, as you grow, of growing into trouble. It also led to our platform. Instead of doing joint ventures with other major industry participants and relying on a partner's expertise, the chief executive actually got to know the US marketplace. So we learned how to operate in this new environment, including how to build, what it costs, where to go, what retailers to include, how to lease, etc. So the US experience actually led to Westfield's platform of staying in-house while expanding in foreign markets.[7]

Phase 2: Diversification outside the real estate industry, 1985–9

The second phase of diversification began during the mid-1980s. At this point in time, according to Peter, Westfield "was still not that big or that diversified. We had four or five malls in the United States . . . The majority of the assets were in Australia."

The company began to experiment with diversification into other industries. As the initial investments in major retailers and an Australian oil company were successful, in 1986 Westfield Capital was created as a vehicle for long-term equity investments in companies not in the shopping center industry. This diversification was seen as a means of protecting the core shopping center business. "With the formation of Westfield Capital Corporation, Frank found himself in an electrifying new environment . . . Markets were bullish, cash was

---

[6] Quoted in Margo, *Frank Lowy*, 185.   [7] Interview with Peter Lowy.

available, deals were being done on an enormous scale."[8] The media seemed like an attractive area for investment.

Westfield Capital entered the media industry in September 1986 by buying an 18 percent stake in Northern Star, a small regional company that wanted to grow. When the Australian government proposed a law in November 1986 that would prohibit one company from owning both print and electronic media after June 1987, Frank Lowy and Northern Star/Westfield Capital made a bid for the television holdings of Rupert Murdoch's News Corporation: Channel Ten in Sydney and Channel Ten in Melbourne. The Lowy/Northern Star bid was selected, despite higher offers, based on Frank's credentials and his reputation as a person who would honor his word.[9] The deal was concluded in February 1987.

Channel Ten was not the only major network to change ownership that year. Channel Nine in Sydney and Melbourne had been purchased in January, and Channel Seven was purchased in July. The owners of each network adopted a strategy of pursuing increased ratings and market share.

Frank was experiencing discomfort, however, because Channel Ten was the first Westfield investment that had been critically challenged by analysts. The question was raised: "What's a shopping center developer doing in television?"[10]

Management capable of running a national network was needed at Northern Star. Frank began to learn how difficult it was to find and attract top talent in the television industry. Eventually he selected Ian Gow, who had been involved in the growth of Channel Nine. Frank's son, Peter, was placed in a financial oversight role. The new management team was charged with raising Channel Ten's ratings.

The worldwide stock market crash in October 1987 caused a sharp drop in the market capitalization of Westfield Capital, as well as a collapse of media share prices in Australia. Northern Star had reached an agreement in August that year to buy some additional media properties that would help the television network have broader national coverage. Because Lowy had a reputation for sticking with deals, he was unwilling to pull out of the deal after the stock market

[8] Margo, *Frank Lowy*, 204.   [9] Margo, *Frank Lowy*, 210.
[10] Margo, *Frank Lowy*, 211.

crashed. To complete the deal, Northern Star had to take on debt that caused it to be over-leveraged.

1988 was a difficult year. "Frank was edgy about his position, his family's position and the viability of the company."[11] Channel Ten's TV ratings were low. Investment in strong programming seemed to be needed. In addition, Channel Ten needed programming to replace a contract with Warner that Channel Ten had lost to Channel Nine shortly before Northern Star became the owner. Frank sought help from contacts in the United States so as to make connections in Hollywood. This led to meetings with Lew Wasserman, in which Frank sought to negotiate an exclusive deal with MCA for programming. A deal was reached. Looking back, it appears that the requirement to accept weak programming as part of the ten-year deal was harmful to Channel Ten's ratings.

By now Peter Lowy was beginning to question the wisdom of the strategy of trying to make Channel Ten the number one station in Australia. He advocated reducing operating costs and accepting lower ratings, in order to start producing net income. Frank was not convinced, however.[12]

By the time of a scheduled financial review in January 1989, Frank recognized that he needed to extricate Westfield from Channel Ten in order to save the core shopping center business. He had "finally realized that, in the light of the history of errors, the management [of Channel Ten] was incapable of turning the company around. The time had come for him to cut his losses and plan his exit."[13]

Although it required a large personal investment to exit honorably, in the summer of 1989 he acted decisively to make the break. He authorized the head of Westfield Capital to work out a plan for exiting the business and gave him a budget of A$200 million to accomplish this. On September 1, 1989, the exit was completed.[14]

Lessons from Channel Ten and the foundation for future expansion

Although the venture into the media business was a major distraction, and ultimately a significant business failure for the Lowys and

---

[11] Margo, *Frank Lowy*, 219. [12] Margo, *Frank Lowy*, 226.
[13] Margo, *Frank Lowy*, 228. [14] Margo, *Frank Lowy*, 236–40.

Westfield, they did learn some lessons that were ultimately to prove invaluable to Westfield's future success.

Never bet the company
Westfield's experience with expansion diversification into media was a financial disaster. It almost resulted in the loss of the company. Unknowingly, the Lowys had bet the company. They resolved never to do that again.

Do your "homework"
A second lesson learned by Westfield and the Lowy family was the need for "extreme due diligence." Frank had always insisted on careful analysis in connection with shopping center deals, but he had invested in the media business without his usual caution. In effect, Westfield had inadvertently abandoned one of its core competencies, and its "winning formula."

Out of the ashes of Channel Ten, the Lowys had a renewed dedication to due diligence and developed a comprehensive approach that became the "new" (more precisely, reinstated) success formula for Westfield's expansion in the US shopping center business.

Follow the money
Another lesson learned by the company concerned the financial performance of its investments. David, the eldest son of Frank, summed up the learning this way: "The television episode was a milestone. The family learned a big but very simple lesson: in a business more money has to come in than goes out. If more cash comes in than goes out over a defined period, you're okay. If that's not happening, you get out. It's as simple as that."[15]

Managing failure

It was not as simple as that, however. On October 24, 2006, Frank addressed a group of the most senior leaders of Westfield in Sydney in connection with the Westfield Executive Development

---

[15] Quoted in Margo, *Frank Lowy*, 241.

Programme. He reflected back on the lessons from the Channel Ten experience as a result of the attempted diversification into media business. He said that that this experience was a great lesson in managing failure.

Frank pointed out that not all business decisions result in success; some are inevitably failures. He discussed what he had learned in dealing with the problems of Channel Ten, and identified four related steps Westfield had taken to address these problems: (1) recognize the problem; (2) marshal your resources; (3) focus on the problem; and (4) "take the 'hit'" and move on.

First, recognize that there is a problem. It does not help to ignore a problem and hope that it will disappear. Second, marshal all your resources, human as well as financial, to deal with the problem. You cannot afford to take it lightly. Third, focus, focus, focus! Focus on the problem to the exclusion of virtually everything else. It demands all your attention, and must be focused upon until it is resolved. Finally, be prepared to accept the cost of the mistake. Attempt to minimize your regret. Treat it as a business decision and move on.

There was a further aspect of the experience of dealing with failure: learn from your mistakes. After the process of dealing with the problem is over, ask what you should have done differently, and plan to remember that in the future.

Westfield's experience with the failure of the diversification into media was a critical incident in the company's history, psyche, and style. It was an expensive lesson, but it provided the foundation for a subsequent period of great success and a reemphasis on the winning formula that Westfield had developed in its early years. It led the company to place great value on attention to detail, and very careful analysis and financial planning.

As noted above, a related lesson of the experience with Channel Ten was the need to devote a very senior person to the due diligence process. It is worth restating Peter's words in connection with what was learned from the Channel Ten experience: "[U]nless someone extremely senior in the organization can dedicate the time and resources to a modest investment to understand the market, you run the risk, as you grow, of growing into trouble."

By 1989 Westfield was done with Channel Ten. It was ready to refocus on its core business and move on to other opportunities.

Phase 3: participating in industry consolidation in the United States, 1989–2000

In 1990 Peter, who had been closely involved with his father in the television venture, moved with his family to Los Angeles to become involved with Westfield's American shopping center holdings. These holdings had expanded in 1985 by adding three malls purchased from the retailer Macy's. From 1985 to 1987 the youngest Lowy son, Steven, gained experience in the United States by managing one of these malls. At the time of the purchase from Macy's, Westfield's US holdings were managed as individual properties, taking advantage of the strategic value in each center and its surrounding community. In 1991, however, shortly after Peter's arrival, there was a collapse of the real estate market in the United States. Peter and other Westfield managers led an effort to cut operations substantially in order to weather the storm.

The collapse of the real estate market also led to opportunities for Westfield to continue its expansion into the US market. It was a classic case of preparation meeting opportunity. Preparation by Westfield had been occurring since the early 1970s, when Westfield first decided to enter the US market. Westfield's solid operations in the United States, combined with financial strength based on its core business in Australia, helped prepare it to take advantage of a significant consolidation in the US shopping center industry that took place in the mid- to late 1990s. As in the classic Peter Sellers movie *Being There*, Westfield was "there" when the recession began in the United States in the early 1990s. As Peter states, "We happened to have a business in Australia that was extremely strong and had equity, which means we were able to play in the consolidation of the mall industry that happened over the next ten years."

In the early 1990s Frank was contacted by a Dutch property investor, Rodamco, Europe's largest property investment fund. Having analyzed the Australian market, Rodamco selected Westfield and wanted to invest in some of Westfield's Australian properties. A deal was successfully executed. "This was a strong vote of confidence in Westfield, which, by all measures, had recovered from its problems in the 1980s."[16] Recognizing that Rodamco was also an investor in the

---

[16] Westfield Publishing, 2000, *The Westfield Story: The First 40 Years*, Sydney, Westfield Publishing, 107.

US shopping center market, Frank began to think about the fund as a potential partner. To shore up the family's financial position, Frank decided to sell the very profitable Garden State Plaza (one of the former Macy's centers, which Westfield had greatly enhanced in value through strategic redevelopment). Rodamco would purchase one half of the shopping center and Westfield Holdings, the Australian company, would purchase the other half.

Dan Neidich of Goldman Sachs, who had been closely involved in the Macy's sale of shopping centers to Westfield, was impressed with the significant improvements in financial results that Westfield had engineered at the Garden State Plaza. When the property investment arm of Prudential Insurance Company of America put the CenterMark Properties up for sale, Goldman Sachs selected Westfield as a partner to place a bid for the centers. Another partner was General Growth Properties, Inc., one of the United States' largest real estate investment trusts. The partnership closed the purchase for $1 billion in February 1994. Westfield and General Growth Properties each took a 40 percent share in the investment, with Goldman Sachs taking the balance (20 percent).

Westfield's winning formula: extreme due diligence

One reason that Westfield was ultimately so successful in its acquisitions was a methodology that had been developed for conducting an extremely detailed and comprehensive due diligence review of every individual center in a portfolio of properties before a bid was made. Frank and Peter Lowy had learned the importance of due diligence from the Channel Ten debacle.

For the CenterMark transaction, Peter brought together a team of fifty people to conduct in-depth due diligence with each of the eighteen centers in a period of six weeks. The team's comprehensive "play book" included:

- deploying a legal team that read every word of every legal document and lease associated with each center;
- conducting a review of two-year financials for each mall, as well as the mall's budget for the current year and proposed budget for the upcoming year;
- modeling the major terms of every individual shop lease for each center in order to forecast a future revenue stream;

- conducting an analysis of all receivables; and
- having a separate development team determine the potential for expansion and redevelopment at each center and produce rough plans, along with estimated costs, yields, and returns.

Peter summarizes the results of this process: "We did due diligence on a purchase like it had never been done before in the US. Center-Mark was a company with eighteen malls and 3,000 tenants. Within six weeks we had every lease modeled, we had our own models built, and we had every potential development scoped out. We knew the company and its earnings better than the people who ran it."[17]

Westfield was selected to manage the new properties. The addition of the CenterMark malls tripled Westfield's US space under management. "The rewards were rapid. In August 1994, Westfield announced a 29.4 percent improvement in net profits due largely to the US acquisitions. The company's assets under management were split 50:50 between the United States and Australia."[18]

"After a patient, seventeen-year presence in the United States, Westfield was one of the largest owner/managers of regional shopping malls in the country and placed in the top five owner/managers of regional malls in the world."[19]

In late 1995 Westfield increased its stake in CenterMark and prepared to buy out its two partners, Goldman Sachs and General Growth. A new Westfield American Trust public offering was successfully sold in Australia in 1996. This was the first time that capital was raised in Australia for a pure foreign investment in real estate. Next an initial public offering (IPO) for Westfield America, Inc., was offered on the New York Stock Exchange in May 1997.

The CenterMark transaction was the first of a series of deals in a consolidation of the shopping center industry in the United States. Other events in the consolidation of the shopping mall industry took place in the 1990s. Simon Properties merged with DeBartolo. Then General Growth bought Homemart, and Simon bought CPI.

The completion in November 1998 of the purchase of the TrizecHahn portfolio of twelve shopping centers further solidified Westfield's prominence and position in the US shopping center

---

[17] Interview with Peter Lowy.   [18] *Westfield Story*, 108.
[19] Margo, *Frank Lowy*, 282.

industry. With this acquisition, Westfield became the biggest shopping center owner in the state of California, with twenty centers. The acquisition reflected Westfield America's investment strategy of acquiring and developing regional shopping malls that are geographically clustered in stable and economically strong markets.[20] Also in November 1998 Westfield branded its North American shopping centers as Westfield Shoppingtowns (the same name used in Australia) and advertised the brand through a multimedia campaign. The *Annual Report* shared the brand strategy:

The goal is to make the brand Westfield Shoppingtown synonymous with more than just great shopping. A Shoppingtown, as the name suggests, is also an important centre of community activity – a new version of Main Street – that is safe, comfortable, accessible and convenient.[21]

Phase 4: becoming a global company, 2001–present

In August 2001 Westfield Holdings purchased a 23.9 percent stake in Rodamco North America (a Dutch-owned public company), which owned forty-one shopping centers in the United States. When Rodamco management was not willing to discuss a merger, Westfield initiated a takeover. Peter Lowy and other Westfield executives spent nine months in the Netherlands pursuing the takeover battle. In a discussion of the deal, it became clear to Frank, Peter, and other Westfield senior executives that something had changed. As Peter states:

Even though we had been operating in the US since 1977, New Zealand since 1997 and in the UK since 2000, we never really thought of the business or our industry in a global context until our takeover battle with Rodamco North America in 2001. In that situation, you had an Australian company trying to take over a Dutch company listed on the Amsterdam Stock Exchange which owned malls in the US. Our competition was not just the company itself but also a number of US REITs. At the end of the day, after a successful conclusion, we invested Aussie dollars to buy stock in euros and own assets in US dollars.[22]

---

[20] *Annual Report*, 1998, New York, Westfield America Trust, 11.
[21] *Annual Report*, 1998, 14.
[22] From a speech by Peter Lowy at a REIT symposium at New York University on March 17, 2006.

When all aspects of the deal were completed, Westfield had added twenty-three US shopping centers to its portfolio. Also in 2001 Westfield purchased an interest in two additional US shopping centers. By the end of that year Westfield America Trust held a portfolio of sixty-three US shopping centers that generated retail sales of approximately $14 billion per year. The Lowys recognized that real estate had become a global business and that Westfield had become a global company.

Organizational changes as an outgrowth of strategy

Once the acquisition of Rodamco North America had been finalized, Westfield management started to think about how to manage this bigger enterprise. As Peter states, "The issues now are what do you need to do to structure and finance this mammoth enterprise?"[23]

At the time, Westfield's structure included two publicly traded REITs and a publicly traded management company. This structure had allowed the business to grow to this point, but the Lowys realized that the structure would need to change to facilitate future growth. As Peter puts it:

We started to look at the structure of the company with the two REITs and the property management company. We had just invested $2.5 billion in acquisitions, giving us a US portfolio that was extremely diverse. In the meantime, we had invested in the UK in a much smaller transaction in 2000, and we were looking to expand further in the UK. How were we going to do this? How were we going to compete? How are we going to compete with Simon [Simon Properties], for instance? It was clear to us that the structure that we had, which had helped us be successful from 1979 to 2002, was now going to weigh upon itself and limit growth.

In 2004 a merger was initiated to convert three Westfield companies into one. A major reason for this move was to lower the weighted cost of capital with a consolidated stream of financing. It also created a company with the size to embark upon transactions that would not have been possible previously. The new Westfield, after what was termed "the stapling," was a single, vertically integrated, internally managed global REIT. It had the size and financial strength to compete globally.

---

[23] Interview with Peter Lowy.

Following the restructuring, Westfield continued its expansion and diversification. This time it chose to expand in the United Kingdom. Westfield had made a small purchase there in 2000. This was a strategic purchase designed to follow the Westfield formula (as originally used in the United States) of entering into a new market in a small way in order to learn how to operate there.

In 2004, having learned more about operating in the United Kingdom, Westfield was ready to expand the scope of its European assets and operations. At that time Westfield already owned part of seven retail centers in the United Kingdom. The company did not own any of the centers outright, however. Westfield's interest was in acquiring some of the properties owned by the UK company Chelsfield. Chelsfield was a property investment company that focused upon a small number of high-value development projects. Westfield was particularly interested in acquiring an ownership position in White City, located in London, which was being developed and expected to become one of the preeminent shopping sites in Europe. Although Westfield's initial overtures were rebuffed, an opportunity arose subsequently for Westfield to purchase Chelsfield's entire property portfolio. This transaction was consummated in 2006.

This purchase of Chelsfield's properties, and particularly White City, has positioned Westfield as one of the premier shopping center developers in Europe and further enhanced its position as the leading developer in the world. In addition, it has provided Westfield with some major competitive advantages vis-à-vis the potential competition, such as Simon Properties, which does not have a presence in the United Kingdom.

Phase 5: the future

Westfield was now faced with the challenge of what it means to operate as a global company. What should the company's future strategy be? Should it be pursuing business in additional countries? In Peter's words, "Now that we are a global company, what should our strategy be? This is what we are struggling with and talking about now. Is it staying in markets you currently are in, or rushing off to emerging markets such as India, or China? What is actually globalization?

Lessons from Westfield's experience in diversification

This section steps back from the details of the Westfield case and offers some lessons for planning and managing change. Why has Westfield been so successful in real estate development expansion and diversification and why did it stumble when it diversified into the media? On the surface, the reason might seem to be that Westfield was successful when it "stuck to its knitting" and focused on shopping centers, and unsuccessful when it ventured too far from its core business. A deeper look, however, suggests that Westfield not only ventured away from its core business, but also departed from what might be termed its "core strategy" of "small incremental steps and investments to get on the learning curve." This is examined below.

The value of small incremental steps and investments

Westfield's use of incremental steps and investments over a period of time was, clearly, a successful strategy for expansion and diversification into the US market. It gave the company time to get on the learning curve and avoid making big bets until it was knowledgeable about the market. In addition, it gave Westfield time to develop its tactical play book for due diligence. Westfield had none of these advantages when it entered into the media market. It made a huge investment in a new business with limited knowledge and experience. Not only did it enter an unfamiliar business, it did so hastily without the proper experience of small incremental investments and steps to facilitate learning what it was getting into.

In pursuing a strategy of small incremental investments into the US market, Westfield avoided the problems encountered by many companies from Australia, which went overseas with big plans and lost a ton of money. As Peter says, "Our company was a reasonable size when it first started overseas and it made a modest investment, so if it did not work we weren't fully exposed." In addition, although the investment was modest in financial terms, states Peter:

[s]enior management (aka my father) spent a large amount of his time on this seemingly small investment. [. . .] By spending so much of his time with Trumbull and paying the price to understand the business, we really understood what we needed to do to be successful. And David [Peter's older brother] was there too.

The bottom line to this lesson is this, in Peter's words: "Focusing Frank's time and energy on a modest investment in a major market over time allowed the company to have the potential to have growth that it otherwise would not have had."

It was the strategic vision of Frank to identify the potential for Westfield to expand overseas and diversify. It was the tactic of making incremental small investments and moving in small steps that made it a reality.

Personal involvement in strategic due diligence

Another lesson from the Westfield experience concerns the role of what might be termed "strategic due diligence," or the process of learning about a new market. This refers to the way Westfield expanded in the United States and, later, in the United Kingdom.

There were people who questioned the wisdom of what Frank, and through him Westfield, were doing. As Peter says, "I am sure there were times when people asked him, 'You know it is one center and it is $25 million and you have a portfolio of $300 million, so what are you doing worrying about this one center on the other side of the world?' But that was his strategic vision."

The Lowy success formula can be summarized as follows: carefully invested, ability for the upside, huge potential for knowledge, with one of the most senior people in the company doing the investigation and learning. In this initial instance, Frank did not pick a senior executive. He himself was personally engaged in the strategic due diligence. The result, according to Peter, was that, "because he (Frank Lowy) understood the business, knew the country, knew the market, the chief executive is fully engaged. Now you can invest!"

When the opportunity to expand in the United States arose in the 1990s, this approach was reinforced by the company's experience with Channel Ten. As Peter states: "One lesson from the Channel Ten experience was that we need to know a business intimately before making a major commitment." Peter personally led the comprehensive due diligence effort that preceded the bid for the CenterMark properties.

This tactic of personal involvement in leading a strategic change effort has been used successfully by other executives as well. For example, Harvey Golub, then CEO at American Express, led that company's effort to embrace the Internet by getting involved in a "hands-on" way.

Planning growth and strategic change

Sometimes strategic change occurs by grand design, and sometimes by incremental steps. Sometimes it even occurs almost by accident.

The transformation of Westfield from an Australian shopping center company into a global enterprise was not by grand design; it was the product of a series of rational and reasonable incremental steps, leading to an epiphany that the company had metamorphosed to become a truly global enterprise. As Peter says about the transformation of Westfield from an Australian shopping center company into a global enterprise, "It would be fair to say that it was not with a grand design. We took advantage of opportunities, and then the accumulation of opportunities led to a moment of insight which led to a design." Lowy also states: "It was a series of strategic transactions, and each transaction led to the case for the next transaction. And Rodamco was the culmination."

The limits of the incremental approach to planning diversification

Although this incremental approach to managing Westfield worked very well for many years, and continues to work, there are other tools that might have helped Westfield avoid the disaster of Channel Ten. Specifically, Westfield never really engaged in long-range strategic planning of the most fundamental kind, focusing upon questions such as "Who are we?" (business definition), "What do we want to become?" (strategic mission), and "What are our core competencies?"

These are the kinds of issues addressed in chapter 2, which presents a template for planning change, including vision change, such as that embraced by Westfield. Using this template and asking the kinds of questions mentioned above might have led Westfield to avoid entry into the media business. If so, it would also have led to avoiding the uncomfortable answer to the question "What's a shopping center developer doing in television?"[24] Alternatively, if Westfield had still

[24] Margo, *Frank Lowy*, 211.

decided to enter the media business, it would have had a better rationale for why it was doing so.

Westfield, and Frank in particular, need to be credited for the way they handled their exit from the media business. The four-step process identified by Frank for Westfield is an excellent template for leading change in any company faced with a major problem.

Avoiding "the Midas syndrome"

Another potential lesson from the Westfield experience concerns the problem of what might be termed "the Midas syndrome." Many companies, after experiencing uninterrupted success over a relatively long period of time, begin to believe that they have the "Midas touch" – that is, that everything they "touch" will turn to gold. Unfortunately, this is a very seductive trap, and it has led many companies into financial problems and even ruin. They forget what they did to get where they are. In part, this is what happened to Westfield. They "forgot" to use Frank's "winning formula" of "extreme due diligence" in the case of Channel Ten.

The educational value of going it alone

According to Peter Lowy, the successful entry into the US real estate market also led to what he termed Westfield's "platform."

Instead of doing joint ventures, instead of relying on someone else to execute in the market, the chief executive actually knew the marketplace. So we learned how to build, what it costs, where to go, how to go, what the stores are, how to lease, what the market is. So, that actually led to our platform of, in essence, going it alone in these foreign markets.[25]

---

[25] Interview with Peter Lowy.

Leading strategic change: lessons learned from practice

In Part II of this book we presented a series of case studies of organizations that have been engaged in a variety of aspects of strategic and/or organizational change. In Part III we step back from the specific cases examined, and draw lessons from the experiences of the various companies (cases) presented in Part II about leading and managing strategic and organizational change.

Our approach will be to use the case studies as "data" to derive insights and lessons about the leadership and management of strategic and organizational change. We conclude this section with suggestions for "taking the integrative model forward."

13 | *Lessons and insights from case studies of change*

Introduction

In Part II we examined nine case studies of strategic change using a "stand-alone" or "vertical" analysis. In this chapter we look at the cases studies as a set and undertake a "horizontal" analysis across the different cases.

In order to derive these insights, we look at the cases from a number of different perspectives. A primary purpose of this chapter, then, is to identify specific lessons about change and change management that can be gleaned from this sample of nine companies.

We conclude this chapter with some thoughts for researchers and scholars about "taking forward the integrative framework" that was proposed in Part I.

Some lessons about the nature of change

In this section, we look at the nature of the change process in terms of what we have learned from the case studies. We examine the different but related aspects of the cases, including the catalyst for change, the overall purpose or objective of the change process, the type of change (including the focus and magnitude of change), and the duration of change. We also identify and examine aspects of the barriers to change that have been encountered.

The catalyst for or driver of change

A catalyst for or driver of change is the trigger, in a sense, for the change process. There appear to be three different catalysts for change in our sample: (1) problems created by organizational growth; (2) the recognition of a "new" market or market opportunity; and

Case	Challenges of organizational growth	Recognition of new market opportunity	Environmental changes
Countrywide	X	X	X
Starbucks	X	X	
Indian Oil			X
Tashman	X		X
IndyMac Bank	X		X
Infogix	X	X	X
Pardee Homes	X		X
Tata Steel			X
Westfield		X	X

Exhibit 13.1 Drivers of change

(3) environmental changes (including increased competition, changes in customers and customer needs, the "globalization" of markets, among others).

As shown in exhibit 13.1, in all but one case – Starbucks – a primary driver of change was the environment in which the company operated. In particular, companies either felt competitive pressure to change (Countrywide, Indian Oil, and Tata Steel) or anticipated that increasing competition would adversely affect their business in the future (Tashman, IndyMac Bank, Infogix, Pardee Homes, Westfield). This strongly suggests that the environment in which a company operates is a key driver of the need to change.

In four cases – Countrywide, Starbucks, Infogix, and Westfield – a driver of change was the identification of "new" market opportunities. For Countrywide, this meant diversifying its products and services beyond mortgages. For Starbucks, this meant changing the business concept from that of a local roaster to a "coffee café" and rolling this concept out nationally. For Infogix, the new opportunity came in the form of creating an entirely new "industry" in information integrity.

Finally, for Westfield, it meant identifying the opportunity to become a global company.

Company growth and the problems associated with managing a much larger business were the drivers of change for four companies – Countrywide, Starbucks, Infogix, and Pardee Homes. In particular, these companies each faced challenges with respect to having an effective planning process, a structure that supported the company's strategy, a performance management system that promoted the achievement of the company's goals, and a well-managed culture.

The analysis of the companies in our sample – presented in exhibit 13.1 – suggests that companies may have multiple drivers of change. For example, in Countrywide's case, change was driven by growth, the environment, and the recognition of new market opportunities.

Purpose or objective of the change process

In our sample, there appear to be three different objectives or purposes of the change process – in a sense, representing the response to the catalyst for change. These are: (1) the transformation of the original business concept; (2) "getting closer to the customer" – i.e., better meeting customer needs; and (3) improving overall organizational effectiveness.

For the four companies – Countrywide, Starbucks, Infogix, and Westfield – that identified a major new market opportunity, the overall purpose of the change process was to transform their original business concept in order to focus on these opportunities. Two other companies – Indian Oil and Tata Steel – also focused on transforming their original business concept, but in these cases this was in response to current and/or anticipated changes in their markets.

It is interesting to note that, with the exception of Starbucks (a company that had identified and was working to grow an entirely "new" business), all the companies in the sample had as one of their objectives "getting closer" to their customers or better meeting customer needs – e.g., through providing additional products/services, improving customer service, etc. The catalyst for this change was changes in the environment – including changes in competition. At Indian Oil, for example, this focus on the customer was made very explicit through the language used to describe the focus for each year of its change process – "Customer Care Year," "Customer Delight Year," "Customer Service Excellence Year."

Tashman, meanwhile, had a strong focus on understanding changing customer needs and identifying ways to provide the best service in a changing environment. At Tata Steel and Pardee Homes, the focus was on creating internal systems that would help the company provide better customer service. Countrywide, IndyMac Bank, and Infogix focused on identifying new products/services to provide to existing and new customers. Westfield's focus was on understanding customer needs in new markets and identifying ways to provide its products to these new customers. Clearly, a focus on maintaining and/or improving customer satisfaction is a key objective in many change processes.

A final objective of the change process in our sample was to improve or enhance organizational effectiveness. All the companies in our sample were, in some way, focused either on developing new or on improving existing internal systems including operational systems, planning and performance management systems, culture management systems, and creating a more effective structure. At Countrywide, Infogix, IndyMac Bank, and Pardee, the focus was on creating more effective planning and performance management systems, and on creating a structure that would support effective operations (including reducing silos and pushing decision making to the "right level" of the company). At Starbucks, the focus was on creating an effective planning process that would ensure everyone was on the same page with respect to the long-term vision of the company. At Indian Oil, Tashman, and Tata Steel, a strong focus was placed on culture management and on training people to support the new culture. At Westfield, following its attempt to diversify into media, the focus was placed on developing and effectively using a due diligence process that would promote effective decision making. This suggests that an objective of many, if not all change processes, relates to improving internal organizational capabilities – regardless of the catalyst for change.

Type of change

Another lesson suggested by the case studies is that organizations frequently face the need to make what might be termed "compound" changes – that is, they need to make multiple changes simultaneously. For example, Starbucks was focused on transforming from a local roaster to a coffee café, on transforming to a more professionally managed company as a response to its growth, and on developing, refining, and implementing the day-to-day systems needed to support these transformations/transitions. This was also true of Infogix. Tashman was making a transformation to professional management and developing systems and processes to meet its changing customer needs. Indian Oil and Tata Steel were focused on transforming their culture in order to compete better in a changing market, and were using training and performance management systems to support this transformation. Countrywide and IndyMac Bank were simultaneously undergoing transformations to professional management, modifying their products and services, and expanding into new markets.

The cases also suggest that companies involved in making strategic changes have to focus on implementing these strategic changes through making operational changes. At Westfield, for example, the success of the decision to expand globally (a strategic change) involved changing/refining/effectively using a due diligence process that supported effective decision making. At Tata Steel, Countrywide, Indian Oil, and Infogix, the success of the strategic transformation was dependent upon making changes in day-to-day systems such as training and the ongoing monitoring of performance.

Exhibit 13.2 summarizes the cases examined according to the magnitude and focus of change using a version of the change typology matrix introduced in chapter 1.

Duration of change

The management of all the companies in the sample recognized that the types of changes that they were making would require time, and were willing to make the investment of this time to support the success of the change process. One of the aspects demonstrated by the cases, however, is that complex change requires a great deal of time – typically more time than originally envisioned. Even in the smallest of the companies in our sample (Tashman), two plus years were required for the initial phase of change. Indian Oil had a three-year-plus plan for becoming more customer-oriented – with each year in the process

Focus of change

Organization	Strategic			Operational		
	Transformational	Major	Incremental	Transformational	Major	Incremental
Countrywide	Changing business concept – from mortgage provider to provider of financial services	Implementation of new planning process		Creating a planning department to oversee process Priority Objective Committees	Training in strategic planning	
Starbucks	Changing the business concept – from local roaster to coffee café Transforming to a professionally managed company	Developing and implementing management systems		Implementing a strategic planning process	Creating day-to-day systems to support transformation	Defining the vision and "guiding principles"

Exhibit 13.2 Application of the change typology matrix to the nine case studies

		Heavier focus on customers and customer satisfaction	Change in how leaders are identified and selected · Organizational restructuring · Rewards and recognition based on performance (rather than other factors)	Strategic HR initiatives · Systems created to monitor progress against key initiatives · Involvement of all key stakeholders in process	Training programs adapted to support transformation
Indian Oil	Changing the business concept – from distributor of petroleum products to a strategic marketing organization · Culture change to support business transformation – "Focus on people, and they will focus on the business"	Heavier focus on customers and customer satisfaction	Change in how leaders are identified and selected · Organizational restructuring · Rewards and recognition based on performance (rather than other factors)	Strategic HR initiatives · Systems created to monitor progress against key initiatives · Involvement of all key stakeholders in process	Training programs adapted to support transformation
Tashman	Changing the business concept – from a manufacturers' representative agency in the hardware and home improvement industry to an innovation, "best in class" professionally managed sales and service business			Proactively maintaining key metrics and "special projects" updates – using systems to track performance	Refining training process to support transformation and superior customer service · Refinement of communication processes

Exhibit 13.2 (*cont.*)

Organization	Strategic			Operational		
	Transformational	Major	Incremental	Transformational	Major	Incremental
IndyMac Bank	Changing business concept – from mortgage company to a bank Making the transformation to a professionally managed company	Increased focus on planning and culture management				Refinement of systems to track and use information on customer needs and market conditions Specific goal setting
Infogix	Changing business concept and creating a new market – information integrity Adopting Deming philosophy – and impact on culture and structure Discontinuing quotas and other numerical objectives linked to incentives and compensation	Project Oxygen Aligning customer unit leaders along industry lines Reorganization by geographical location		Performance optimization and planning system Elimination of formal performance evaluations and salary adjustments tied to performance evaluation		

Exhibit 13.2 (*cont.*)

Company					
Pardee Homes	Changing decision-making style and process Refining planning process and structure	Articulation of cultural principles	Transitioning from a functional to a matrix and divisional structure	Creating goal-oriented incentive compensation	Introduction of team norms Semi-annual meetings Field visits by senior management and company newsletter to promote more open communication
Tata Steel	Becoming the low-cost producer Implementation of new technology Changes in company culture			Development of tools – stories and other forms of communication – to support culture change Implementing TQM training to support greater focus on company effectiveness and efficiency	
Westfield	Transforming from an Australian to a global company				Modifying/better deploying due diligence process to support effective decision making

Exhibit 13.2 (*cont.*)

identified by a specific name. At the other end of the spectrum, the structural transformation at Pardee Homes required almost a decade to complete. The transformation of Westfield from an Australian to a global player required almost a quarter of a century. In brief, the greater the scope of the change the longer it will take to accomplish it.

This factor is important in creating the appropriate organizational mindset or expectations about the nature and duration of the change process. Since change can create turmoil, it is important for people to understand the magnitude of the anticipated change and the expected length of time it might take to be accomplished. We have seen many examples of boards that tire of change and change leaders in midstream. For example, the removal of Carly Fiorina at Hewlett-Packard might have been premature.

The implication is that management must be prepared for a significant period of change; it will probably take longer than originally envisioned. In addition, a lengthy period of time can itself be an ingredient in a successful transformation, because management then has the time to understand the full dynamics of the changes involved and digest them appropriately. In the case of Westfield, the successful transformation from a uni-national to a global player took almost a quarter-century from the initial steps to its fruition. This allowed management to proceed in small, digestible steps. In contrast, the Westfield foray into TV ended in almost total disaster. The whole process was relatively quick from start to finish. The lesson is that time for learning may well be an essential ingredient in successful change management.

Barriers to change

Another perspective from which to examine the cases is in terms of the barriers to change encountered in each company. The barriers to change are summarized in exhibit 13.3. As seen in this exhibit, there is a great deal of variation in the nature of the barriers encountered – both in terms of the type of barrier and the levels (organizational, group, and/or individual) at which the barriers were present.

At the organizational level, a major barrier to change for some of the larger companies in our sample – in particular Countrywide, Indian Oil, and Tata Steel – was the belief that, because they had been successful in the past, this success would continue into the future.

Organization	Predominant type of barrier		
	Organizational	Group	Individual
Countrywide	Belief that success in the past would support success in the future Focused more on short than long term	Organizational silos	
Starbucks	Feeling that "we are what we are" (and we've been successful), so we don't need to change	Board pressure to change/adjust vision	
Indian Oil	Extended success that breeds inertia	"Groupthink" among unions	Changes perceived as threat to individual employees
Tashman	Top management's knowledge of and comfort with existing structure and decision-making processes		
IndyMac Bank	Top management's knowledge of and comfort with existing structure and decision-making processes	Functional silos	
Infogix	Top management's knowledge of and comfort with existing structure and decision-making processes	Functional silos	Problems in understanding and embracing Deming philosophy – including rewarding teams rather than individuals
Pardee Homes	Top management's knowledge of and comfort with existing structure and decision-making processes	Functional silos	"Super project managers" who did not wish to lose control over organizational functioning
Tata Steel	Extended success that breeds inertia		Fear of job loss due to new technology
Westfield	Lack of understanding of new business (media)		

Exhibit 13.3 Barriers to change in the nine case studies

The leaders of the change effort, in these cases, needed to convince their organizations that this was no longer the case. Starbucks faced a somewhat similar barrier, in the belief that "we are what we are, so why change?" In this case, the leaders of the change effort needed to show their company and their board that staying the same would result in limited or no growth.

At the group level, "silos" constituted a barrier to successful change that needed to be managed by Infogix, Pardee Homes, and Country-wide. In these companies, groups, project teams, and/or divisions operated as independent entities, with a focus on what was best for the group, team, or division rather than what was best for the company as a whole. Part of the change that needed to take place in these cases, therefore, was to redefine the structure and culture of the company so as to better align the goals of all groups, teams, and divisions.

Finally, at the individual level, the "fear" of change and the impact that it might have on one's position and role was most evident in the description of Tata Steel's transformation to being a low-cost producer. It is probably safe to assume, however, that this barrier to change was also present in some of the other cases – even though it has not been discussed explicitly. At Tata Steel, this barrier was overcome through training and communication programs.

Some lessons about leading change

This section identifies some potential lessons for the leaders of change – ranging from how they define their roles, to the emphasis that needs to be placed on specific organizational systems during the change process, to the investment (in terms of both time and money) required to promote successful change.

Recognize and effectively deploy multiple roles in leading change

Much of the previous literature on change deals with the role of leadership as though it is a one-dimensional construct. There is a leader or "champion" of change. There is "a change master." Unfortunately, this would appear to be too simplistic: it seems to be based upon a romantic notion of a heroic leader.

What we actually observe in most cases of organizational change is that there are examples of both individual leadership and leadership teams rather than merely single individuals. For example, the change efforts at Countrywide, Starbucks, Tashman, and Indian Oil were led by teams of people; while at Infogix, Pardee Homes, and IndyMac Bank the leadership does seem to be that of a single individual.

In addition to the issue of a single leader as opposed to a team, leaders can adopt different "roles." Change seems to involve a number of roles or tasks, including "sponsorship," "blessing," and "execution." Change programs require a sponsor or champion. This is someone who is the prime mover toward the change. At Countrywide, this was Stanford Kurland; at Starbucks, it was variously Howard Schultz, Orin Smith and Howard Behar; at IndyMac Bank, it was Michael Perry; at Infogix, it was Madhavan Nayar; and at Tashman, it was Rich Tashman.

In addition to the sponsor of change, under certain circumstances there can also be a need for the change to be embraced or "blessed" by another powerful organizational figure. At Countrywide, Angelo Mozilo (CEO) needed to bless the changes, even though they were led by Kurland. Similarly, even though the transformation to professional management at Starbucks was led by Smith and Behar, it had to be "blessed" or embraced by Schultz.

Where the change sponsor is the CEO or company leader, there is less need for the change to be blessed by others. We have encountered situations, however, in which a change was sponsored by a CEO, but was then actively subverted by other high-ranking executives. In one case, for example, the CEO had a vision that would have transformed the company from a single consumer product to a broader lifestyle product company. This would have required significant risk on the part of the company and significant risk on the part of senior management. Most of the senior managers were between fifty and sixty years of age, relatively settled in their careers and lives, and did not want to assume the burden of additional effort. They were comfortable. The CEO was faced with passive and active resistance with respect to his new vision. Ultimately, he decided that he did not want to deal with the potential conflict that he saw could emerge and he did not want to replace the existing team. As a result, he abandoned his vision for taking the company to the next level. The company continues to be a reasonably successful organization, but it has never achieved its full potential.

What we have observed in the case studies is that the role of the leader in change is to identify the issues, clarify the goals for the change, provide "support" (both resources and sponsorship), and monitor progress against goals. In brief, effective change typically requires sponsorship and blessing, the clarification of goals, and support for the process, but not necessarily involvement in execution. Another aspect is to "measure" the results of the change at the end of the process.

Lesson: successful change typically requires more than one "leader."

Focus on management systems and culture

As should be evident by now, in most of the cases examined in this book the companies were focused on making significant, transformational changes. To support these changes, leaders focused on taking their companies' management systems (i.e., planning, performance management, structure, and/or leadership development systems) and/or culture management systems to the "next level" of development. In brief, the transformations described could not have been completed successfully in the absence of changes to these systems.

At Countrywide, a significant amount of effort was focused upon modifying the company's planning infrastructure and process and on developing the systems – including the training of personnel in all divisions – to ensure that the "new" process was embraced by all personnel. Similarly, the leadership of Starbucks, Tashman, IndyMac Bank, Infogix, and Pardee Homes also used planning as a tool to support the company's change efforts.

Indian Oil, Tashman, IndyMac Bank, Infogix, and Pardee Homes used performance management systems to support the change process. At Indian Oil, the reward and recognition system was changed from one in which employees were rewarded regardless of performance to one in which employees were recognized and rewarded based on performance – with a particular focus on providing effective customer service. At Tashman, IndyMac Bank, and Pardee Homes, performance against goals was continually and consistently tracked – to promote greater accountability and performance. At Infogix, the focus was on teamwork and systems and on changing the reward system so that teams, rather than individuals were rewarded for performance against goals (consistent with the Deming philosophy).

Changes in structure played a key supporting role in the change process at Indian Oil, Infogix, and Pardee Homes. In all cases, the changes in structure were intended to help the company "get closer to its customers." In all three companies, this was accomplished, in part, by creating structures in which those "in the field" had greater decision-making authority. At Infogix, the "new" structure – with units headed by "Group Leaders" rather than people with more traditional "management" titles – was intended to help all employees embrace the transformation to a team-based approach (as defined by Deming).

At Indian Oil and Pardee Homes, a focus was also placed on identifying and developing leaders/managers who could support, help implement, and operate within the "new" environment created by the change. At Indian Oil, potential leaders were identified and then given additional training. At Pardee, the focus was on taking current leaders to the "next level" and helping them embrace their more expanded role as decision makers.

Changing and effectively managing the company's culture played a key role in supporting change at all the companies examined in this book. At Indian Oil and Tata Steel, management of the company's new culture was a specific focus of the change effort. In particular, these companies developed specific training programs to help employees understand and embrace the "new" culture, identified and rewarded those who embraced the new culture, and created systems to monitor progress in changing the company's culture. At Countrywide and Infogix, the "new" culture needed to support both the new business concept (diversified financial services and information integrity, respectively) and the idea that "we are one company" versus silos. At Starbucks and Pardee Homes, the culture (which, at Starbucks, was defined in terms of guiding principles) needed to support the transformation to professional management. Finally, at Westfield, the culture needed to support becoming a global enterprise.

Lesson: management systems and corporate culture are key levers in the change process – particularly when the magnitude of change is transformational.

Create and use "symbols" to communicate and help individuals understand the objectives of change

Many of the change leaders in our sample developed and used various "symbols" (including new language, specific position titles, new company names, etc.) to help all the employees understand the change.

Countrywide, Infogix, and Pardee Homes changed their corporate names. At Countrywide, the new name was intended to communicate to all employees and to all customers that the focus was now on diversified financial services, as opposed to simply mortgages. At Infogix (formally Unitech Systems), the name change reflected the new industry being created by the company – information integrity. Finally, at Pardee Homes, the name change from Pardee Construction was intended to help both employees and customers understand the focus that Pardee placed on its "homeowners."

At Indian Oil, the increased focus on the customer was conveyed by embedding "customer" and "change" in many aspects of the organization. Each year of the change process was labeled in terms of the customer – "Customer Care Year" (year 1), "Customer Delight Year" (year 2), and "Customer Service Excellence Year" (year 3). "Customer Ambassadors" were created and specific leaders were identified as "champions of change." While somewhat less formal, Tata Steel also used language as an important part of their change management process.

Lesson: find ways – through symbols (including the language used) – to communicate and reinforce the change.

Continually communicate with staff about the change and the change process

In every case presented in this book, one of the keys to managing the change successfully was that leaders created ways to communicate continually with employees throughout the change process.

At Countrywide, Starbucks, and IndyMac Bank, this communication took place in the context of the strategic planning process. At Tashman and Infogix, there was constant communication up, down, and across the organization as the changes were being implemented. At Indian Oil and Tata Steel, everyone at the company (at Indian Oil, this included trade union leaders) was invited to provide input and feedback on the changes being implemented. At Pardee Homes, the change leaders made frequent visits to the "field" to discuss the change, address questions, and solicit input. The intent of all these efforts was to help create buy-in to the changes taking place.

Lesson: communicate, communicate, communicate!

Don't be afraid to seek outside expertise

With the exception of Westfield, all the companies in our sample used outside experts to support their change processes. Countrywide, Starbucks, Tashman, IndyMac Bank, and Infogix brought in outside help to assist in taking their planning processes to the new level. Indian Oil and Pardee Homes sought outside expertise to help them develop a structure that would support the change process. Tata Steel used outside expertise to assist in changing its culture and developing training programs to support this change.

Lesson: don't be afraid to ask for help.

Be willing to invest resources in the change process

In all the cases discussed in this book, the leaders of the change process were willing to invest resources – including their own time, the time of employees throughout their companies, and money – to make the change process work. At Countrywide, Starbucks, IndyMac Bank, and Infogix, time and other resources were invested in developing and implementing a "new" strategic planning process and related performance management systems that would support the change. At Indian Oil, Tashman, Tata Steel, and Pardee Homes, resources (both time and money) were invested in developing and implementing employee and leadership training programs, so as to support the objectives of the change process and to help employees throughout the company understand the "new" culture (another desired outcome of the change process). At Westfield, resources were invested in ensuring that the due diligence process was effectively executed – resulting in better decision making.

Lesson: change requires resources.

Maximize involvement in the change process

The case studies suggest that maximizing employee involvement in the change process is another key determinant of success. At

Countrywide, for example, this meant training teams in the new strategic planning process and asking them to develop plans to support the overall mission of the company. At Indian Oil, this meant involving managers, employees (in general), and union leaders in the change toward a greater focus on customers. At Tata Steel, employees from throughout the company were asked to help craft the new vision and culture. The evidence regarding the impact of employee involvement on successful change in these case studies supports previous research on the role of participation and involvement in change, as was described in chapter 3.

Lesson: to the greatest extent possible, involve those who will be affected by it in planning for and implementing the change.

Stay the course

While it will sometimes be extremely difficult to do – as is most keenly evident in the case of Schultz standing up to his board at Starbucks – successful change requires a strong commitment on the part of the change leaders. As described throughout this book, resistance to change is the rule rather than the exception.

At Countrywide, Indian Oil, and Tata Steel, the leaders of change needed to find ways to help their organizations understand that, just because they had been successful in the past, that didn't necessarily mean that success would continue in the future. At Starbucks, Schultz and his team needed to stay focused on their vision, even when there was extreme pressure from the board to abandon it. At IndyMac Bank, Perry focused on helping his team understand and embrace the need to promote greater accountability for performance. At Infogix, Nayar focused on helping his team embrace the Deming philosophy and create systems to support it. At Pardee Homes, the change leaders needed to be willing to listen to the concerns of their employees, while at the same time continuing to reinforce their vision and take the steps to make it a reality. At Westfield, the leaders needed to help everyone embrace the vision of becoming a global company, while at the same time understanding the need to be proactive in identifying and effectively taking advantage of market opportunities.

Lesson: change requires a total commitment by its leaders – they can't give up.

Taking the integrative framework forward

In the first two sections of this chapter we identified the lessons learned from our case studies – with respect to leading change – from the practitioner's perspective. That is, we focused on providing suggestions to the leaders of change. In this section our focus is primarily on the lessons learned from a "theoretical" or scholarly perspective, and on the "next steps" for taking the frameworks and models presented in this book forward.

Although our primary intention in this book has been to provide a framework and a set of tools for practitioners, we are also keenly aware of the interest of researchers in this field. We fully expect that our models will be critiqued as a basis for furthering scholarly progress in the field of change management and leadership. This section is primarily addressed to scholars and practitioners who are steeped in the literature of change management. (The appendix provides references for further reading aimed at both practitioners and "academics".)

In Part I we proposed an integrative framework for leading strategic and organizational change that consisted of three levels: (1) theoretical concepts/frameworks for managing change; (2) an actionable model for planning for and managing change; and (3) the leadership capabilities required to implement the change management process successfully (defined at level 2). We now examine how the components of this framework were used by leaders within the companies in our sample, and identify areas of future research and work.

Level 1: theoretical concepts/frameworks for managing change

The case studies in our sample provide few insights into the knowledge that leaders had of the theoretical concepts/frameworks for successfully leading change discussed in chapter 1. Nonetheless, the change management process within all the studies reflects the focus that leaders placed on identifying the outcomes they wanted to achieve and on managing the process to achieve these outcomes. In many cases, leaders were also focused on identifying and finding ways to manage the barriers to successful change. There did not seem to be a focus on identifying the "type" of change required – using something like the change typology matrix proposed in chapter 1.

We would suggest that using a "change typology" may be beneficial to practitioners in the change planning process. It would assist them in identifying – up-front – what will be required, and at what levels of their organizations, to support a successful change effort.

For scholars and researchers, there are many "phases of change" models (component/construct 2 of Level 1) that can and have been tested – including Lewin's (which was described in chapter 1). In addition, the impact of measurement (component/construct 3 of level 1) has been well researched. It is the second component/construct of our framework – the typology of change – on which we suggest researchers and scholars might concentrate their efforts. The focus of this research might include examining questions such as these.

- Is the typology "valid"? That is, are there, in fact, three dimensions that identify the "type of change"?
- Do change efforts fall into one segment or multiple segments of the typology?
- What is the relationship between the different types of change and the leadership/processes required to manage that specific type of change successfully?

Level 2: an actionable model for planning and managing change

Most of the leaders of the companies that underwent the change processes described in Part II of this book used a template to plan for and execute change. Many of them used the framework presented in chapter 2 – including Countrywide, Starbucks, IndyMac Bank, Infogix, and Pardee Homes.

With one exception – the unsuccessful Westfield diversification into the media business from the shopping center business – all the cases cited are examples of successful change processes. This seems to suggest an association between the use of a systematic process of change and the success of the change. As noted in chapter 12, West-field's unsuccessful effort to diversify into TV could have benefited from the use of a formal planning process. This is a hypothesis for further investigation.

We do not claim that our model is the only model for successfully planning for and managing change, or that it is a perfect model, or even that it is the best possible model among competing alternatives.

We merely point out that our model has actually worked in several different types of companies, dealing with several different aspects of strategic and organizational change.

It was noted earlier that there are a number of models for leading the change process. John Kotter, for example, has proposed an eight-stage process of leading what he terms "major change," which he defines as a transformation.[1] Although his approach has reasonable "face validity" (that is, it appears sensible and logical on reading it), there are no case examples of change cited to demonstrate either its utility or its empirical validity.

Another well-known change model is that proposed by David Nadler and Michael Tushman.[2] This model is intended for diagnosing organizational behavior – as opposed to identifying a process to plan for and lead organizational change. Tushman and Nadler view the environment as a force affecting change, and in that sense it is an input to change. In viewing their model, it appears that the organization must *respond* to environmental change.

Their change process includes "the task, people, the formal organization, and the informal organization." These four constructs reflect the prevailing paradigm of organizational analysis at the time that their model was developed (the late 1970s).

It should also be noted that a more recent version of the original Nadler–Tushman model was published by Nadler in 1998 in a book dealing with organizational change.[3] In this version, however, Nadler has deleted the four factors of the transformation process and replaced them with a more global construct, labeled "the operating organization."

Although it is extremely difficult to carry out empirical research testing a framework for managing strategic and organizational change – such as that presented in chapter 2 and those cited above – it is not impossible. We have cited several empirical examples of companies using versions of this approach as part of their actual processes of planning and leading strategic and organizational change. This provides significant support for these proposed models and frameworks.

---

[1] Kotter, *Leading Change*, 20–1.

[2] Nadler, D. A., and M. L. Tushman, 1980, "A model for diagnosing organizational behavior," *Organizational Dynamics*, 9(2), 35–51.

[3] Nadler, D. A., 1998, *Champions of Change*, San Francisco, Jossey-Bass, 31.

A next step would be for other researchers/practitioners to apply the models in actual situations and assess the results. This would then lead to insights for the validation and possible further refinement of the models and frameworks.

Level 3: leadership capabilities

In chapter 3 we suggest that there are four capabilities – which comprise a leadership molecule – that need to be present to support successful change: (1) creating, communicating, and managing the vision; (2) managing corporate culture; (3) developing and managing systems; and (4) managing operations. As shown in exhibit 13.4, these capabilities were present in many of the case studies examined in this book – although it wasn't necessarily the case (as was suggested in chapter 3) that three or more individuals were needed to form the molecule.

Given that the theoretical VCSO model (or the hypothesis that there are, in fact, four distinct capabilities needed to support successful change) has not yet been empirically tested, this creates a number of research possibilities. One is to explore whether these four capabilities are truly distinct. A second is to examine whether these four are, in fact, the capabilities required by change leaders – or if there are others. A third is to explore what can be done to develop individual change leadership capabilities in these four areas – vision, culture management, systems, and operations. Researchers might also focus on how the four (and/or other) leadership capabilities actually manifest themselves in companies where change is and is not successful. In other words, they might explore the relationship between specific leadership capabilities and the success or otherwise of change.

The integrative framework as a whole and its components

Another potential avenue for research would be to investigate the integrative framework as a whole – examining the impact of each level on the success of a change effort. This might lead to the identification of other factors that should be included. Furthermore, research might focus on the individual components of the frameworks, including such variables as the length or duration of the change process, the magnitude of change, the types of change (strategic or organizational), and the like.

Case	Vision	Culture	Systems	Operations
Countrywide	Stanford Kurland, Angelo Mozilo	Angelo Mozilo	Stanford Kurland	Dave Sambol
Starbucks	Howard Schultz	Howard Schultz	Orin Smith	Howard Behar
Indian Oil	IOC leadership	IOC leadership	Director HR	
Tashman	Rich Tashman	Stan Tashman	Rich Tashman	Ty Olson
IndyMac Bank	Michael Perry	Michael Perry	Michael Perry and senior management	
Infogix	Madhavan Nayar	Madhavan Nayar		
Pardee Homes	Michael McGee, Hal Struck	Michael McGee, Hal Struck	Michael McGee, Hal Struck	Department heads and regional managers
Tata Steel	Entire company	Entire company		
Westfield	Frank Lowy Peter Lowy	Frank Lowy		

Exhibit 13.4 Leadership capabilities present in the nine case studies
Note: The information is this table is derived from that presented in each case and is based on the authors' analysis. In some cases, there was not enough information to identify whether the capability was or was not present. In these cases, the segment has been left blank.

In a sense, our proposed framework provides a potential "paradigm" for the change management process. This could lead to a program of research conducted by many different scholars.

Conclusion

This book has presented a framework or lens that leaders of change can use to understand and manage the change process. The framework includes three levels – theoretical concepts/frameworks for managing change, a practical framework for planning for and managing change, and identification of the leadership capabilities that need to be present to support successful change. We have identified criteria for effective or successful change and have examined the issue of measuring change.

Another contribution made by this book has been to help define a language or vocabulary of change. This is a set of constructs that we believe will be useful in thinking about and planning change. These include the original typology of change presented in chapter 1, as well as the notions of instrumental and ultimate change discussed in this chapter. Moreover, to assist in the systematic planning of strategic and organizational change, we have developed the model described in chapter 2.

This book has also examined nine case studies of actual organizational change. Although the number of companies is limited, there is still value in formulating some preliminary insights and propositions that can be tested empirically in future research. We have done that in this chapter.

Ultimately, change is created through a process of leadership in organizations. This involves the planning and execution of change programs. What we have seen is that, just as each situation is different, each company's approach or response to change is also different. Nevertheless, there are some common underlying aspects of the successful management of change in organizations.

We do not claim that our models for planning and leading organizational change are "perfect," or that they are the only models available in the literature. We do believe, however, that they work, as we have cited in the case examples discussed throughout this book.

It is our hope that this book will make a valuable contribution to the increased probability of managing change successfully and to avoiding the inevitable pitfalls of change.

Appendix
References for further reading
on leading change

Practitioner-oriented

Abrahamson, E., 2000, "Change without pain," *Harvard Business Review*, 78(4), 75–9.

2003, *Change without Pain: How Managers Can Overcome Initiative Overload, Organizational Chaos, and Employee Burnout*, Boston, Harvard Business School Press.

2004a, "Avoiding repetitive change syndrome," *Sloan Management Review*, 45(2), 93–5.

2004b, "Using creative recombination to manage change," *Employment Relations Today*, 30(4), 33–41.

Beer, M., 1987, "Revitalizing organizations: change process and emergent model," *Academy of Management Executive*, 1(1), 51–5.

2000, "Lead organizational change by creating dissatisfaction and realigning the organization with new competitive realities," in E. A. Locke (ed.), *Blackwell Handbook of Principles of Organizational Behavior*, Oxford, Blackwell, 370–86.

2001, "How to develop an organization capable of sustained high performance: embrace the drive for results–capability development paradox," *Organizational Dynamics*, 29(4), 233–47.

Beer, M., R. A. Eisenstat, and B. Spector, 1990a, "Why change programs don't produce change," *Harvard Business Review*, 68(6), 158–66.

1990b, *The Critical Path to Corporate Renewal*, Boston, Harvard Business School Press.

Beer, M., and N. Nohria, 2000, *Breaking the Code of Change*, Boston, Harvard Business School Press.

Beer, M., and A. E. Walton, 1987, "Organization change and development," *Annual Review of Psychology*, 38, 339–67.

Cohen, D. S., 2002, *The Heart of Change Field Guide: Tools and Tactics for Leading Change in Your Organization*, Boston, Harvard Business School Press.

Ginsberg, A., and E. Abrahamson, 1991, "Champions of change and strategic shifts: the role of internal and external change advocates," *Journal of Management Studies*, 28(2), 173–90.

Huber, G. P., and W. H. Glick, 1993, *Organizational Change and Redesign*, New York, Oxford University Press.

Huy, Q. N., 2001, "In praise of middle managers," *Harvard Business Review*, 79(8), 72–9.

Huy, Q. N., and H. Mintzberg, 2003, "The rhythm of change," *Sloan Management Review*, 44(4), 79–84.

Kotter, J. P., 1996, *Leading Change*, Boston, Harvard Business School Press.

Kotter, J. P., and D. S. Cohen, 2002, *The Heart of Change*, Boston, Harvard Business School Press.

Kotter, J. P., and L. A. Schlesinger, 1979, "Choosing strategies for change," *Harvard Business Review*, 57(2), 106–14.

Nadler, D. P., and M. Nadler, 1998, *Champions of Change*, San Francisco, Jossey-Bass.

Senge, P., A. Kleiner, C. Roberts, G. Roth, R. Ross, and B. Smith, 1999, *The Dance of Change: The Challenges to Sustaining Momentum in Learning Organizations*, New York, Doubleday.

Tushman, M. L., 1974, *Organizational Change: An Exploratory Study and Case History*, Ithaca, NY, New York State School of Industrial and Labor Relations, Cornell University.

Tushman, M. L., and C. A. O'Reilly, 2002, *Winning through Innovation: A Practical Guide to Leading Organizational Change and Renewal*, Boston, Harvard Business School Press.

Academic-oriented

Amis, J., T. Slack, and C. R. Hinings, 2004, "The pace, sequence and linearity of radical change," *Academy of Management Journal*, 47(1), 15–39.

Anderson, P., and M. L. Tushman, 1990, "Technological discontinuities and dominant designs: a cyclical model of technological change," *Administrative Science Quarterly*, 35(4), 604–33.

Argyris, C., 1991, "Teaching smart people how to learn," *Harvard Business Review*, 69(3), 99–109.

Bartunek, J. M., C. A. Lacey, and D. R. Wood, 1992, "Social cognition in organizational change: an insider–outsider approach," *Journal of Applied Behavioral Science*, 28(2), 204–33.

Bartunek, J. M., D. M. Rousseau, J. W. Rudolph, and J. A. DePalma, 2006, "On the receiving end: sensemaking, emotions and assessments of an organizational change initiated by others," *Journal of Applied Behavioral Science*, 42(2), 182–206.

Brown, S. L., and K. M. Eisenhardt, 1997, "The art of continuous change," *Administrative Science Quarterly*, 42(1), 1–34.

1998, *Competing on the Edge: Strategy as Structured Chaos*, Boston, Harvard Business School Press.

Cobb, A. T., K. C. Wooten, and R. Folger, 1995, "Justice in the making: toward understanding the theory and practice of justice in organizational change and development," *Research in Organizational Change and Development*, 8, 243–95.

Coch, L., and J. R. P. French, Jr., 1948, "Overcoming resistance to change," *Human Relations*, 1(4), 512–32.

Cohen, M. D., J. C. March, and J. P. Olsen, 1972, "A garbage can model of organizational choice," *Administrative Science Quarterly*, 17(1), 1–25.

Cummings, T., and C. Worley, 2004, *Organization Development and Change*, 8th edn., New York, South Western College Publishing.

Dent, E. B., and S. G. Goldberg, 1999, "Challenging 'resistance to change,'" *Journal of Applied Behavioral Science*, 35(1), 25–41.

Ethiraj, S. K., and D. Levinthal, 2004, "Bounded rationality and the search for organizational architecture: an evolutionary perspective on the design of organizations and their evolvability," *Administrative Science Quarterly*, 49(3), 404–37.

Frohman, A. L., 1997, "Igniting organizational change from below: the power of personal initiative," *Organizational Dynamics*, 25(3), 39–53.

Gersick, C., 1991, "Revolutionary change theories: a multi-level exploration of the punctuated equilibrium paradigm," *Academy of Management Review*, 16(1), 10–36.

1994, "Pacing strategic change: the case of a new venture," *Academy of Management Journal*, 37(1), 9–45.

Greenwood, R., and C. R. Hinings, 1993, "Understanding strategic change: the contribution of archetypes," *Academy of Management Journal*, 36(5), 1052–81.

Greenwood, R., R. Suddaby, and C. R. Hinings, 2002, "Theorizing change: the role of professional associations in the transformation of institutionalized fields," *Academy of Management Journal*, 45(1), 58–80.

Greve, H. R., 1998, "Performance, aspirations, and risky organizational change," *Administrative Science Quarterly*, 43(1), 58–86.

Hannan, M. T., and J. Freeman, 1984, "Structural inertia and organizational change," *American Sociological Review*, 49(2), 149–64.

Kanter, R. M., 1983, *The Change Masters*, New York, Simon & Schuster.

2003, "Leadership and the psychology of turnarounds," *Harvard Business Review*, 81(6), 58–67.

Keck, S. L., and M. L. Tushman, 1993, "Environmental and organizational context and executive team structure," *Academy of Management Journal*, 36(6), 1314–44.

Lau, C. M., and R. W. Woodman, 1995, "Understanding organizational change: a schematic perspective," *Academy of Management Journal*, 38(2), 537–54.

Lawrence, P. R., 1954, "How to deal with resistance to change," *Harvard Business Review*, 32(3), 49–57.

Lewin, K., 1947, "Frontiers in group dynamics 1. concept, method and reality in social science: social equilibria and social change," *Human Relations*, 1(1), 5–41.

March, J. G., 1991, "Exploration and exploitation in organizational learning," *Organization Science*, 2(1), 71–87.

Marshak, R. J., 2002, "Changing the language of change: how new contexts and concepts are challenging the ways we think and talk about organizational change," *Strategic Change*, 11(5), 279–86.

McGrath, C., and D. Krackhardt, 2003, "Network conditions for organizational change," *Journal of Applied Behavioral Science*, 39(3), 324–34.

Meyer, A. D., A. S. Tsui, and C. R. Hinings, 1993, "Configurational approaches to organizational analysis," *Academy of Management Journal*, 36(6), 1175–95.

Meyerson, D. E., and M. A. Scully, 1995, "Tempered radicalism and the politics of ambivalence and change," *Organization Science*, 6(5), 585–600.

Morgan, G., 1997, "Unfolding logics of change: organization as flux and transformation," in *Images of Organization*, 2nd edn., London, Sage, 251–300.

Morrison, E. W., and S. L. Robinson, 1997, "When employees feel betrayed: a model of how psychological contract violation develops," *Academy of Management Review*, 22(1), 226–56.

Nutt, P., 1986, "Tactics of implementation," *Academy of Management Journal*, 29(2), 230–61.

Pascale, R., M. Millemann, and L. Gioja, 1997, "Changing the way we change," *Harvard Business Review*, 75(6), 127–39.

Pettigrew, A. M., 1990, "Longitudinal field research on change: theory and practice," *Organization Science*, 1(3), 267–92.

Pettigrew, A. M., R. W. Woodman, and K. S. Cameron, 2001, "Studying organizational change and development: challenges for future research," *Academy of Management Journal*, 44(4), 697–713.

Piderit, S. K., 2000, "Rethinking resistance and recognizing ambivalence: a multidimensional view of attitudes toward an organizational change," *Academy of Management Review*, 25(4), 783–94.

Rajagopalan, N., and G. M. Spreitzer, 1997, "Toward a theory of strategic change: a multi-lens perspective and integrative framework," *Academy of Management Review*, 22(1), 48–79.

Reichers, A. E., J. P. Wanous, and J. T. Austin, 1997, "Understanding and managing cynicism about organizational change," *Academy of Management Executive*, 11(1), 48–59.

Robertson, P. J., D. R. Roberts, and J. I. Porras, 1993, "Dynamics of planned organizational change: assessing empirical support for a theoretical model," *Academy of Management Journal*, 36(3), 619–34.

Romanelli, E., and M. L. Tushman, 1994, "Organizational transformation as punctuated equilibrium: an empirical test," *Academy of Management Journal*, 37(5), 1141–66.

Sastry, A. M., 1997, "Problems and paradoxes in a model of punctuated organizational change," *Administrative Science Quarterly*, 42(2), 237–75.

Schweiger, D. M., and A. S. DeNisi, 1991, "Communication with employees following a merger: a longitudinal field experiment," *Academy of Management Journal*, 34(1), 110–35.

Spreitzer, G. M., and R. E. Quinn, 1996, "Empowering middle managers to be transformational leaders," *Journal of Applied Behavioral Science*, 32(3), 237–61.

Staw, B. M., L. E. Sandelands, and J. E. Dutton, 1981, "Threat-rigidity effects in organizational behavior: a multilevel analysis," *Administrative Science Quarterly*, 26(4), 501–24.

Tetenbaum, T. J., 1998, "Shifting paradigms: from Newton to chaos," *Organizational Dynamics*, 26(4), 21–32.

Tushman, M. L., and P. Anderson, 1986, "Technological discontinuities and organizational environments," *Administrative Science Quarterly*, 31(1), 439–65.

Tushman, M. L., and C. A. O'Reilly, 1996, "Ambidextrous organizations: managing evolutionary and revolutionary change," *California Management Review*, 38(4), 8–30.

Van de Ven, A. H., and M. S. Poole, 1995, "Explaining development and change in organizations," *Academy of Management Review*, 20(3), 510–40.

Weick, K. E., and R. E. Quinn, 1999, "Organizational change and development," *Annual Review of Psychology*, 50, 361–86.

Woodman, R. W., 1989, "Organizational change and development: new arenas for inquiry and action," *Journal of Management*, 15(2), 205–28.

Index